Finally a book that looks at this largely overlooked topic. It's an essential read for all business practitioners to understand that we can do better than CSR-type paternalism. And trade unionists will enjoy crucial insights into how the rise of CSR can help improve their operations in the second decade of the new millennium.

Dirk Matten, *Professor, York University, Canada*

Preuss, Gold and Rees have assembled a fine collection of studies on a timely yet understudied topic: the link between trade unions and corporate social responsibility (CSR). By comparing insights from a wide range of European countries, this volume provides a systematic overview of how different trade unions relate to CSR.

Frank G.A. de Bakker, *Associate Professor, VU University Amsterdam, the Netherlands*

Corporate Social Responsibility and Trade Unions

Growing interest in corporate social responsibility (CSR) has focused attention on the relationship between businesses and key stakeholders, such as NGOs and local communities. Curiously, however, commentators on CSR rarely discuss the role of trade unions, while commentators on employment relations seldom engage with CSR. This situation is all the more remarkable since unions are a critically important social actor and have traditionally played a prominent role in defending the interests of one key stakeholder in the company, the employee.

Written by dedicated experts in their field, this book addresses a key gap in the literature on both CSR and employment relations, namely trade union policies towards CSR, as well as union engagement with particular CSR initiatives and the challenges they face in doing so. The research covers 11 European countries which, when taken together, constitute a representative sample of industrial relations structures across the continent.

This book will be essential reading for scholars, students and practitioners of international business, employment relations, public policy and CSR. Its foreword is written by Philippe Pochet and Maria Jepsen, Directors of the European Trade Union Institute in Brussels.

Lutz Preuss is Reader in Corporate Social Responsibility at the School of Management, Royal Holloway, University of London, UK.

Michael Gold is Professor of Comparative Employment Relations at the School of Management, Royal Holloway, University of London, UK.

Chris Rees is Professor of Employment Relations at the School of Management, Royal Holloway, University of London, UK.

Routledge Research in Employment Relations

Series editors: Rick Delbridge and Edmund Heery
Cardiff Business School, UK

Aspects of the employment relationship are central to numerous courses at both undergraduate and postgraduate level.

Drawing from insights from industrial relations, human resource management and industrial sociology, this series provides an alternative source of research-based materials and texts, reviewing key developments in employment research.

Books published in this series are works of high academic merit, drawn from a wide range of academic studies in the social sciences.

1 **Social Partnership at Work**
Carola M. Frege

2 **Human Resource Management in the Hotel Industry**
Kim Hoque

3 **Redefining Public Sector Unionism**
UNISON and the future of trade unions
Edited by Mike Terry

4 **Employee Ownership, Participation and Governance**
A study of ESOPs in the UK
Andrew Pendleton

5 **Human Resource Management in Developing Countries**
Pawan S. Budhwar and Yaw A. Debrah

6 **Gender, Diversity and Trade Unions**
International perspectives
Edited by Fiona Colgan and Sue Ledwith

7 **Foucault, Governmentality, and Organization**
Inside the factory of the future
Alan McKinlay and Philip Taylor

8 **New Unions, New Workplaces**
A study of union resilience in the restructured workplace
Andy Danford, Mike Richardson and Martin Upchurch

9 **Partnership and Modernisation in Employment Relations**
Edited by Mark Stuart and Miguel Martinez Lucio

10 **Partnership at Work**
The quest for radical organizational change
William K. Roche and John F. Geary

11 **European Works Councils**
Pessimism of the intellect, optimism of the will?
Edited by Ian Fitzgerald and John Stirling

12 **Employment Relations in Non-Union Firms**
Tony Dundon and Derek Rollinson

13 **Management, Labour Process and Software Development**
Reality bytes
Edited by Rowena Barrett

14 **A Comparison of the Trade Union Merger Process in Britain and Germany**
Joining forces?
Jeremy Waddington, Marcus Kahmann and Jürgen Hoffmann

15 **French Industrial Relations in the New World Economy**
Nick Parsons

16 **Union Recognition**
Organising and bargaining outcomes
Edited by Gregor Gall

17 **Towards a European Labour Identity**
The case of the European Work Council
Edited by Michael Whittall, Herman Knudsen and Fred Huijgen

18 **Power at Work**
How employees reproduce the corporate machine
Darren McCabe

19 **Management in the Airline Industry**
Geraint Harvey

20 **Trade Unions in a Neoliberal World**
British trade unions under New Labour
Gary Daniels and John McIlroy

21 **Diversity Management in the UK**
Organizational and stakeholder experiences
Anne-marie Greene and Gill Kirton

22 **Ethical Socialism and the Trade Unions**
Allan Flanders and British industrial relation reform
John Kelly

23 **European Works Councils**
A transnational industrial relations institution in the making
Jeremy Waddington

24 **The Politics of Industrial Relations**
Labor unions in Spain
Kerstin Hamann

25 **Social Failures of EU Enlargement**
A case of workers voting with their feet
Guglielmo Meardi

26 **Trade Unions and Workplace Training**
Issues and international perspectives
Edited by Richard Cooney and Mark Stuart

27 **Men, Wage Work and Family**
Edited by Paula McDonald and Emma Jeanes

28 **Gendering and Diversifying Trade Union Leadership**
Edited by Sue Ledwith and Lise Lotte Hansen

29 **Gender and Leadership in Trade Unions**
Gill Kirton and Geraldine Healy

30 **Minimum Wages, Pay Equity, and Comparative Industrial Relations**
Edited by Damian Grimshaw

31 **The Transformation of Employment Relations in Europe**
Institutions and outcomes in the age of globalization
Edited by James Arrowsmith and Valeria Pulignano

32 **Financial Services Partnerships**
Labor-management dynamics
Peter J. Samuel

33 **Voice and Involvement at Work**
Experience with non-union representation
Edited by Paul J. Gollan, Bruce E. Kaufman, Daphne Taras and Adrian Wilkinson

34 **Corporate Social Responsibility and Trade Unions**
Perspectives across Europe
Edited by Lutz Preuss, Michael Gold and Chris Rees

Corporate Social Responsibility and Trade Unions

Perspectives across Europe

Edited by
Lutz Preuss, Michael Gold
and Chris Rees

LONDON AND NEW YORK

First published 2015
by Routledge
2 Park Square, Milton Park, Abingdon, Oxon OX14 4RN

and by Routledge
605 Third Avenue, New York, NY 10017

First issued in paperback 2020

Routledge is an imprint of the Taylor & Francis Group, an informa business

British Library Cataloguing in Publication Data
A catalogue record for this book is available from the British Library

Library of Congress Cataloging in Publication Data
Corporate social responsibility and trade unions: perspectives across Europe/edited by Lutz Preuss, Michael Gold and Chris Rees.
pages cm. – (Routledge research in employment relations)
Includes bibliographical references and index.
1. Labor unions–Europe. 2. Social responsibility of business–Europe. 3. Industrial relations–Europe. I. Preuss, Lutz
HD6657.C67 2014
658.4'08–dc23 2014014163

ISBN 13: 978-0-367-73965-2 (pbk)
ISBN 13: 978-0-415-85681-2 (hbk)

Typeset in Sabon
by Wearset Ltd, Boldon, Tyne and Wear

Contents

Contributors

Jesús Cambra-Fierro, PhD, is Professor of Marketing and Head of the Department of Marketing at the University Pablo de Olavide, Sevilla. He is a member of the research group Generes. His research topics are related to strategic marketing, SMEs and business ethics. He has published research papers in leading international journals, such as *Journal of Business Ethics*, *International Small Business Journal*, *Industrial Marketing Management* and *Management Decision*, amongst others.

Xavier Coller is Professor of Sociology at the University Pablo de Olavide, Seville and holds a PhD in Sociology from Yale University. He has been visiting fellow at Warwick University, University of California (Berkeley), Yale University, Harvard University, Georgetown University and University of Montpellier 1. He has authored over 70 works on social theory, research methods, collective identities, political elites and complex organizations. He is the winner of several international awards, among them the 2003 Sussman Dissertation Award (Yale University), and an honourable mention in the 2003 Seymour Martin Lipset Award (Society for Comparative Research, Princeton University).

Jan Czarzasty is Associate Professor in the Institute of Philosophy, Sociology and Economic Sociology, at the Warsaw School of Economics (SGH), and a correspondent to the *Working Conditions and Industrial Relations Observatory* (EurWORK), formerly EIRO. His research interests include industrial relations, social dialogue and organizational culture. He is Assistant-Chief Editor of the 'Warsaw Forum of Economic Sociology'. He has published in journals such as the *British Journal of Industrial Relations*, *European Journal of Industrial Relations* and *Human Resources Development International.* He recently co-edited a book, *Organizowanie związków zawodowych w Europie. Badania i praktyka* (Trade Union Organizing in Europe. Research and Practice) (2014).

Sabina Du Rietz is Assistant Professor in the Department of Accounting, Auditing and Law at the Norwegian School of Economics. She holds a doctorate from Stockholm University School of Business. Her current research addresses questions around corporate governance in social and environmental issues, such as the role of governance technologies like accounting and corporate accountability enforced by investors and trade unions.

Michael Gold is Professor of Comparative Employment Relations in the School of Management at Royal Holloway, University of London. He is editor of *Employment Policy in the European Union: Origins, Themes and Prospects* (Palgrave, 2009), and has published extensively in the areas of European employment policy, employee participation, self-employment and British industrial relations in the 1970s. A former journalist, he worked at Incomes Data Services and Industrial Relations Services, and was a consultant editor for the European Industrial Relations Observatory. He is currently a visiting professor at the University of Westminster.

Urša Golob is Associate Professor of Marketing Communication at the Faculty of Social Sciences, University of Ljubljana. Her research interests focus on corporate social responsibility, corporate communication and marketing. Her work has been published in international journals like *European Journal of Marketing*, *Public Relations Review*, *Journal of Business Research*, *Journal of Marketing Communications* and *Systemic Practice and Action Research*. In 2013 she co-edited a special issue of *Corporate Communications: An International Journal* on facets of CSR communication. She is also a co-author of a book chapter on CSR and dialogue in the *Handbook of Communication and Corporate Social Responsibility* (Wiley Blackwell, 2011).

Thomas Gualtieri is a journalist with *El País*, the leading Spanish daily newspaper. He holds an MSc in Comparative Employment Relations and Human Resource Management, earned with distinction from the London School of Economics and Political Science. He is a PhD student (currently on leave) at the department of Labour Law of Pompeu Fabra University, Barcelona. His dissertation at LSE, about Italian industrial relations, has been published by *Quaderni di Rassegna Sindacale*, the journal of Cgil, the main Italian trade union. His research interests are international and comparative industrial relations, with a special focus on southern Europe, and corporate social responsibility.

Axel Haunschild is Professor of Work and Employment Studies at Leibniz University of Hannover, Germany. He held Visiting Professorships at Royal Holloway, University of London and the University of Innsbruck, Austria. His research interests include changing forms of work, employment and organization, creative industries, CSR from an industrial relations perspective, organizations and lifestyles and organizational boundaries. He has published in journals such as *Human Relations*, *Journal of Organizational Behavior*, *British Journal of Industrial*

Relations and *International Journal of Human Resource Management.* He is on the International Advisory Board of the journal, *Work Employment and Society.*

Christelle Havard is Associate Professor in Human Resource Management in the Burgundy School of Business, France. She is member of the research team 'Management and Responsible Innovation'. Her teaching areas are human resource management, change management and industrial relations. Her research topics include change management, human resource management and corporate social responsibility. She has been working with André Sobczak on unions and corporate social responsibility in France and is currently working on responsible management. She has published in the *Journal of Business Ethics* and the *European Journal of Industrial Relations*, amongst others.

Virginija Jurėnienė is a historian, and Professor in the Department of Philosophy and Culture Studies at Kaunas Faculty of Humanities, University of Vilnius. Her research focuses on gender issues, civil rights and culture tourism and cultural heritage. Individually and in collaboration with other researchers, she has published about 100 papers in national and international volumes and monographs (as the editor and co-editor): *Lithuanian Women's Movement at the end of 19th – the middle of the 20th centuries* (2006), *Map of Creative Industries/Social, Economic Analysis in Kaunas Region (County)* (2010), *Restructuring: Theory and Practice* (2012), *Sustainable Development: Poland, Lithuania, Ukraine* (2013).

Florian Krause is a PhD student and Lecturer at the Institute for Work and Employment Studies, Leibniz University of Hannover, Germany. He studied economics and philosophy at the University of Trier. In his PhD project, he focuses on business ethics and the roots of rationality in organizations. Other research interests include CSR from an industrial relations perspective, and philosophical and organizational issues around the environment, sustainability, diversity, working time and voluntary work. He is a member of the Transatlantic Doctoral Academy on Corporate Responsibility (TADA).

Anna-Maija Lämsä is Professor of Human Resource Management at the School of Business and Economics of Jyväskylä University, Finland. Her research interests are in ethical approaches to management, leadership and organizations, CSR, and gender, leadership and careers. She researches these topics in different socio-cultural contexts. Her work has appeared in journals such as *Journal of Business Ethics*, *International Journal of Human Resource Management*, *Business Ethics: A European Review*, *Scandinavian Journal of Management*, *Baltic Journal of Management* and *Gender in Management: An International Journal.* She has published three textbooks in Finland and won the Edita award for her textbooks in 2005.

Matthew Lloyd-Cape is a PhD student at the Doctoral School of Political Science, Public Policy and International Relations at Central European University, Budapest, Hungary. His research interests focus on industrial relations in global production networks, international union organizing and global governance. His PhD is a study of cross-border union organizing in the furniture sector in the USA, Sweden, Russia and Poland. Prior to writing his PhD, Matthew worked as a project manager and researcher in the international development sector, with experience of working for NGOs in Southern Africa, the South Pacific and Central America.

Céline Louche is Associate Professor at Audencia Nantes School of Management, France. Her research focuses on the areas of sustainability and corporate responsibility. It builds on organizational, network and strategic analyses to understand how businesses undergo a transformation towards sustainability. Before joining academia, she worked as Sustainability Analyst for Responsible Investment at the Dutch Sustainability Research Institute. She is the author of several articles, book chapters and books, the most recent being *SRI in the 21st Century: Does it Make a Difference for Society?* (2014). In 2005–2006 she was involved in a research project into trade union attitudes on CSR, which was led by Eurocadres.

Iguácel Melero-Polo is a PhD student in the Department of Marketing Management at the University of Zaragoza. She is a member of the research group, Generes, recognized by the government of Aragon. Her research interests include the study of consumer behaviour, customer-firm relationships and the measurement of customer value. She has published research papers in both local and international journals, such as *Service Business*, *Innovation*, *Management Policy and Practice* and *Universia Business Review*. She has attended and presented research papers to several international conferences, such as the European Marketing Academy Conference and Marketing Science Conference.

Aurelija Novelskaitė is an Associate Professor of Sociology and Social Research Methodology at Kaunas Faculty of Humanities, the University of Vilnius and a Senior Researcher at the Lithuanian Social Research Centre. Her research interests encompass research and academic ethics, gender issues in science, and ethical practices in organizations. Individually and in collaboration with other researchers, she has published about 30 papers in national and international volumes and several books as well as textbooks. As an expert, she has been contributing to developing the Lithuania's national strategy on gender equality in science.

Klement Podnar is Associate Professor of Marketing Communication at the Faculty of Social Sciences, University of Ljubljana. His research interests lie in corporate marketing and communication, corporate social responsibility and organizational identification. He is the associate editor of *Journal of Promotion Management* and a member of the editorial board of several other international journals. His research has appeared in several book chapters and journals such as *Journal of Business Research*, *European Journal of Marketing*, *Journal of Public Policy and Marketing*, *Corporate Communications: An International Journal*, *Journal of Communication Management*, *Corporate Reputation Review* and *Journal of Marketing Communications*.

Lutz Preuss is Reader in Corporate Social Responsibility in the School of Management at Royal Holloway, University of London. He holds a doctorate from King's College London. His research addresses various questions around corporate social responsibility, particularly cross-national differences in approaches to CSR. His work – some 50 journal articles and book chapters – has appeared in journals such as *Academy of Management Review*, *Journal of Business Ethics*, *International Journal of Human Resource Management*, *Public Administration* and *Entrepreneurship and Regional Development*. In 2005–2006 he was involved in one of the early studies into trade union attitudes on CSR, co-ordinated through the European trade union umbrella body, Eurocadres.

Raminta Pučėtaitė is an Associate Professor of Business Ethics and Corporate Social Responsibility at Kaunas Faculty of Humanities, Vilnius University in Lithuania and an adjunct professor of Organizational Ethics and Human Resource Management at Jyväskylä University School of Business and Economics, Finland. Her research focuses on ethical issues in human resource management, research and academic ethics, values management and organizational innovation in a post-Soviet context. She has published in national and international volumes, including *Journal of Business Ethics*, *Business Ethics: A European Review* and the *Baltic Journal of Management*.

Chris Rees is Professor of Employment Relations in the School of Management at Royal Holloway, University of London. His research interests are in international and comparative employment relations and in employee involvement, voice and representation. He is co-editor (with Tony Edwards) of the book, *International Human Resource Management: Globalisation, National Systems and Multinational Companies* (3rd edition due 2015), and he has published in journals such as *Organization Studies*, *Work Employment and Society*, *Human Resource Management*, *European Journal of Industrial Relations*, *Employee Relations* and *Transfer*. He is on the Associate Board of the journal, *Work Employment and Society*.

André Sobczak is Professor and Associate Dean for Research at Audencia Nantes School of Management. He is the founding director of Audencia's Institute for Global Responsibility and the holder of the Chair on CSR within SMEs. Editor of the academic journal, *Responsible Organization Review*, he has published various articles on CSR as an organizational learning process and the importance of engaging stakeholders. He has published a textbook on managing CSR and acts as a consultant on CSR strategies for public and private organizations.

Miroslav Stanojević is Professor of Industrial Relations at the Faculty of Social Sciences, University of Ljubljana. He holds a PhD in Sociology from the University of Ljubljana. His research includes the sociology of work and industrial relations, the marketization of state-regulated societies and the transformation of industrial relations in Slovenia. He is engaged in networks dealing with trade unions, employment relations and HRM research in the EU and central and eastern European countries. He has published in journals such as *European Journal of Industrial Relations*, *Politics and Society*, *Europe–Asia Studies* and *Transfer*.

Soilikki Viljanen has an MSc from the University of Jyväskylä School of Business and Economics, in which her thesis focused on CSR from the trade union point of view, as well as an EMBA degree from the executive education programme, Advance, at the same university. She is currently a PhD student, specializing in management and leadership. Her research interests are in CSR, stakeholder management, organizational trust and women managers and professionals in engineering. She has a long and extensive work experience in trade unions in the engineering sector.

Foreword

Since the global economic and financial crisis, we have all become increasingly aware of the serious weaknesses that affect corporate practices across the whole of Europe. While the shareholder model of corporate governance has come under particular criticism – for encouraging excessive executive pay, an uncontrolled bonus culture and disengaged investors – restructuring and rationalization have created job insecurity and undermined confidence in companies, particularly multinational companies, everywhere. Calls for a more 'responsible capitalism' echo across Europe alongside the campaigns for the 'sustainable company' advocated by the European Trade Union Confederation (ETUC) and European labour movement more generally.

Against the backdrop of various recent initiatives from the European Commission, which are generally aimed at less but 'better' regulation of companies, the European labour movement has argued forcibly that regulation of employee participation across the EU is disjointed and that we need a fundamental 'EU framework instrument' on workers' rights. To inform this debate, we require a detailed understanding of how companies operate more broadly and how unions can influence forms of corporate social responsibility (CSR) in a turbulent and globalising world. We need to know in particular how strengthening workers' rights within companies would link in and produce synergies with all the other areas of corporate policy – on the environment, relationships with suppliers and ethical trading initiatives amongst others – which would together create genuinely 'sustainable companies'.

For these reasons we greatly welcome this book, which is – as far as we know – the first systematic attempt to analyse the varying perspectives adopted towards CSR by European trade unions. It focuses on union engagement with CSR in 11 EU member states, drawn from all corners of Europe, and in doing so it provides a nuanced overview, outlining why some unions have adopted a more conciliatory or even proactive approach than others. Based on extensive interviews, the book examines policies and attitudes across a range of unions in each country and explains how engagement varies with historical, political and institutional traditions in each national context.

We consider that this book will prove to be essential reading for everyone – academics, campaigners, policy-makers, practitioners and trade unionists – who believes that the future of economic and social progress in Europe depends on a more accountable and responsive private sector in industry and services.

Philippe Pochet
General Director of the European Trade Union Institute (ETUI)
Maria Jepsen
Director of the Research Department of ETUI

Acknowledgements

We are grateful to our contributors for their patience and understanding during the long process of planning, assembling and editing this book. Their prompt replies and good humour made our task as editors much easier. We are also grateful to all our trade union respondents across Europe who kindly gave their time to be interviewed. Without them, there wouldn't have been a book at all!

We should like to thank the editorial staff at Routledge for their detailed and helpful responses to our enquiries, particularly in the final stages of preparing the manuscript.

Thanks too to the Academy of Business in Society (ABIS) for funding the meeting that brought all our contributors together for two days in May 2012 to discuss preliminary findings from our interviews. This meeting helped to generate the team spirit that underpinned our subsequent collaboration.

We also appreciate the support given us by the School of Management at Royal Holloway, University of London, particularly for funding our research costs.

Abbreviations

ABVV-FGTB	General Federation of Belgian Labour, Algemeen Belgisch Vakverbond, Fédération Générale du Travail de Belgique
ACLVB-CGSLB	General Confederation of Liberal Trade Unions of Belgium, Algemene Centrale der Liberale Vakbonden van België, Centrale Générale des Syndicats Libéraux de Belgique
ACV-CSC	Confederation of Christian Trade Unions, Algemeen Christelijk Vakverbond, Confédération des Syndicats Chrétiens
AGM	annual general meeting
AHFSz	Audi Hungary Independent Union, Audi Hungaria Fuggetlen Sakszervezet
Akava	Confederation of Unions for Professional and Managerial Staff in Finland, Akava
Alternativa	Slovene Union of Trade Unions Alternativa, Slovenska zveza sindikatov Alternativa
ASzSz	Autonomous Trade Union Confederation, Autonóm Szakszervezetek Szövetsége
BITC	Business in the Community
CCOO	Workers' Commissions; Comisiones Obreras
CEC	continental European capitalism
CEO	chief executive officer
CEOE	Spanish Confederation of Employers' Organizations, Confederación Española de Organizaciones Empresariales
CEPYME	Spanish Confederation of Small and Medium-Sized Companies, Confederación Española de la Pequeña y Mediana Empresa.
CERSE	National Council for Corporate Social Responsibility, Consejo Estatal de Responsabilidad Social de las Empresas
CFDT	French Democratic Confederation of Labour, Confédération Française Démocratique du Travail
CFE-CGC	French Confederation of Managers – General Confederation of Executives, Confédération Française de l'Encadrement – Confédération Générale des Cadres

CFTC	French Confederation of Christian Workers, Confédération Française des Travailleurs Chrétiens
CGB	Christian Trade Union Federation of Germany, Christlicher Gewerkschaftsbund Deutschland
CGT	General Confederation of Labour, Confederación General del Trabajo [Spain]
CGT	General Confederation of Labour, Confédération Générale du Travail [France]
CGT-FO	General Confederation of Labour – Workers' Force, Confédération Générale du Travail – Force Ouvrière
CIG	National Union of Galicia, Confederación Intersindical Galega
CME	co-ordinated market economy
CSI-CSIF	Central Independent Union of Public Sector Employees, Central Sindical Independiente y de Funcionarios
CSR	corporate social responsibility
DBB	German Civil Service Federation, Deutscher Beamtenbund
DFID	Department for International Development (UK)
DGB	Confederation of German Trade Unions, Deutscher Gewerkschaftsbund
DIRSE	Spanish Association of Social Responsibility Managers, Asociación Española de Directivos de Responsabilidad Social
DME	dependent market economy
EF	Forum of Experts on Corporate Social Responsibility, Foro de Expertos sobre la Responsabilidad Social Empresarial
ÉFÉDOSzSz	Union of Workers in the Building Materials Industry, Az Építö, Fa, és Építöanyagipari Dolgozók Szakszervezeteinek Szövetsége
EIRIS	Ethical Investment Research and Information Service
ELA-STV	Basque Workers' Solidarity, Eusko Langileen Alkartasuna-Solidaridad de los Trabajadores Vascos
EMU	European Monetary Union
EPSU	European Federation of Public Service Unions
ESF	European Social Fund
ESS	Economic and Social Council, Ekonomsko-socialni svet
ÉSzT	Confederation of Trade Unions for Professionals, Értelmiségi Szakszervezeti Tömörülés
ETI	Ethical Trading Initiative
ETUC	European Trade Union Confederation
ETUI	European Trade Union Institute
EU	European Union
Eurocadres	Council of European Professional and Managerial Staff
EWC	European Works Council
FCRSE	Citizens' Forum on Corporate Social Responsibility, Forum Citoyen pour la Responsabilité Sociale des Entreprises

FDI	foreign direct investment
FETICO	Federation of Independent Commerce Sector Workers, Federación de Trabajadores Independientes de Comercio
FNE	Natural Environment France, France Nature Environnement
FNV	Dutch Labour Movement Federation, Federatie Nederlandse Vakbeweging
FOB	Responsible Business Forum, Forum Odpowiedzialnego Biznesu.
FRDO-CFDD	Federal Council for Sustainable Development, Federale Raad voor Duurzame Ontwikkeling, Conseil Fédéral du Développement Durable
FSU	Unitary Union Federation, Fédération Syndicale Unitaire
FZZ	Trade Unions Forum, Forum Związków Zawodowych
FZZPOZiPS	Federation of Healthcare and Social Care Employee Unions, Federacja Związków Zawodowych Pracowników Ochrony Zdrowia i Pomocy Społecznej
GDP	gross domestic product
GFA	global framework agreement
GMB	large general union in the UK
GNP	gross national product
GRI	Global Reporting Initiative
GUF	Global Union Federation
ICT	information and communications technology
ICTWS	Institutional Characteristics of Trade Unions, Wage Setting and Social Pacts
ICTWSS	Institutional Characteristics of Trade Unions, Wage Setting, State Intervention and Social Pacts
IF Metall	Industrial and Metalworkers' Union, Industrifacket Metall
IFA	International Framework Agreement
IG BCE	Mining, Chemical and Energy Workers' Union, Industriegewerkschaft Bergbau, Chemie, Energie
IG Metall	Metalworkers' Union, Industriegewerkschaft Metall
ILO	International Labour Organization
INE	National Institute of Statistics, Instituto Nacional de Estadística
IRDO	Institute for the Development of Social Responsibility, Inštitut za razvoj družbene odgovornosti
ISO	International Organization for Standardization
IUF	International Union of Food Workers
JEREMIE	Joint European Resources for Micro to Medium Enterprises
JHL	Trade Union for the Public and Welfare Sectors, Julkisten ja hyvinvointialojen liitto
KNG	Chemical, Non-metal and Rubber Industries Trade Union of Slovenia – Sindikat kemične, nekovinske in gumarske industrije Slovenije

KNSS	Confederation of New Trade Unions of Slovenia, Konfederacija novih sindikatov Slovenije
KÖVET	Hungarian Association of Environmentally Aware Management, Egyesület a Fenntartható Gazdálkodásért
KP	Confederation of Labour, Konfederacja Pracy
KS-90	Trade Union Confederation 90 of Slovenia, Konfederacija sindikatov 90 Slovenije
KSJS	Confederation of Public Sector Trade Unions, Konfederacija sindikatov javnega sektorja
LAB	Nationalist Workers Commissions, Langilen Abertzaleen Batzordeak
LCPDPSF	Lithuanian Chemical Industry Workers' Trade Union Federation, Lietuvos chemijos pramonės darbuotojų profesinių sąjungų federacija
LDF	Lithuanian Labour Federation, Lietuvos darbo federacija
LEDPSF	Lithuanian Federation of Energy and Electrical Workers' Trade Unions, Lietuvos energetikos darbuotojų profesinių sąjungų federacija
LIGA	Democratic Confederation of Free Trade Unions, LIGA
LME	liberal market economy
LMP	Lithuanian Food Industry Trade Union, Lietuvos maistininkų profesinė sąjunga
LO	Swedish Trade Union Confederation, Landsorganisationen i Sverige
LPSDPS	Lithuanian Trade Union of the Workers in Service Field, Lietuvos paslaugų sferos darbuotojų profesinė sąjunga
LPSK	Lithuanian Trade Union Confederation, Lietuvos profesinių sąjungų konfederacija
LSE	Law for a Sustainable Economy, Ley de Economía Sostenible
MDOS	Network for Corporate Social Responsibility Slovenia, Mreža za družbeno odgovornost Slovenije
MME	mixed market economy
MNC	multi-national company
MOSz	National Council of Trade Unions, Szakszervezetek Orszagos Tanacsa
MPF	Lithuanian Federation of Forest and Forest Industry Workers' Trade Unions, Lietuvos miško ir miško pramonės darbuotojų profesinių sąjungų federacija
MSzOSz	National Confederation of Hungarian Trade Unions, Magyar Szakszervezetek Országos Szövetsége
MSzP	Hungarian Socialist Party, Magyar Szocialista Párt
NAVĮT	National Network of Responsible Enterprises, Nacionalinis atsakingo verslo įmonių tinklas
NBS	national business system
NGO	non-governmental organization

NGTT	National Economic and Social Council, Nemzeti Gazdasági és Társadalmi Tanács
NSZZ Solidarność	Independent Self-Governing Trade Union 'Solidarity', Niezależny Samorządny Związek Zawodowy 'Solidarność'
OECD	Organization for Economic Co-operation and Development
OÉT	National Interest Reconciliation Council, Országos Érdekegyeztető Tanács
OPZZ	All-Poland Alliance of Trade Unions, Ogólnopolskie Porozumienie Związków Zawodowych
ORSE	Observatory on Corporate Social Responsibility, Observatoire de la Responsabilité Sociétale des Entreprises
PCE	Communist Party of Spain, Partido Comunista de España
PERGAM	Confederation of Trade Unions PERGAM, Konfederacija sindikatov PERGAM
PKPP	Polish Confederation of Private Employers 'Lewiatan', Polska Konfederacja Pracodawców Prywatnych 'Lewiatan'
PP	Popular Party, Partido Popular
PSOE	Spanish Socialist Workers' Party, Partido Socialista Obrero Español
R&D	research and development
SACO	Swedish Confederation of Professional Associations, Sveriges akademikers centralorganisation
SAK	Central Organisation of Finnish Trade Unions, Suomen Ammattiliittojen Keskusjärjestö
SASK	Trade Union Solidarity Centre of Finland, Suomen Ammattiliittojen Solidaarisuuskeskus
SDGD	Trade Union of Construction Industry Workers of Slovenia, Sindikat delavcev gradbenih dejavnosti Slovenije
SDPZ	Union of Transportation and Telecommunication Workers of Slovenia, Sindikat delavcev prometa in zvez Slovenije
SDT	Social Dialogue Round Table, Mesa de diálogo social
SEKO	Swedish Union for Service and Communication Employees, Facket för service och kommunikation
SEPLA	Spanish Union of Airline Pilots, Sindicato Español de Pilotos de Líneas Aéreas
SERV	Social and Economic Council of Flanders, Sociaal-Economische Raad van Vlaanderen
SKEI	Trade Union of the Metal and Electrical Industry of Slovenia, Sindikat kovinske in elektro industrije Slovenije
SME	small and medium-sized enterprise

Solidarnost	Union of Workers' Solidarity Confederation, Zveza delavcev Solidarnost
SRI	socially responsible investment
STTK	Finnish Confederation of Professionals, Toimihenkilökeskusjärjestö
SZEF	Forum for the Co-operation of Trade Unions, A Szakszervezetek Együttműködési Fóruma
TCO	Swedish Confederation of Professional Employees, Tjänstemännens Centralorganisation
TEK	Academic Engineers and Architects in Finland, Tekniikan Akateemiset
TUAC	Trade Union Advisory Committee
TUC	Trades Union Congress (UK)
TUSO	Trade Union Share Owners (UK)
UGT	General Union of Workers, Unión General de Trabajadores
UK	United Kingdom
UN	United Nations
UNCTAD	United Nations Conference on Trade and Development
UNDP	United Nations Development Programme
UNIZO	Union of Self-Employed Entrepreneurs, Unie van Zelfstandige Ondernemers
UNSA	National Union of Autonomous Unions, Union Nationale des Syndicats Autonomes
US(A)	United States (of America)
USO	Federation of Workers' Unions, Unión Sindical Obrera
USS	an association of unaffiliated French unions, Union Syndicale Solidaires
UT	trade union of the company 'Utenos trikotažas', AB 'Utenos trikotažas' profesinė sąjunga
UWE	Walloon Union of Companies, Union Wallonne des Entreprises
VASAS	Hungarian Union of Iron Workers, Vas-és Fémmunkások
Ver.di	Confederation of Service Sector Unions, Vereinigte Dienstleistungsgewerkschaft
VoC	varieties of capitalism
ZNP	Polish Teachers' Union, Związek Nauczycielstwa Polskiego
ZRP	Polish Crafts Union, Związek Rzemiosła Polskiego
ZSSS	Association of Free Trade Unions of Slovenia, Zveza svobodnih sindikatov Slovenije
ZZG	Trade Union of Miners in Poland, Związek Zawodowy Górników w Polsce
ZZMK	Trade Union of Locomotive Drivers in Poland, Związek Zawodowy Maszynistów Kolejowych w Polsce

1 The rise of corporate social responsibility as a challenge for trade unions

Lutz Preuss, Michael Gold and Chris Rees

Introduction

Corporate social responsibility (CSR) is a concept that has been adopted extensively by societal actors in business, public policy and non-governmental organizations (NGOs). CSR has diffused to all corners of the globe over the past decades, far beyond its origins in the United States (Visser and Tolhurst 2010). This trend is illustrated in part by the emergence of CSR-related institutions at the transnational level, such as the United Nations Global Compact, CSR guidance document ISO 26000 from the International Standards Organization and the sustainability reporting framework from the Global Reporting Initiative (GRI) (Leipziger 2010). Additionally, the global financial crisis has brought the issue of the legitimacy of corporate power into sharp relief (Werhane *et al.* 2011), making private corporate responsibility a core matter of public concern (Brammer *et al.* 2012).

In the wake of such developments, renewed attention has been devoted to the relationship between business and its key stakeholders, whether these are NGOs (Seitanidi and Crane 2009) or local communities (Bowen *et al.* 2010). Curiously, however, one societal actor is frequently absent in such discussions, namely trade unions. Such an omission is remarkable for two reasons. First, as the role of unions has traditionally been to defend the interests of the employee stakeholder, they should be part of the discussion of business–stakeholder relations. This is particularly important at a time when labour is affected by an increase in competition over international labour costs that in many industrialized nations has led to significant employment losses. Second, unlike trade unions, NGOs often do not have elected officials and do not necessarily consult their membership when they draw up their policies (Nye 2001). For this reason, many NGOs, although more often invited to participate in CSR discourse, appear to be less democratic than trade unions. The time is thus ripe to examine in greater detail what trade unions make of the rise of CSR.

We examine this question across 11 European countries, namely Belgium, Finland, France, Germany, Hungary, Lithuania, Poland,

Slovenia, Spain, Sweden and the United Kingdom. Our approach draws loosely upon the 'national business systems' and 'varieties of capitalism' literatures, which highlight national variation in the way key institutions – such as the state, the legal system and the industrial relations system – combine to embed social and economic structures and norms within particular 'national logics' (Hollingsworth and Boyer 1997; Whitley 1999; Hanké *et al.* 2007). While not seeking to make an explicit theoretical contribution to this literature, our book aims to examine the nature of CSR, and trade union responses to it, through a broadly comparative institutionalist lens.

The rise of CSR

The rise of CSR is the result of several societal trends that have come together in the last few decades. With regard to changes in the political arena, many governments in industrialized nations have experienced a relative erosion of their powers, not least their ability to control multinational companies (MNCs) (Vogel 2010). This has been accompanied by important changes in civil society. There is a growing awareness in many countries of environmental problems and persisting social inequalities, coupled with new opportunities to address such concerns in ways that go beyond traditional party politics (Beck 2000). A crucial change in the economic sphere is the increasing mobility of corporations and the enhanced significance of financial markets for corporate success (Froud *et al.* 2006). Magnified by media scrutiny and advances in information technology, these pressures have led to an expectation that business should – in addition to benefiting from novel opportunities in the wake of globalization – assume a more beneficial social role.

CSR has been defined as 'the responsibility of enterprises for their impacts on society', which requires companies to 'have in place a process to integrate social, environmental, ethical, human rights and consumer concerns into their business operations and core strategy in close collaboration with their stakeholders' (European Commission 2011: 6). In turn, a stakeholder in an organization is 'any group or individual who can affect, or is affected by, the achievement of the organization's objectives' (Freeman 1984: 46). Less formulaic conceptualizations of CSR have been offered by authors like Carroll (1991), whose 'pyramid of CSR' starts with a company's economic responsibilities, after which it should meet its legal responsibilities as well as ethical responsibilities, and finally engage in philanthropic activities. Business in the Community, a London-based CSR organization, suggests five material areas of CSR, namely: workforce, environment, marketplace, community and human rights (BITC 2000). While these conceptualizations of CSR give frequent attention to employees, trade unions are only occasionally explicitly recognized as stakeholders (e.g. Clarkson 1995; Basu and Palazzo 2008).

The reasons commonly advanced as to why companies should engage in CSR fall into three broad categories. Prominent among these is the 'business case for CSR', according to which investment in social and environmental initiatives leads to financial benefits for the firm in terms of stronger consumer loyalty, higher employee satisfaction, enhanced brand reputation, preferential access to input markets or a better standing with regulators (Carroll and Shabana 2010; Porter and Kramer 2006). However, empirical studies into the link between corporate social and financial performance have so far proved inconclusive (Orlitzky *et al.* 2003; Peloza 2009). Another category of arguments is more normative. With a starting position in moral philosophy, these argue that businesses should take account of CSR as it is 'the right thing to do' (Hartman *et al.* 2007: 374). Yet this perspective has been less able to offer concrete advice on how companies should manage these responsibilities. Finally, there are sociological accounts which centre around the notion of a 'licence to operate', the idea that business needs tacit or even explicit permission from society to operate, and that this licence can be revoked if a firm were found wanting in terms of its social or environmental performance (van Marrewijk 2003; Lynch-Wood and Williamson 2007).

As a form of private regulation, CSR has led to the evolution of a wide range of instruments (Leipziger 2010). At the voluntary end of this range, many companies have adopted codes of conduct to manage employee behaviour or stakeholder engagement. As one of the most widespread CSR tools, codes of conduct have been adopted by 92 per cent of the largest 250 companies worldwide (KPMG 2008). Beyond the level of the individual company, codes are also promoted by a number of business interest groups, such as the Caux Principles adopted by the Caux Roundtable, a group of senior business leaders from North American, European and Japanese companies (Barkemeyer *et al.* 2014). CSR has also led to the emergence of a sizeable support industry. Key players here are the International Standards Organization (ISO), which has produced tools like the environmental management standard ISO 14001 and the CSR guidance document ISO 26000, and the Global Reporting Initiative (GRI), which developed guidelines for social and environmental reporting to make CSR performance comparable between firms and over time (Leipziger 2010). Corporate take-up of these tools is again voluntary, although adherence to them can be certified by external parties. Meanwhile, the United Nations adopted the UN Global Compact, consisting of 10 principles of responsible business practice. Other UN initiatives with a focus on business are the Guiding Principles on Business and Human Rights and the Principles for Responsible Investment.

At the more mandatory end of the range of CSR initiatives, a number of national governments have engaged in measures to shape the emerging CSR debate. Governments can play various roles in CSR, from requiring minimum standards for business performance, through facilitating collaboration between the public sector, the private sector and civil society, to endorsing best practice examples (Fox *et al.* 2002). For example, dialogue between the governments of the US and the UK, companies in the extractive and energy sectors as well as NGOs led to the Voluntary Principles on Security and Human Rights. Such efforts are complemented at the supranational level. Here, the European Commission has published a range of official documents on CSR, starting with the green paper *Promoting a European Framework for Corporate Social Responsibility* (Commission of the European Communities 2001). In later documents, such as the Communication *Implementing the Partnership for Growth and Jobs: Making Europe a Pole of Excellence on Corporate Social Responsibility* (Commission of the European Communities 2006) and *A Renewed EU Strategy 2011–14 for Corporate Social Responsibility* (European Commission 2011), the Commission has sought to present CSR as part of a set of initiatives to stimulate growth and employment within the EU. The Organization for Economic Co-operation and Development (OECD) has produced Guidelines for Multinational Enterprises, which cover a range of CSR issues, such as human rights, employment conditions, environmental protection, consumer interests and taxation. The International Labour Organization (ILO) has adopted several hundred conventions and recommendations covering a broad spectrum of labour-related subjects in addition to its Tripartite Declaration of Principles on Multinational Enterprises and Social Policy. Being supra-national organizations, the European Commission, the OECD and the ILO first and foremost address the national governments of their member countries, which are expected to translate the various initiatives into national law. Beyond this, however, their stipulations are increasingly being taken up by companies, not least in their codes of conduct (Preuss 2010).

Situated between voluntary and mandatory initiatives, CSR also entails a wide range of more or less binding commitments. Of particular interest here are International Framework Agreements (IFAs), also called Global Framework Agreements (GFAs), between companies and trade unions, usually between multinational corporations and international union federations. Early examples of such agreements were concluded between French food manufacturer Danone and the International Union of Food Workers (IUF) in the early 1990s. Such agreements are voluntary for companies to enter but, once concluded, contain binding clauses regarding corporate adherence to international labour standards across all the company's sites (ETUC 2013; Hammer 2005). IFAs thus address some of the shortcomings of purely voluntary CSR tools, such as codes of conduct, in terms of enabling monitoring and providing accountability (Pearson and Seyfang 2001).

The trade union movement has not remained aloof from these developments. In 2002, Eurocadres, the Council of European Professional and Managerial Staff, initiated a project on 'Responsible European Management' to collect examples of best practice on CSR for use by its members and wider audiences. The project 'systematically bridges the old social models and the new ones' (Eurocadres 2006: 5). Somewhat less sanguinely, the European Trade Union Confederation (ETUC) published a report entitled *European Trade Unions and Corporate Social Responsibility* in 2004. It concluded that, while many unions admitted to a lack of knowledge of the concept, overall 'European trade union organisations are still extremely cautious when it comes to talking about ... CSR' (ETUC 2004: 6). The main reason for this reserved attitude was that CSR was seen as privatization of the law, which can reduce the role played by the social partners. An updated mapping exercise of ETUC member unions in 2013 found that the 'concept has become a "reality" ... that must be incorporated and appropriated [and that] can, under certain conditions, have positive "effects" on society' (ETUC 2013: 5). Under the auspices of the European Trade Union Institute (ETUI), a group of academics and trade unionists have recently advanced the concept of the 'sustainable company', a company 'that would be economically successful, that would care for social interests inside and outside of the company, that would respect worker rights and that would be environmentally friendly' (Vitols and Kluge 2011: 10).

Thus CSR has had a somewhat curious evolution. On the one hand, it has become a global phenomenon which is not only practised by businesses from all continents but is also promoted by national governments, intergovernmental organizations and civil society organizations (Visser and Tolhurst 2010). On the other hand, it has remained an ambiguous concept that is open to a multitude of interpretations (Rowley and Berman 2000; Windsor, 2006). Here, references to societal expectations or to mandatory responsibilities have led to the earlier grounding of CSR in the voluntary behaviour of companies (McWilliams and Siegel 2001) increasingly being questioned as 'a rather limited approach to understanding the social responsibilities of business' (Brammer *et al.* 2012: 5). Hence, a number of scholars are now calling for more integrated studies of the interface between business and society (Crouch 2006; Aguilera and Jackson 2010).

Trade unions and CSR

Given the global rise to prominence of CSR, what has been said about trade union positions on this topic? Some unions have evidently been sceptical that CSR can deliver what it promises (Preuss *et al.* 2006; Salzmann and Prinzhorn 2006; Segal *et al.* 2003). For example, ETUC (2011: 3) expressed concern that CSR may be 'just the proverbial good tree that hides a forest of bad practices. It is not enough to "invite" companies to act responsibly; more concrete/binding measures are needed.' Unions are particularly critical of the voluntary nature of CSR. For example, the Dutch union FNV argues: 'The voluntary character of guidelines and definitions – good as they may be – is simply not good enough. Ecologically speaking, businesses very often have a clear self-interest. For social aspects, in many cases this interest is scarcely present' (quoted in ETUC 2013: 31). Unions have thus emphasized the importance of tools that allow the verification of CSR claims, such as CSR labels, mandatory information and auditing (Nordestgaard and Kirton-Darling 2004; Preuss *et al.* 2006).

Moving beyond scepticism, other unions have opted for a limited engagement with the concept, where they try to align CSR with the traditional aims of the union movement (Preuss *et al.* 2006). Although noting limitations arising from the voluntary nature of CSR commitments, the European Federation of Public Service Unions (EPSU) 'encourages unions and EWCs [European works councils] to put CSR on the agenda of meetings with companies' (EPSU no date). Similarly, the British union GMB demanded some time ago that CSR 'must be based on the development of quality employment, with the ongoing development of workers' skills and qualifications through training and lifelong learning' (2001: 1). ETUC has more recently noted that 'the practice [of CSR] has become more widespread with several member unions having taken ownership of the topic and others having built on their expertise and broadened the scope of their activities' (ETUC 2013: 41).

Finally, there are unions that have embraced CSR in a broader sense, i.e. by supporting CSR aspects that go beyond the immediate interests of their members. Trade unions have thus addressed social and environmental challenges through being vocal about the negative social consequences of technological development or through giving a voice to social concerns that counter market values (Dewey 1998). An example here is the Ethical Trading Initiative (ETI), a collaboration between major UK-based retailers, NGOs and trade unions, which has also been endorsed and financially supported by the UK Department for International Development (Williams 2009). Among other measures, the ETI adopted a Base Code, a set of clauses for labour conditions in international supply chains, which all member companies must adopt (Preuss 2009). Established in 1997, the ETI has grown to become 'one of the most prominent multi-stakeholder organisations in Europe' (Hughes 2001: 422).

National varieties of CSR

Our starting point for mapping varying trade union approaches to CSR is the national business systems and varieties of capitalism literatures (Whitley 1999; Hollingsworth and Boyer 1997; Hall and Soskice 2001; Hanké *et al.* 2007). Whitley (1999: 33) defines national business systems as 'distinctive patterns of economic organization that vary in their degree and mode of authoritative co-ordination of economic activities, and in the organization, and interconnections between owners, managers, experts, and other employees'. He distils a number of key features that differentiate national business systems from each other, such as the scope for autonomy that managers have from owners, the amount of co-ordination that takes place between firms and sectors, and the degree of interdependence and trust that exists between employers and employees. On this basis, he distinguishes, with reference to Europe, between a compartmentalized business system, like that of the UK, a collaborative business system, such as in Germany, and a co-ordinated industrial district, as found in northern Italy.

In terms of the varieties of capitalism strand of the literature, Hall and Soskice (2001) similarly compare a liberal market economy, such as the UK, with a co-ordinated market economy, like Germany. Hanké *et al.* (2007) expanded this typology to cover a state-controlled economy, such as post-war France, and a compensating state, like Italy or Spain (see also Hollingsworth and Boyer 1997, for a comparable typology). Since the political and economic transition in eastern Europe, these literatures have expanded from their initial focus on western Europe to cover these countries too. For example, King (2007) refers to the much greater reliance on foreign investors in eastern European countries like Hungary and Poland to characterize these countries as 'liberal dependent post-Communist capitalism'.

Central to all these models is the idea that a nation's comparative economic advantage is shaped by the degree to which its key institutions complement each other. In a liberal market economy, for example, fluid labour markets, easy access to stock market capital, arm's length competitive relations and supply-and-demand price signalling complement each other to create optimum conditions for radically innovative firms (Hall and Soskice 2001). However, these ideas have also been criticized on a number of accounts. Not least, they are said to be too static, focusing on path dependencies at the national system level and thereby downplaying conflict between societal actors as well as variation within nations. Perhaps most significantly, there is concern with the tendency to portray firms as passive, that is, as merely 'takers' of institutions rather than as autonomous agents who also 'make' institutions (Crouch 2005). This literature has also been criticized for failing to give sufficient attention to the forces of convergence that result from globalization (Panitch and Gindin 2003).

We combine a broadly national business systems/varieties of capitalism approach with an institutionalist one. Institutional theory seeks cognitive and cultural, rather than economic or efficiency-driven, explanations of social and organizational phenomena (DiMaggio and Powell 1983). It is concerned with the processes through which institutions – defined as 'humanly devised constraints that structure human interaction' (North 1994: 360) – are shaped through regulative, normative and cultural-cognitive processes (Scott 2008), so that they 'become taken for granted by members of a social group as efficacious and necessary; thus [serving] as an important causal source of stable patterns of behavior' (Tolbert and Zucker 1996: 179).

Rather than seeking to advance theory in these areas, our book draws on these concepts in order to provide a broad picture of the nature of CSR across 11 European countries, indicating how CSR might reflect distinctive economic patterns and historical developments. This comparative institutionalist approach helps to examine how the boundaries between business and society are constructed in different ways in different national settings (Brammer *et al.* 2012). We thus seek to contribute to an emergent body of literature which applies institutional theory to the study of CSR in a cross-national comparative fashion (e.g. Gjølberg 2009; Jackson and Apostolakou 2010). In a key contribution to this literature, Matten and Moon (2008) argue that, unlike the explicit forms of CSR found in liberal market economies, CSR in co-ordinated market economies, where the social responsibilities of business are more strongly defined by law or are subject to binding negotiations with labour unions, is likely to be more implicit within institutional settings. Such 'implicit' CSR can take a variety of forms, whether it is German CEOs emphasizing the societal value of manufacturing or South Korean ones defining CSR in terms of its contribution to national development (Witt and Redding 2012). Given the contested nature of CSR – not least entailing 'a paradox between a liberal notion of voluntary engagement and a contrary implication of socially binding responsibilities' (Brammer *et al.* 2012: 10) – it remains unclear how stakeholder pressure on corporations to maintain their legitimacy plays out in different national settings.

The comparative institutionalist perspective has furthermore been applied to the embryonic literature on trade union engagement with CSR. In the US context, it has been argued that structural features of the political and industrial relations systems have encouraged a narrow union agenda that focuses on material gains for union members as opposed to wider societal challenges (Obach 2004). Across Europe, national differences in union attempts to define CSR have been identified. Reflecting a relatively secure power base in the country's corporatist system, the German trade union confederation DGB (Deutscher Gewerkschaftsbund), for example, put forward a rather instrumental position on CSR when it argued: 'A structured dialogue between companies and other "stakeholders" will only come into existence when socially responsible action becomes relevant for the economic performance of companies and in particular for the profit expectations of their shareholders' (DGB, 2001: 11).

Whilst there is undoubtedly a developing literature on union responses to the rise of CSR, much of it is either based on secondary data, chiefly analyses of union documents (e.g. Preuss *et al.* 2006; Preuss 2008), or, where it includes primary data, covers either individual countries (e.g. Burchell and Cook 2006) or only a small selection of countries (e.g. France, Germany and the UK in Delbard 2011). What is lacking is a comprehensive study that goes beyond individual or small numbers of countries. As a step in this direction, this book adopts a pan-European perspective and covers 11 European countries. In particular, its individual chapters seek to describe differing national patterns of trade union engagement with CSR and thus to more clearly illuminate the varying ways in which CSR is both related to and embedded within broader institutional arrangements.

Methodology

As there is a relative scarcity of research into trade union engagement with CSR, the contributions in this book utilize the case study research methodology (Eisenhardt 1989; Yin 2014). Using such an exploratory approach, the book aims to examine the question of what conditions seem to lead unions to adopt which approach to CSR. Case organizations were selected through theoretical replication as they reflect key characteristics of national business systems as identified in the literature review (Yin 2014). Following the comparative institutionalist literature, we selected the following 11 countries:

- the United Kingdom – a liberal market economy
- Germany – a co-ordinated market economy
- France – a state-led market economy
- Belgium – one of the smaller western European countries
- Sweden and Finland – Nordic economies
- Spain – a southern European economy
- Hungary, Poland, Lithuania and Slovenia – eastern European transition economies.

Within each country, national trade union confederations and sector level unions were approached. Different sectors display very different trajectories in global capitalism in terms of domestic versus global markets, quality product versus low-wage competition, as well as value creation in Europe versus outsourcing (Quack *et al.* 2000). In line with the varieties of capitalism approach, we would expect such national and sectoral differences to lead to differences in union engagement with CSR.

The data for the study were collected through semi-structured interviews as well as complementary sources of evidence, like union documents. Where possible, interviews were conducted face-to-face, but in a minority of cases by telephone. They were undertaken by country teams composed of academic scholars working on the intersection of industrial relations and CSR. The teams were fully fluent in the respective local language and had a good insight into the topic before commencing their interviews. The data were collected between October 2011 and March 2013. In total, the researchers carried out 77 interviews with 76 respondents, lasting a total of 97 hours 45 minutes.

The schedule of interview questions utilized a funnel model (Voss *et al.* 2002). It started with broad and open-ended questions, like recent developments around CSR in the individual country, and proceeded to more detailed ones, such as where CSR expertise resides within a union or how its engagement with the concept has come about. The schedule was discussed by all the researchers and then translated into the local languages by the individual country teams. The data documentation and coding process entailed recording the interviews and transcribing their content shortly after the event. To reduce data into categories, the raw data as presented by the informants were coded manually according to the criteria of the conceptual framework. Once coding was completed for all interviews, the data were re-ordered in accordance with construct categories and then re-arranged in summary display. The analysis was undertaken first within and then between cases (Eisenhardt 1989). To strengthen the reliability of the data analysis process, all the teams involved in the project came together in a two-day workshop in May 2012 to discuss their respective findings. One of the key strengths of this book, therefore, is that it was planned in a harmonized way. Since all the chapters are based on the same interview schedule, the reader can easily compare and contrast findings between countries.

Conclusions

The question of how trade unions engage with the rise of CSR is clearly important, but remains under-researched. It is important for society, as it is concerned with a key impact of business on society. Since CSR seems to have become the internationally dominant approach to organizing business–society relations, it is pertinent to consider the extent to which the regulation of social and environmental externalities of economic activity – traditionally the remit of government – should, and can be, driven by various stakeholders, rather than being left to corporate initiative alone. The question of trade union engagement with CSR is furthermore important for employees, since it concerns collective choices regarding the 'best' way of protecting the interests of this key stakeholder. Not least, it is important for trade unions themselves. Here a 'certain paradox in union attitudes to CSR' has been identified (Segal *et al.* 2003: 18): although CSR concerns initiatives that have traditionally fallen, at least partly, into the remit of trade unions, the initiative to develop CSR has come more or less entirely from management, and there is thus a danger of unions being left out of the debate on the future of CSR.

It is against this backcloth that our book examines union attitudes towards CSR across Europe. Bringing together researchers from 11 European countries, the book offers a representative sample of national institutional contexts and industrial relations structures across the continent. Following this introduction, Chapters 2 to 12 present the empirical evidence from the individual countries. Here we distinguish three key areas: first, how trade unions *understand* CSR; second, what *policies* unions adopt towards CSR, particularly aspects covering employment relations;

and, third, how they *engage* with such policies, that is, what steps they take to ensure that such policies are implemented and enforced. Finally, Chapter 13 provides a summary of our key findings and offers some reflections on the major themes that have emerged from our study.

References

Aguilera, R.V. and Jackson, G. (2010) 'Comparative and international corporate governance', *Annals of the Academy of Management*, 4, 485–556.

Barkemeyer, R., Holt, D., Preuss, L. and Tsang, S. (2014) 'What happened to the development in "sustainable development"?', *Sustainable Development*, 22(1): 15–32.

Basu, K. and Palazzo, G. (2008) 'Corporate social responsibility: a process model of sensemaking', *Academy of Management Review*, 33(1): 122–136.

Beck, U. (2000) *What is Globalization?*, Cambridge: Polity Press.

BITC (2000) *Winning with Integrity: A Guide to Social Responsibility*, London: Business in the Community.

Bowen, F., Newenham-Kahindi, A. and Herremans, I. (2010) 'When suits meet roots: the antecedents and consequences of community engagement strategy', *Journal of Business Ethics*, 95(2): 297–318.

Brammer, S., Jackson, G. and Matten, D. (2012) 'Corporate social responsibility and institutional theory: new perspectives on private governance', *Socio-Economic Review*, 10(1): 3–28.

Brammer, S. and Pavelin, S. (2005) 'Corporate community contributions in the United Kingdom and the United States', *Journal of Business Ethics*, 56(1): 15–26.

Burchell, J. and Cook, J. (2006) 'It's good to talk? Examining attitudes towards corporate social responsibility dialogue and engagement processes', *Business Ethics: A European Review*, 15(2): 154–170.

Campbell, J.L. (2007) 'Why would corporations behave in socially responsible ways? An institutional theory of corporate social responsibility', *Academy of Management Review*, 32(3): 946–967.

Carroll, A.B. (1991) 'The pyramid of corporate social responsibility: toward the moral management of organizational stakeholders', *Business Horizons*, 34(4): 39–48.

Carroll, A.B. and Shabana, K.M. (2010) 'The business case for corporate social responsibility: a review of concepts, research and practice', *International Journal of Management Reviews*, 12(1): 85–105.

Clarkson, M.B.E. (1995) 'A stakeholder framework for analyzing and evaluating corporate social performance', *Academy of Management Review*, 20(1): 92–117.

Commission of the European Communities (2001) *Green Paper – Promoting a European Framework for Corporate Social Responsibility, COM(2001) 366 final*, Brussels: Commission of the European Communities.

Commission of the European Communities (2006) *Implementing the Partnership for Growth and Jobs: Making Europe a Pole of Excellence on Corporate Social Responsibility, COM(2006) 136 final*, Brussels: Commission of the European Communities.

Crouch, C. (2005) *Capitalist Diversity and Change: Recombinant Governance and Institutional Entrepreneurs*, Oxford: Oxford University Press.

Crouch, C. (2006) 'Modelling the firm in its market and organizational environment: methodologies for studying corporate social responsibility', *Organization Studies*, 27(10): 1533–1551.

Delbard, O. (2011) 'Social partners or full-fledged stakeholders? Trade unions and CSR in Europe (France, Germany and the UK)', *Society and Business Review*, 6(3): 260–277.

Dewey, S. (1998) 'Working for the environment: organized labor and the origins of environmentalism in the United States: 1948–1970', *Environmental History*, 3(1): 45–63.

DGB (2001) *DGB Stellungnahme zum Grünbuch der Europäischen Kommission 'Europäische Rahmenbedingungen für die soziale Verantwortung der Unternehmen'*, Düsseldorf: Deutscher Gewerkschaftsbund.

DiMaggio, P.J. and Powell, W.W. (1983) 'The iron cage revisited: institutional isomorphism and collective rationality in organizational fields', *American Sociological Review*, 48(2): 147–160.

Eisenhardt, K.M. (1989) 'Building theory from case study research', *Academy of Management Review*, 14(4): 532–550.

EPSU (no date) *CSR: More Than a Public Relations Exercise?*, Brussels: European Federation of Public Service Unions. www.epsu.org/a/122 [accessed 18 March 2014].

ETUC (2004) *European Trade Unions and Corporate Social Responsibility*, Brussels: European Trade Union Confederation.

ETUC (2011) *ETUC Resolution on a Renewed EU Strategy 2011–14 for Corporate Social Responsibility (CSR)*, Brussels: European Trade Union Confederation.

ETUC (2013) *Corporate Social Responsibility – Union Thinking on the EU Strategy 2011–2014 for Corporate Social Responsibility*, Brussels: European Trade Union Confederation.

Eurocadres (2006) *A Curriculum for Responsible European Management (REM)*, Brussels: Council of European Professional and Managerial Staff.

European Commission (2011) *A Renewed EU Strategy 2011–14 for Corporate Social Responsibility, COM(2011) 681 final*, Brussels: European Commission.

Fox, T., Ward, H. and Howard, B. (2002) *Public Sector Roles in Strengthening Corporate Social Responsibility: A Baseline Study*, Washington, DC: World Bank.

Freeman, R.E. (1984) *Strategic Management: A Stakeholder Approach*, Boston: Pitman.

Froud, J., Johal, S., Leaver, A. and Williams, K. (2006) *Financialization and Strategy: Narrative and Numbers*, London: Routledge.

Gjølberg, M. (2009) 'The origin of corporate social responsibility: global forces or national legacies', *Socio-Economic Review*, 7(4): 605–637.

GMB (2001) *Responding to the EU Commission Green Paper*, London: GMB.

Hall, P. and Soskice, D. (2001) *Varieties of Capitalism: The Institutional Foundations of Comparative Analysis*, Oxford: Oxford University Press.

Hammer, N. (2005) 'International framework agreements: global industrial relations between rights and bargaining', *Transfer: European Review of Labour and Research*, 11(4): 511–530.

Hanké, B., Rhodes, M. and Thatcher, M. (2007) 'Introduction: beyond varieties of capitalism', in B. Hanké, M. Rhodes and M. Thatcher (eds) *Beyond Varieties of Capitalism: Conflict, Contradictions and Complementarities in the European Economy*, Oxford: Oxford University Press.

Hartman, L.P., Rubin, R.S. and Dhanda, K.K. (2007) 'The communication of corporate social responsibility: United States and European Union multinational corporations, *Journal of Business Ethics*, 74(4): 373–389.

Hollingsworth, J.R. and Boyer, R. (1997) 'Coordination of economic actors and social systems of production', in J.R. Hollingsworth and R. Boyer (eds) *Contemporary Capitalism: The Embeddedness of Institutions*, Cambridge: Cambridge University Press.

Hughes, A. (2001) 'Multi-stakeholder approaches to ethical trade: towards a reorganisation of UK retailers' global supply chains?', *Journal of Economic Geography*, 1(4): 421–437.

Jackson, G. and Apostolakou, A. (2010) 'Corporate social responsibility in Western Europe: an institutional mirror or substitute?', *Journal of Business Ethics*, 94(3): 371–394.

King, L.P. (2007) 'Central European capitalism in comparative perspective', in B. Hanké, M. Rhodes and M. Thatcher (eds) *Beyond Varieties of Capitalism: Conflict, Contradictions and Complementarities in the European Economy*, Oxford: Oxford University Press.

KPMG (2008) *KPMG International Survey of Corporate Responsibility Reporting 2008*, Amstelveen, NL: KPMG International.

Leipziger, D. (2010) *The Corporate Responsibility Code Book*, 2nd edn, Sheffield: Greenleaf Publishing.

Lynch-Wood, G. and Williamson, D. (2007) 'The social licence as a form of regulation for small and medium enterprises', *Journal of Law and Society*, 34(3): 321–341.

Matten, D. and Moon, J. (2008) '"Implicit" and "explicit" CSR: a conceptual framework for a comparative understanding of corporate social responsibility', *Academy of Management Review*, 33(2): 404–424.

McWilliams, A. and Siegel, D. (2001) 'Corporate social responsibility: a theory of the firm perspective', *Academy of Management Review*, 26(1): 117–127.

Nordestgaard, M. and Kirton-Darling, J. (2004) 'Corporate social responsibility within the European sectoral social dialogue', *Transfer: European Review of Labour and Research*, 10(3): 433–451.

North, D.C. (1994) 'Economic performance through time', *American Economic Review*, 84(3): 359–368.

Nye, J.S. (2001) 'Globalization's democratic deficit: how to make international institutions more accountable', *Foreign Affairs*, 80(4): 2–6.

Obach, B.K. (2004) 'New labor: slowing the treadmill of production?', *Organization and Environment*, 17(3): 337–354.

Orlitzky, M., Schmidt, F.L. and Rynes, S.L. (2003) 'Corporate social and financial performance: a meta-analysis', *Organization Studies*, 24(3): 403–441.

Panitch, L. and Gindin, S. (2003) 'American imperialism and EuroCapitalism: the making of neoliberal globalization', *Studies in Political Economy*, 71/72: 7–38.

Pearson, R. and Seyfang, G. (2001) 'New hope or false dawn? Voluntary codes of conduct, labour regulation and social policy in a globalizing world', *Global Social Policy*, 1(1): 49–78.

Peloza, J. (2009) 'The challenge of measuring financial impacts from investments in corporate social performance, *Journal of Management*, 35(6): 1518–1541.

Porter, M.E. and Kramer, M.R. (2006) 'Strategy and society: the link between competitive advantage and corporate social responsibility', *Harvard Business Review*, 84(12): 78–92.

Preuss, L. (2008) 'A reluctant stakeholder? On the perception of CSR among European trade unions', *Business Ethics: A European Review*, 17(2): 149–160.

Preuss, L. (2009) 'Ethical sourcing codes of large UK-based corporations: prevalence, content, limitations', *Journal of Business Ethics*, 88(4): 735–747.

Preuss, L. (2010) 'Codes of conduct in organisational context: from cascade to lattice-work of codes', *Journal of Business Ethics*, 94(4): 471–487.

Preuss, L., Haunschild, A. and Matten, D. (2006) 'Trade unions and CSR: a European research agenda', *Journal of Public Affairs*, 6(3/4): 256–268.

Preuss, L., Haunschild, A. and Matten, D. (2009) 'The rise of CSR: implications for HRM and employee representation', *International Journal of Human Resource Management*, 20(4): 975–995.

Quack, S., Morgan, G. and Whitley, R. (2000) *National Capitalisms, Global Competition, and Economic Performance*, Amsterdam: John Benjamins Publishing.

Rowley, T. and Berman, S. (2000) 'A brand new brand of corporate social performance', *Business and Society*, 39(4): 397–418.

Salzmann, O. and Prinzhorn, J. (2006) 'Unions: on the backseat of corporate sustainability', in U. Steger (ed.) *Inside the Mind of the Stakeholder: The Hype behind Stakeholder Pressure*, Basingstoke: Palgrave.

Scott, W.R. (2008) *Institutions and Organizations: Ideas and Interests*, Thousand Oaks, CA: Sage.

Segal, J.P., Sobczak, A. and Triomphe, C.A. (2003) *Corporate Social Responsibility and Working Conditions*, Dublin: European Foundation for the Improvement of Living and Working Conditions.

Seitanidi, M.M. and Crane, A. (2009) 'Implementing CSR through partnerships: understanding the selection, design and institutionalisation of nonprofit-business partnerships', *Journal of Business Ethics*, 85(S2): 413–429.

Tolbert, P.S. and Zucker, L.G. (1996) 'The institutionalization of institutional theory', in S.R. Clegg, C. Hardy and W.R. Nord (eds) *Handbook of Organization Studies*, London: Sage.

van Marrewijk, M. (2003) 'Concepts and definitions of CSR and corporate sustainability: between agency and communion', *Journal of Business Ethics*, 44(2/3): 95–105.

Visser, W. and Tolhurst, N. (2010) *The World Guide to CSR: A Country-by-Country Analysis of Corporate Sustainability and Responsibility*, Sheffield: Greenleaf.

Vitols, S. and Kluge, N. (eds) (2011) *The Sustainable Company: A New Approach to Corporate Governance*, Brussels: European Trade Union Institute.

Vogel, D. (2010) 'The private regulation of global corporate conduct: achievements and limitations', *Business and Society*, 49(1): 68–87.

Voss, C., Tsikriktis, N. and Frohlich, M. (2002) 'Case research in operations management', *International Journal of Operations and Production Management*, 22(2): 195–219.

Werhane, P., Hartman, L., Archer, C., Bevan, D. and Clark, K. (2011) 'Trust after the global financial meltdown', *Business and Society Review*, 116(4): 403–433.

Whitley, R. (1999) *Divergent Capitalisms: The Social Structuring and Change of Business Systems*, Oxford: Oxford University Press.

Williams, P. (2009) 'The Ethical Trading Initiative: Tenth Anniversary Conference', *Development in Practice*, 19(3): 424–426.

Windsor, D. (2006) 'Corporate social responsibility: three key approaches', *Journal of Management Studies*, 43(1): 93–114.

Witt, M.A. and Redding, G. (2012) 'The spirits of corporate social responsibility: senior executive perceptions of the role of the firm in society in Germany, Hong Kong, Japan, South Korea and the United States', *Socio-Economic Review*, 10(1): 109–134.

World Bank (2003) *Company Codes of Conduct and International Standards: An Analytical Comparison. Vol. 1: Apparel, Footwear and Light Manufacturing, Agribusiness, Tourism*, Washington, DC: World Bank.

Yin, R.K. (2014) *Case Study Research: Design and Methods*, 5th edn, Thousand Oaks, CA: Sage.

2 Belgium

Unions questioning the added value of CSR

Céline Louche

> CSR is our core business but I don't think companies see it that way. I think on the contrary they try to exclude us.... They don't have any interest in involving the trade unions in their own CSR initiatives ... as result, there is a growing mistrust among the trade unions towards the three letters: 'C.S.R.'
>
> (ABVV-FGTB, General Federation of Belgian Labour)

Introduction

Lack of trust is most probably what would best characterize the perception of corporate social responsibility (CSR) by trade unions in Belgium. The unions recognize the importance and relevance of CSR as a concept, but regret the way it is being used or misused by many companies, often as a marketing tool more than anything else. Moreover, they feel that there is a gap between the way unions define CSR and the way it is being defined by companies. Trade unions want concrete actions and clear results. Unfortunately they feel that CSR often remains at the level of rhetoric. Another element leading to mistrust is the feeling of substitution: CSR might provide a legitimate bypass to avoid dialogue with trade unions, rather than reinforce it. This scepticism has emerged progressively over the last few years. Although the unions have never been highly engaged in the CSR community and initiatives in Belgium, in the early 2000s they were generally more positive and hopeful with regard to CSR. However, the attitude of trade unions towards CSR is not homogenous. As we see below, there is one noticeable exception – the Christian union branch in Leuven – that views CSR as a way to rethink the role and relationship of trade unions with businesses.

Belgium has a strong trade union tradition and a high level of employee unionization, certainly one of the highest in Europe. The unions are known for their capacity for negotiation, which takes place at three levels: the company, the business sector and, at the highest level, the negotiation of intersectoral agreements. Although trade unions may have lost some of their political power, they still play a critical role in Belgian industrial relations. However, their mobilizing force may be weakened by the numerous divisions that characterize Belgium in terms of languages, communities and regions, which are sources of internal tension but have also helped to develop a culture of negotiation and compromise. Within this context, CSR has become more of a dividing than a unifying force within trade unions, which have remained absent from debates at government, company or multi-stakeholder levels. Although they do not reject the concept, they prefer to remain at a certain distance.

National business system

Belgium has a small, open economy with a highly productive and skilled workforce, a high GNP and high exports per capita. It is traditionally mainly a Catholic country, although the position of the Catholic Church has declined significantly over recent decades (Heene *et al.* 2003). The business landscape in Belgium is characterized by a limited a number of large companies and a very high number of small and medium-sized enterprises (SMEs). More than 91 per cent of the companies in Belgium were micro enterprises in 2010. SMEs represented 65.7 per cent of employment and 58.2 per cent of the value added in 2010 (European Commission 2012). Although a majority of these SMEs are family businesses, they are important players on the international market too. It is also interesting to note that a majority of the large companies in Belgium belong to foreign groups such as Microsoft and Randstad.

Belgium is an example of a co-ordinated market economy (CME) in the sense of the varieties of capitalism literature (Hall and Gingerich 2004; Hall and Soskice 2001), or of continental European capitalism (CEC) according to Amable (2003). Both typologies stress the importance of stable political and social relations. Traditionally, social actors are more likely to seek compromise than try to impose their views using disruptive strategies (Faniel 2011).

Belgium presents some interesting features in relation to economic, linguistic, political and regional divides, which have led to six reforms of the state structure, the first one being in 1970. Throughout the reforms, Belgium evolved from a unitary state to a federal state with communities, regions and language areas. Belgium consists of three regional governments (Flanders, Wallonia and Brussels) and three linguistic communities (Flemish-, French- and German-speaking). These divides have resulted in a complicated federal state apparatus with extensive political and cultural autonomy for regions and language communities, formalized in the new Constitution of 1993.

According to political studies, this complex structure reduces the probability that government policies will affect business decisions negatively (Dekocker *et al.* 2012). The Belgian federal state is very decentralized down to regional structures, which in turn lessens the potential for conflict at the national or federal level (Swenden *et al.* 2006; Dekocker *et al.* 2012). The national/regional divides affect all aspects of Belgian society. For example, employment law is still decided at national level but the division between the communities has an impact on the relationships between the unions. The regions also determine environmental objectives as well as appropriate policy instruments, and carry out enforcement (O'Brien *et al.* 2001). Another consequence is the asymmetry that results from 'the use of territory and language as the criteria on which the division and delegation of responsibilities is based' (Dekocker *et al.* 2012: 12). Therefore it is possible to have different political orientations at national and regional levels. A further result of the divides is that all the bodies and organizations connected with industrial relations have both French and Flemish names and abbreviations.

As Dekocker *et al.* (2012) have argued, the political divide needs to be understood in the context of changing economic activities along the regional axes. Belgium has a long and established history of social and collective responsibility which is the result of centuries of occupation (until 1830) by diverse foreign powers (Heene *et al.* 2003). Until the middle of the twentieth century, the heavy, large-scale steel and coal mining industries were the most important economic activities in Belgium, especially in Wallonia. Flanders was characterized rather by SMEs and more diversified activities. But during the twentieth century the Belgian economy faced a significant change with the move of wealth creation and economic activities from Wallonia to Flanders.

Industrial relations system

The economy and the industrial relations system in Belgium can be characterized by the size of the country, which is rather small (an estimated 11 million inhabitants in 2012). It provides a relatively equal distribution of income, high union density, a well-structured collective bargaining system, and unions and employers' organizations engaged with political decision-making processes. The country's institutionalized 'pyramid of negotiation' creates high trust between the parties (Vilrokx and Leemput 1998) and a multi-layered system of collective bargaining, with employers and unions negotiating collective agreements at intersectoral, sector and company level (Dekocker *et al.* 2012). Agreements at one level cannot be less favourable than those at higher levels.

According to the database of Institutional Characteristics of Trade Unions, Wage Setting and Social Pacts (ICTWSS), trade union density in Belgium was 52 per cent in 2012, which makes Belgium one of the most highly unionized countries in the European Union. The density level has remained stable since the 1980s (Faniel 2011). The high density can be explained by the role trade unions play in the administration of unemployment schemes and in the day-to-day payment of unemployment benefits. The drawback of the system is that the union membership is quite old. Many workers become union members, for instance, in order to access certain services (such as unemployment benefits and legal counselling) or to be protected if they face problems at work.

Belgium has a strong trade union tradition. This is partly for historical reasons, as industrialization began very early. Indeed, the three main trade union confederations have been in existence for over 100 years. However, the first forms of workers' organization, the corporatist *mutualités* of craftsmen, developed in the middle of the nineteenth century. Trade unionism in Belgium is not synonymous with union activism. Belgian unions have lost much of their capacity to be heard through the media and in the political field, even though the political parties are historically close to them (Faniel 2011). The Belgian situation presents some distinctive features, especially regarding linguistic and regional tensions, that have a direct impact upon trade unions. At the beginning of the 2010s, the trade unions were searching for new developments, new positioning and a renewal of their practices. Nonetheless, trade unions and employers' associations remain powerful organizations. Meeting places where trade unions or representatives of workers can exert influence on managerial decision-making exist at many different levels: at the plant and enterprise level through works councils or trade union committees especially for addressing health and safety issues at work, at industry level through the joint committees, and at national intersectoral level through the National Labour Council.

In Belgium there are three active trade union confederations. Since 1958, the Confederation of Christian Trade Unions (ACV-CSC) has remained the most important, with 1,665,217 members in 2010. The General Federation of Belgian Labour (ABVV-FGTB), which was set up in 1945 by Socialist, Communist and Anarcho-Syndicalist unions, had 1,503,748 members in 2010. The smallest is the General Confederation of Liberal Trade Unions (ACLVB-CGSLB) with 274,308 members in 2010.

Belgian trade unions are not organized on a craft or occupational basis, and industrial unions prevail. Both the Socialist and Christian unions have separate sections for white-collar workers, regardless of the sector to which they belong (Blanpain 2010). The ACV-CSC and ABVV-FGTB have essentially the same structure; both are federations of national trade unions organized along sectoral lines and are decentralized at the regional and local level.

Belgium is characterized by union pluralism. But what makes the Belgian trade union landscape different from other countries is the dominance of the Christian confederation (Pasture 1994; Faniel 2011) and the existence of a 'liberal union' (Vandaele 2012). Despite union pluralism, confederations often try to adopt common positions on major issues and to act jointly in a so-called 'common front' (Faniel 2011).

The evolution of CSR

CSR is a relatively recent concept in Belgium, although the not-for-profit sector has a long history in the country. An embryonic form of CSR can be traced to the emergence of trade unions in the second half of the nineteenth century alongside a developing charitable attitude among some entrepreneurs. CSR is framed within the European, and more specifically continental, model of the welfare state, where relationships between the social partners are anchored in law. This is reflected strongly in the legal framework developed by the government.

CSR in Belgium reflects the complexity of the country, with initiatives organized at both national and regional levels. Already in the early 1990s a number of environmental laws and initiatives had started to emerge. The federal framework for sustainable development was launched in May 1997 (Graham *et al.* 2011). This provided an institutional consultation and co-operation process across the various ministries concerned in order to prepare, monitor and assess the federal sustainable development plan that has to be adopted by the federal government every four years. It was also during this period that the Federal Council for Sustainable Development (FRDO-CFDD) was established. This serves as an advisory body to the federal government on sustainable development policies and as a forum to stimulate debate amongst the representatives of civil society. The first Federal Plan for Sustainable Development was adopted in 2000 and revised in 2004 and 2008.

From 2000 to 2008, CSR was strongly promoted by the government and other stakeholders. The early 2000s saw the number of CSR networks and initiatives increase quite significantly and include a broad range of stakeholders such as business, government, trade unions and not-for-profit organizations (Graham *et al.* 2011). It was also during this period that employers' organizations such as the Union of Self-Employed Entrepreneurs (UNIZO) in Flanders and the Walloon Union of Companies (UWE) in Wallonia, and organizations for the self-employed and SMEs, started to get actively involved. In 2006 the Belgian federal government adopted the Belgian CSR Reference Framework which was established through a multi-stakeholder consultation. This document was an important landmark as it provided a common basis for all organizations in Belgium. This was followed by the Federal Action Plan in October 2006. However, if the government was driving debates and initiatives in the 2000s, in the 2010s this is less evident.

There is currently no legal obligation for companies to publish a CSR report, but since 1995 companies have been required to include in their annual report a social balance sheet (*bilan social*) consisting of data on the nature and evolution of employment across their operations (including details about the workforce, changes in employment and training). And since 2010, publically listed companies have been required to publish in their annual report a corporate governance declaration including information on their governance structure and remuneration policy, under the 'comply or explain' principle.

CSR practices in Belgium have been influenced by the active presence of many trade unions and the specific evolution of labour-related issues within companies. However, as we shall explain in the following sections, trade unions have been rather slow to participate in CSR issues.

Methods: unions interviewed

The three major trade unions were all approached: ACV-CSC (Christian), ABVV-FGTB (Socialist) and ACLVB-CGSLB (Liberal). However it is important to note that only representatives from the Flemish community were interviewed, despite several attempts to talk to representatives of the French-speaking community.

In total, five face-to-face interviews were conducted in March 2012. Each interview lasted between 1 hour and 1 hour 30 minutes, and was recorded and transcribed. All the officials interviewed were chosen because of their former or present involvement in CSR.

The first interview was conducted with a representative of SERV, the Social and Economic Council of Flanders, which is a joint forum for trade unions and employer organizations. This respondent was in charge of a CSR study conducted in 2007 to introduce the concept of CSR to trade unions as well as to address the role of trade unions with respect to CSR. Three other interviews were conducted with representatives of the Flemish interregional office of the three main trade unions. All three had been involved in the past in discussions of CSR within their own trade unions. A fifth interview was conducted with the ACV-CSC regional office in Leuven. This last respondent was selected because of his personal and exceptional involvement in developing CSR activities within the regional office in Leuven, making ACV-Leuven a Belgian front-runner trade union with regard to CSR. The person interviewed at ACV-Leuven was highly committed to CSR and wanted to make ACV-Leuven a showcase for ACV-CSC at the federal level.

Union understanding of CSR

Although the trade unions have not been very active on the CSR scene, all three regarded CSR as a very important and relevant concept. They were rather supportive of the concept of CSR and described it as their core business or very close to their core business:

> [W]e consider ourselves as the first organization ever to be engaged in promoting CSR although it did not have this name at that time.
>
> (ACV-CSC)

> [I]t is our core business to promote better labour conditions.
>
> (ABVV-FGTB)

> CSR is, of course, about HR and employability, it is our core business. But as a trade union we are also worried about the environmental consequences of what companies do, it is especially linked to health and safety. Therefore CSR is not something strange for trade unions.
>
> (ACLVB-CGSLB)

However, they saw an important discrepancy between the way they understood CSR and the way companies defined and implemented it, and even felt excluded from CSR policy developments within companies. As one of the interviewees said:

> CSR is our core business, but I don't think companies see it that way. I think on the contrary they try to exclude us because they don't have any interest in involving the trade unions in their CSR project.
>
> (ACV-CSC)

From the interviews, it seems that the trade unions in Belgium have a rather ambiguous relationship with CSR. One the one hand, they were rather positive and in favour of the concept of CSR. It was almost natural to them. On the other hand, they were not actively involved in the CSR scene and did not have an active position and engagement with CSR. One of the interviewees regretted the limited involvement of trade unions in the CSR discussion, but was also unsure how to generate interest within his union (from both the top and among the members).

The lack of involvement of Belgian unions in CSR may be explained by two main factors: an ill-defined concept and the way CSR is being used within companies. Together these factors contribute to a sceptical attitude towards CSR and, in particular, a lack of trust. With respect to the first factor, the problem of definition, CSR remains a very fuzzy and vague notion among the trade unions. They referred to the European Commission definition as well as to the document that was published by SERV in 2007. They made a clear distinction between CSR and sustainable development, the first being at the corporate level and the latter a more 'holistic concept'. One of them said: 'To me CSR is only one part of sustainable development, only one part' (ACV-CSC). The lack of definition of CSR is a major problem for the trade unions. Although they regard CSR as a very relevant and important concept, they have difficulties in communicating it to their members. Indeed their members, the workers, do not know about the concept of CSR, which is not to say that they do not care about it – on the contrary – but they lack the vocabulary to own it for themselves and so become rather lost in the company discourse around CSR. The concept of CSR was perceived as too conceptual and general to appeal to their members:

> CSR is too big, too general. Our representatives, they see lots of clouds in CSR and very little sunshine.
>
> (ABVV-FGTB)

> CSR is always approached as a whole concept, with a lot of different things. Whereas we would like to discuss more concrete things, more concrete issues like diversity management, work-life balance.
>
> (ACLVB-CGSLB)

As a result CSR was perceived as a very remote concept and mainly there for the top management within companies, the people involved in policy-making and strategic plans. It was not there for the workers, and was mainly regarded as an unnecessary 'extra', there only to dilute the 'real problems and issues'. The trade unions felt there was a huge gap between what was being portrayed in CSR policies and what was happening at the workplace. One of the interviewees said that 'CSR is far from the reality' (ACV-CSC).

Although the trade unions did not have a clear definition, they had the feeling that their own understanding of CSR differed considerably from the companies' perspective: 'I think it is a big problem, how we see CSR and how companies deal with it' (ACV-CSC), mentioned one of the interviewees. The trade unions described CSR as a 'principle' while they described companies' approach to CSR more as a 'project', meaning it was not integrated into the company's business strategy.

The second factor is the way CSR is being used by companies. Lack of involvement was not related to a lack of interest, but rather to a certain fear and a lack of trust with respect to the way companies use the concept. In 2007, when SERV organized a conference on CSR to launch their report, all the social partners were present and agreed in their support for CSR. However, the unions regretted the way it was being used, or rather misused, by companies, mainly as a marketing tool:

> It is often used as window-dressing rather than in a serious way. Therefore it is difficult for us to have a clear position. Moreover there is a kind of competition between CSR and issues related to employment. There is a certain tension between the social aspect, the core interest of the trade unions, and environmental issues. It makes it difficult.
>
> (ABVV-FGTB)

> In companies, often reporting is more important than doing CSR. We need to make sure companies go beyond reporting. From the beginning the big risk with CSR is that it becomes only 'communication'.
>
> (ACLVB-CGSLB)

The interviews revealed that unions have the feeling that during the last six years CSR has become an easy, even too easy, way for companies to present themselves as 'responsible organizations'. They said that CSR was being used as a 'trade mark' and as a 'marketing tool', and therefore it had become 'something with little content and meaning'. They did not think that companies were interested in the content or 'what's in it' but rather in the marketing impact. There was a general feeling that the concept of CSR did not add anything new. International Conventions like those adopted by the International Labour Organization are already perceived as sufficient in terms of freedom of association, the right to collective bargaining and all fundamental principles and rights at work. The added-value of CSR was somehow questioned. They also described CSR as a concept that had been defined by and for companies. The name itself does not encourage others to participate in the debate, but instead is rather exclusive:

> Trade unions are not integrated into the CSR dialogue ... CSR is a story from and for the company.
>
> (ABVV-FGTB)

> As a union, I have the impression that CSR is the initiative of the employers who do not ask for the participation of unions. They decide to do it or not, and develop their policies and strategies without involving unions. It is not a reflex to ask unions about their CSR.
>
> (ACV-CSC)

> CSR as a name keeps trade unions out of the debate, there is a problem in the name itself. It is only for companies.
>
> (ACV-CSC)

Another element that added to the mistrust of the CSR concept is the instrumental use of CSR. The unions had the impression that companies tend to hide themselves behind tools like CSR reports, labels or certifications. Although these tools are useful, they are not sufficient in themselves and do not cover the issues that are of real interest to trade unions. However, as one of the interviewees said, neither companies nor trade unions were able to go beyond those tools: 'We [companies and trade unions] need to be more critical' (ACV-CSC).

A last element may be added to these two factors (that is, the ill-definition of the concept and the way it is used by companies), namely CSR as an object of fear. The trade unions maybe fear that their role might be usurped by CSR. Indeed, under the heading of CSR companies engage in issues where trade unions used to have a leading role, such as working hours, working conditions, work life balance and so on. Because of CSR they increasingly feel excluded from those discussions. The interviewees noted that companies tend to involve trade unions less than they used to;

social and employee-related issues were being increasingly discussed internally within the company as part of their CSR policies. The trade unions felt not only excluded but also feared that the debate was shifting from the well-being of people to a question of productivity. They had the impression that CSR, rather than reflecting a social logic, was dominated by a commercial logic and short-term perspective.

Another fear that emerged is that CSR, rather than reinforcing the relationship between trade unions and companies, was widening the gap between the two. One of the interviewees stated that companies did not make the link between CSR and trade unions, either unintentionally or intentionally, but also used CSR as a way to avoid any confrontation with difficult topics and discussions. They all regretted that, although CSR was about stakeholder dialogue, it did not happen in reality and CSR may even have a negative impact on social dialogue between trade unions and companies:

> Sometimes companies organize so called 'stakeholder meetings' and invite a large number of stakeholders, but in those meetings discussions are just impossible.
>
> (ABVV-FGTB)

Union policies on CSR

Trade union policies on CSR do exist but are limited in scope. Documents and information can be found on the trade unions' websites, though during the interviews it seemed that those policies were not well known. None of the three unions has a CSR policy at the regional or national level. The unions do address the three pillars of CSR (social, environmental and economic responsibilities) in their diverse and numerous documents and reports which are available on their websites, including environmental issues, especially climate change. However, these documents do not cover social and environmental impacts on their own governance structures, as organizations. One of the websites of the unions mentioned 'sustainability', but CSR was not to be found. On the other hand, the SERV 2007 conference and the 2010 follow-up publication was known by the three trade unions and referred to as a key document by some of them.

None of the three trade unions has, or has had in the past, a formal structure to deal with CSR. Although around 2007 some of them had nominated an individual to integrate the concept of CSR into his/her work, they had moved to other topics by the end of the decade. Trade unions got involved in the CSR debate because of a potential political interest, an interest which by 2012 seems to have disappeared. Nonetheless, CSR is being addressed within trade unions, but rather at the top level, and it seems to remain a discourse rather than a set of actions. Two of the trade unions, ACV-CSC and ABVV-FGTB, said that sustainability was a recurring theme at their annual meetings, but nothing very concrete:

> Is our trade union proactive on these issues? I think we try, but from a top down level.... But it is on a very conceptual level. We address sustainability at the congress, like the union should promote sustainable development and should promote transition to renewable energy sectors where there is a lot of potential job creation, but it is very theoretical and conceptual. It is very difficult to translate these concepts into instruments or concrete measures – how are you going to realise those things at the level of a company, at the level of the shop-floor?
>
> (ACV-CSC)

The lack of CSR policies is general across the three trade unions. However, it is worth mentioning one exception, a branch of the Confederation of Christian Trade Unions (ACV/CSC) in Leuven. ACV Leuven was more active and engaged in CSR thanks to the interest of one person within the branch, as protagonist. As described below, ACV Leuven is quite an exceptional case among the Belgian unions.

ACV Leuven, a branch of ACV-CSC, has put CSR high on its agenda. The union's local offices have a high degree of autonomy within their own confederation, so the active engagement of ACV Leuven does not necessarily reflect what is happening in other branches or at national or regional levels. Within ACV Leuven, one person decided to dedicate considerable attention and effort to the concept of CSR because of his personal interest in the topic, and he has been championing CSR within ACV Leuven. According to him, CSR challenges trade unions to broaden their views and can therefore help trade unions to change their model and develop their actions. He considers CSR as intrinsically related to the trade unions' *raison d'être* and therefore does not see how unions can neglect or avoid addressing it. Similarly to the other trade unions and his colleagues in ACV-CSC, he started to get involved in CSR in 2007 with the conference organized by SERV, after which ACV Leuven decided to take some concrete actions. CSR became an important issue. In 2008, AVC Leuven organized its annual congress around the topic of CSR which led to the development of an action plan.

Although by 2012 the action plan was far from complete, many initiatives and efforts had been taken, such as CSR training for members, an awareness campaign and CSR policies within ACV Leuven to reduce their own environmental footprint. CSR was again on the agenda of the 2012 annual congress of ACV Leuven. Being tabled twice for the annual congress shows that ACV Leuven takes CSR seriously because of its relevance for companies, but also for the trade union as an organization in its own right.

Just like the other interviewees, the representative of ACV Leuven was very critical of the way CSR is implemented within companies as mainly a management issue, excluding trade unions from any dialogue. However, in contrast to the other interviewees, this was exactly why the ACV Leuven

CSR protagonist wants to be involved: to make sure that the union has a voice, rather than leaving it all to the companies. Rather than neglecting CSR and adopting a passive conformity approach, he argues that trade unions should become more proactive to ensure that CSR is not left entirely to companies: 'That's why unions need to have some knowledge of CSR, to take a more active role' (ACV-CSC Leuven).

Union engagement with CSR

Trade unions in Belgium have had limited involvement in CSR discussions and activities. In 2007 under the initiative of the SERV, trade unions were actively engaged in the debate, though it did not last long. During the interviews, it was made clear that their involvement around 2007, at least from the Flemish perspective, was mainly due to the government push. At that time the Flemish government was rather active and had placed CSR high on the political agenda. However, according to the interviewees, the elected Flemish government from 2009 gave less attention to CSR as it focused more on the 2008 financial crisis, and accordingly the interest of the trade unions decreased. By 2012 the unions seemed to be completely absent from all CSR debates and platforms.

Interestingly, all three unions said that they had received invitations to participate in stakeholder fora organized by the government, either at the regional or national level, or by other organizations like Kauri, a Belgian multi-actor network bringing together a wide range of actors including non-governmental organizations (NGOs) and companies, or Business and Society Belgium, a network organization bringing companies together around CSR issues. However, they all admitted that they did not respond positively to the invitations. They saw no need to attend, and had very low expectations about the outcomes of the discussions.

Once again ACV Leuven is an exception. They have been participating actively in several CSR related events, especially with Kauri. In 2008, when ACV Leuven launched its CSR action plan, the union decided to focus on three main points: first, to know more about CSR; second, to develop the union's competences on CSR; and third, to participate in discussion and debate. The objective was to build knowledge and raise awareness within the union, as they noticed that most members had never heard of CSR, and to become equipped to work proactively and strategically with companies on their CSR policies. The ACV protagonist gave the example of Danone Belgium, which in 2012 decided to appoint a CSR manager. ACV Leuven became aware of this new appointment through the legal documents and reports they receive from the company. ACV Leuven took it as a positive step, and decided to inform the company that as a trade union they wanted to be involved in the decision-making process. This proactive approach was apparently well received by the company.

ACV Leuven started a training programme on CSR for the union representatives present in the company. Although only a four-day programme, it allowed them to be introduced to the concept of CSR, to get acquainted with the vocabulary and the tools around CSR, and especially to feel more at ease in addressing the subject within their companies. As well as the knowledge and awareness programme, ACV Leuven also decided to develop their own CSR policy to integrate CSR into their management practices: 'It would be too easy to say to the companies what they should and should not do. We also need to take our own responsibilities and do it ourselves internally.' They accordingly integrated policies in areas like waste management, recycling, the use of fair trade products, energy consumption and sustainable commuting into their everyday organizational practices.

ACV Leuven remains an exception which so far seems not to be followed by others. In general it appears that trade union actions, just like those of companies, are dominated by short-term issues. In 2012, the trade unions were more concerned with issues related to the financial crisis, such as restructuring and site closure. As one of the interviewees said: 'we don't have time to think about CSR' (ACLVB-CGSLB).

Discussion

There is an ambiguous relationship between the trade unions and CSR. Even though CSR is regarded as an important and relevant concept for companies, the trade unions remain sceptical. Several factors may explain this ambiguity.

First, CSR is perceived as a fine concept but too far removed from reality, as too general and too vague. If the concept is regarded as valuable in terms of the principles it promotes, its implementation is difficult and cumbersome. Moreover, the unions perceive CSR as a rather exclusive concept used by top management, rather than as a concept for all workers. CSR is therefore not adapted to trade union members, who are primarily blue-collar. Overall, CSR is perceived as rhetoric rather than reality. As a result trade unions feel disconnected as they do not see how their work can fit into the concept and above all because they do not see how CSR can help them to address the concrete issues and problems workers meet in their day-to-day jobs. The vocabulary around and about CSR is also not adapted to their members and their activities. CSR often builds on abstract and difficult ideas, words and concepts not adapted to the unions' members.

Second, trade unions feel that CSR is mainly used by companies as a marketing tool and so is more focused on the reputation of the company than on the content and implementation of CSR. They also regret the instrumental and business case approach that companies adopt towards CSR, which clearly emphasises the dominance of commercial logic. This has greatly contributed to the distrust of trade unions with regard to CSR initiatives developed within companies.

Third, unions may fear that CSR threatens their role and sustainability. This is not entirely clear, but some interviewees implied that CSR is perceived as a potential risk for trade unions, in terms of their losing power in social dialogue as well as legitimacy with respect to other stakeholders. Rather than re-thinking their role in social dialogue and seeing CSR as an opportunity to address union concerns, it seems that most unions, with the exception of one, have adopted a rather reactive approach.

Despite all these issues, CSR as a principle is highly supported by the trade unions and none of them denied its relevance. They all recognized that companies are engaging more and more in CSR, and for different motivations, but for the Belgian trade unions it remains unclear how they could be more involved in the movement and indeed whether they want to be more active.

Conclusions

In Belgium, CSR was strongly promoted by the government during the mid-2000s. This political will was a significant driver for the unions to start to think about CSR. Under the impulse of SERV, the Social and Economic Council of Flanders, Flemish trade unions initiated a consultation process involving the country's three trade union confederations to understand better the concept of CSR and its implications for the unions. However, with the exception of one office, ACV Leuven, by 2012 CSR had not taken off within the Belgian unions.

Unions tend to be very sceptical towards CSR, seeing it as a concept that has been developed by and for companies. There is a general distrust of CSR; it is too often used as a marketing tool or a way to 'buy' a good reputation. Moreover, CSR is perceived as a way to bypass the unions rather than reinforcing and stimulating social dialogue. The one exception among the Belgian trade unions, however, regards CSR as an opportunity to question and re-think the role of trade unions and their relationships with companies, and also to start to think about their own social and environmental impacts. ACV Leuven's commitment and engagement might in the future create a new momentum for the unions to regain some interest in CSR. These findings help us to understand better the absence of trade unions in CSR debates and initiatives. CSR is touching on territories that are very sensitive and relate to power struggles. The case of CSR within Belgian trade unions highlights some of these struggles.

References

Amable, B. (2003) *The Diversity of Modern Capitalism*. Oxford: Oxford University Press.

Blanpain, R. (2010) 'Belgium', in R. Blanpain (ed.) *International Encyclopaedia of Laws: Labour Law and Industrial Relations*, Alphen aan den Rijn, NL: Kluwer Law International.

Dekocker, V., Pulignano, V., Léonard, E. and Broeck, M.v.d. (2012) 'The national business system and its applications: reflections from the Belgian experience', *International Business Research*, 5(12): 8–18.

European Commission (2012) *SBA Fact Sheet 2010/11 – Belgium*. Available at http://ec.europa.eu/enterprise/policies/sme/index_en.htm.

Faniel, J. (2011) 'Crisis behind the figures? Belgian trade unions between strength, paralysis and revitalisation', *Management Review*, 23(1): 14–31.

Graham, V., Swaen, V., Louche, C. and Callens, I. (2011) *2011 Barometer of Social Responsibility: Sustainable Development Firmly Rooted in Companies in Belgium*. Brussels: Business and Society Belgium.

Hall, P.A. and Gingerich, D.W. (2004) *Varieties of Capitalism and Institutional Complementarities in the Macroeconomy: An Empirical Analysis (Discussion Paper 04/5)*. Cologne, Germany: Max Planck Institute for the Study of Societies. Available at www.mpifg-koeln.mpg.de

Hall, P.A., and Soskice, D. (2001) 'An introduction to varieties of capitalism', in P. A. Hall and D. Soskice (eds) *Varieties of Capitalism: The Institutional Foundations of Comparative Advantage*. Oxford: Oxford University Press, pp. 1–70.

Heene, A., Langenberg, S. and Dentchev, N.A. (2003) *Corporate Social Responsibility in Belgium*. Working Paper, Ghent University.

O'Brien, P., Carey, D., Høj, J. and Woergoetter, A. (2001) *Encouraging Environmentally Sustainable Growth in Belgium, Economics Department Working Paper No. 300*, Paris: Organisation for Economic Co-operation and Development.

Pasture, P. (1994) *Christian Trade Unionism in Europe since 1968. Tensions between Identity and Practice*, Aldershot: Avebury.

Swenden, W., Brans, M. and De Winter, L. (2006) 'The politics of Belgium: institutions and policy under bipolar and centrifugal federalism', *West European Politics*, 29(5): 863–873.

Vandaele, K. (2012) 'Een vreemde eend in de bijt? De ACLVB in West-Europees en historisch perspectief', in S. Lannoo, C. Devos, M. Mus and J. Faniel (eds) *Liberale vakbond: contradictio in terminis? Een onderzoek naar het profiel en de overtuigingen van de leden van ACLVB*. Gent: Academia Press, pp. 39–63.

Vilrokx, J. and Leemput, J.v. (1998) 'Belgium: The great transformation', in A. Ferner and R. Hyman (eds) *Industrial Relations in Europe*. Oxford: Basil Blackwell, pp. 315–347.

3 Finland

Positive union engagement with CSR

Anna-Maija Lämsä and Soilikki Viljanen

> I certainly see that in Finland [CSR] increases opportunities, that in a way our foundation is so strong, that we've got these strong unions and we've got strong legislation, we've got strong official procedures, so we don't really have to be very afraid.
>
> (JHL, Trade Union for the Public and Welfare Sectors)

Introduction

The institutional system of Finland is an example of the Nordic welfare model. The government and public sector have an important role in social and, to some extent, business activities. The trade unions have been key players in the Finnish system for a long time, with institutionalized patterns of interaction as well as mandatory and codified rights. In addition to collective agreements between employees and employers, the labour market organizations have concluded various other agreements that establish consistent procedures for dealing with general questions about working conditions, such as earnings-related social security insurance. Since the government and the public sector play a crucial role in social activities, the incentive for companies to engage in philanthropy has been traditionally rather low. In recent years, CSR has grown in importance in the eyes of Finnish companies, which have started to make their attachment to it explicit. Increasing globalization of the business environment and deregulation of the business system are important reasons for this phenomenon.

Despite certain reservations, the Finnish trade unions mostly have a positive attitude towards CSR. The unions, which are currently taking steps to make CSR explicit in their policies, have engaged in a number of responsibility initiatives in practice, but have seldom defined the concept precisely. It is commonly accepted amongst the Finnish unions that CSR does not mean a replacement of formal agreements between employers and employees and legally codified employee rights – hence, it is not seen as contrary to their aims but rather as supportive of them. The unions have experienced increasing pressure to engage in CSR as a result of the institutional changes in the business environment that have come with globalized markets. However, they view themselves as having a strong legitimate status in the Finnish institutional system, and do not appear to be experiencing any sense of threat from CSR.

National business system

Finland industrialized relatively late compared with the other Nordic countries. It was only in the mid-1970s that the country caught up economically with the most advanced countries (Pohjola 2003). Since then the Finnish economy has done well (Sala-i-Martin *et al.* 2011). Today Finland is considered a typical Nordic welfare state, still having some characteristics of the co-ordinated market economy (Hall and Soskice 2001). The government and the public sector have an important role in social and, to some extent, business activities (Lilja *et al.* 2009).

Until the 1980s there were several co-ordinating mechanisms over and above the level of individual companies in Finland. For a long time the forestry and paper industries had an important position in the economy. The industries built close relations with the government and influenced it in various ways, both formally and informally (Lamberg and Laurila 2005). The post-war business system in Finland was rather closed and characterized by state-led co-ordination, long-term investment in heavy industries, reliance on cartels, and hierarchical and state-dependent, partly state-owned, corporations (Tainio and Lilja 2003; Moen and Lilja 2004). A crucial feature of the Finnish system was that major banking groups were linked to specific companies, and companies in these groups were provided finance through their banks (Oinas 2005). The banking groups and the state were the focal actors in this centralized national business system (Lilja *et al.* 2011).

From the beginning of the 1990s, there has been a significant reduction in centralized co-ordination across all sectors of the Finnish economy. The Finnish business system changed in significant ways. The collapse of the Soviet Union in 1991, the deep recession in the early 1990s and membership of the European Union in 1995 were important drivers to change. The economy became less concentrated around the forestry and paper industries, and there was rapid growth in information and communications technology (ICT) (Moen and Lilja 2004). One of the major outcomes of this transformation has been that multinational corporations of both Finnish and non-Finnish origin have become focal actors in the economy. The traditional system of banking groups collapsed. This meant the end of the banking spheres of influence over companies and the invigoration of the stock market. Restrictions on foreign ownership of companies based in Finland were abolished (Lilja *et al.* 2009.)

However, today the Finnish national business system forms a model of a knowledge economy that still retains some characteristics of a co-ordinated economy (Lilja *et al.* 2009). The system is characterized by generalist education. Capital markets are well developed and foreign ownership of stock-listed companies has increased significantly over the last few decades. The system of corporate governance in Finland is based on national legislation, European Union (EU) regulation, stock exchange rules and corporate governance codes and, overall, has now been professionalized.

Key features of the Finnish business value system include pragmatism, high risk-aversion and co-operation. Trust, honesty and keeping one's promises are important values, which can be described as important social resources in Finnish society (Kujala 2010). It has been argued that the welfare system has a significant role in the creation and maintenance of trust in Finnish society (Ilmonen and Jokinen 2002). Humanitarian values, co-operation, equality and justice have a high place in the Finnish value system even if it is now argued that Finns' values have become more individualistic and efficiency-oriented (Helkama and Seppälä 2004). However, according to Puohiniemi (2006), Finnish values still stress security and goodwill.

Industrial relations system

Even though the Finnish national business system in general has changed significantly since the beginning of the 1990s, there remain subsystems that have not undergone radical change. According to Lilja *et al.* (2011), one of them is the industrial relations system.

The trade unions have long been key players in Finnish public life. Finnish trade union membership grew rapidly in the 1970s, and by the mid-1990s trade union density had reached about 85 per cent of the labour force. Since then it has declined somewhat, but in 2011 it still stood at 74 per cent, amongst the highest in the EU countries (Vitols 2010). There is general acceptance of the principle of collective regulation of employment negotiated jointly between employees and employers to protect the weaker party (employees). Individual employment contracts are subject to overriding collective agreements concluded between unions and employer organizations which define rates of pay and working conditions. Employers have to comply with collective agreements applicable to their line of business whether or not they are affiliated to the relevant employer organization, and agreements cover all employees, regardless of whether or not they are members of the union. However, in the international context, where the unions cannot rely on the same sort of institutional system as in Finland itself, the situation appears to be more demanding. Here the unions are increasingly networking, negotiating and acting in co-operation with foreign unions, non-governmental organizations (NGOs) and multinational corporations. The challenge to negotiate on working conditions and employee rights with multinational companies has increased.

The aim of the industrial relations system overall is to guarantee minimum conditions for employees' remuneration and working conditions in both the private and the public sectors (Labour Court Establishment 2013). In addition to collective agreements, labour market organizations have concluded several other agreements that establish consistent procedures for dealing with general questions about working conditions. For example, unions take care of most of the unemployment insurance funds that pay earnings-related unemployment benefits (Böckerman and Uusitalo 2006).

The relationship between employers' organizations and the unions in Finland can be described as interdependent and co-operative. In particular, a form of corporatism – co-operation between the political system and the labour market organizations – has long been a crucial feature of Finnish labour relations. Wage bargaining used to be highly centralized at intersectoral level, but it has recently become more decentralized, taking place now at sector level. Traditionally, tripartite co-operation was the pattern for the labour market organizations: centralized incomes policy agreements at confederation level were complemented by collective bargaining at sectoral levels, with some issues, such as working time arrangements, agreed at local level in the workplace. The number of issues negotiable at local and workplace level has been steadily increasing since the early 1990s. However, in 2011, the framework agreement between employers' national confederations and unions was negotiated for two years to try to boost Finland's competitiveness and ensure the best possible development of employment and purchasing power amidst the uncertain global economic climate (Akava 2011).

The evolution of CSR

A central feature of early industrial companies in Finland was their strong paternalism. Finnish industrial activity was generally located in sparsely populated areas (Koivuniemi 2000). The company provided a long and stable working relationship as well as a variety of services for employees and their families, such as housing, health care, canteens, schools, leisure facilities and so on (Lämsä 2007). Takala (1991) contends that paternalism in the form of factory communities can be seen as the model for an early form of corporate social responsibility. Even if employers considered that the economic function of the company was of prime importance, they also considered that the company was responsible for the basic wealth of the community. These attitudes did not die out until the 1960s and 1970s.

In the 1960s, the Finnish government started to build a modern welfare state (Oinas 2005). It was particularly during the 1970s that the country moved rapidly in this direction and the earlier role of companies underpinning socially responsible behaviour was taken over by the government and the public sector. Nowadays, social and welfare services are regarded by many Finns as a universal right for citizens, and they are guaranteed through extensive legislation, although there is also increasing pressure coming from central government to cut costs and privatize the public welfare services. Since the government and the public sector have a crucial role in social activities, the incentive for companies to engage in them is rather low. Finnish businesses have tended to remain relatively uninterested in philanthropy (Juholin 2004).

Extensive labour legislation, together with contracts between employers and employees, provide a variety of economic, social and professional benefits for employees. According to Takala (2004), the ideology of enlightened self-interest is nowadays a common way to understand CSR in Finnish business life. This view is supported by various empirical research results (Panapanaan *et al.* 2003; Juholin 2004; Lämsä *et al.* 2008; Chamber of Commerce 2009; Kujala *et al.* 2011).

Finnish CSR has many components. One crucial element of CSR in Finland is compliance with the law and regulations. Paying taxes is seen as an important way for a responsible company to play its part in meeting community responsibilities and maintaining the welfare state. Other types of voluntary community involvement are seen as important for multinational companies operating in less developed countries. The stakeholder model is understood as a responsible way of doing business (Kujala 2010). In general, traditional Finnish values, such as honesty, trustworthiness, accountability and reliability, can be seen as providing important guiding principles for responsible business activities (Kujala 2004).

These values, together with laws and other formal rules and contracts, largely provide the framework for the current Finnish version of CSR, which could be regarded as being more implicit than explicit in nature (Matten and Moon 2008). However, companies have recently started to make their attachment to CSR more explicit. Both Finnish companies and public authorities have promoted the application and communication of CSR in the form of value statements, codes of conduct, standards, audits and reports (Kourula 2010). This change to make CSR more explicit can be said to have developed only at the start of the 2000s but, according to Lähdesmäki (2012), it has not yet reached small and middle-sized companies (SMEs).

Methods: unions interviewed

We carried out ten interviews between November 2011 and January 2012. All the interviewees were experts on CSR issues in their organizations. Our goal was to take in a broad perspective of Finnish trade unions today. Therefore all three union confederations were interviewed. Additionally, six representatives of sectoral unions were interviewed. These unions were selected because their members either as a whole or in part represent the

ICT sector, a key player nowadays in Finnish business life. The sector is internationalized and faces global challenges of CSR. Finally, a representative of SASK, Suomen Ammattiliittojen Solidaarisuuskeskus (Trade Union Solidarity Centre of Finland), was interviewed. SASK was included as it represents Finnish trade unions in a broader sense by strengthening their role around the world. The interviews lasted between 1 and 2.5 hours. The total length of the interviews was 15 hours 45 minutes.

Representatives of the following unions and union organizations were interviewed:

- SAK, Central Organisation of Finnish Trade Unions – the largest confederation consisting mainly of blue-collar unions organized by industry and representing more than one million members in 20 affiliated trade unions;
- Akava, Confederation of Unions for Professional and Managerial Staff in Finland – the confederation for those with a university, professional or other higher qualification. It has more than 30 affiliates with altogether over half a million members, as well as over 100,000 student members;
- STTK, Finnish Confederation of Professionals – this confederation consists of 18 affiliated trade unions representing approximately 600,000 professional employees in the public sector, private industry and the private services sector;
- TEK, Academic Engineers and Architects in Finland – affiliated to Akava, TEK represents engineers and architects and has about 73,500 members working in the field of technology;
- Metalliliitto, Finnish Metalworkers´ Union – affiliated to SAK, this union represents industrial workers (mainly in technology, the electronic and electrical industries and ICT) and has about 160,000 members;
- JHL, Trade Union for the Public and Welfare Sectors – affiliated to SAK, JHL represents the public and private welfare services sector and has about 240,000 members;
- Sähköliitto, Finnish Electrical Workers' Union – affiliated to SAK, the union represents electrical workers and has about 35,000 members;
- Ammattiliitto Pro, Trade Union Pro – affiliated to STTK, the union represents clerical employees in the private sector and has about 130,000 members;
- Suomen Konepäällystöliitto, Finnish Engineers' Association – affiliated to STTK, the union represents engineering experts and supervisors (mainly in seafaring and power plants) and has about 4,500 members;
- SASK, Trade Union Solidarity Centre of Finland, Suomen Ammattiliittojen Solidaarisuuskeskus – the solidarity and development cooperation organization of Finnish trade unions has approximately 1.6 million members belonging to it through their trade unions.

Union understanding of CSR

The interviewees referred to various concepts when talking about what is involved in CSR, but most of them agreed with the idea that CSR is about sustainable development, compliance with the Conventions and Recommendations of the International Labour Organization (ILO) and environmental responsibility. Even though there was some vagueness in the definitions, the three pillar model of social, environmental and economic responsibilities was recognized in all but one of the unions, with the emphasis being on the social dimension. CSR was also viewed as focusing on company values and practices rather than as something undertaken for philanthropic reasons.

CSR was described in terms of voluntary commitment rather than compliance with the law. Several interviewees agreed on the legitimacy of the European Commission's definition of CSR. According to the definition, to meet their social responsibility, enterprises 'should have in place a process to integrate social, environmental, ethical, human rights and consumer concerns into their business operations and core strategy in close collaboration with their stakeholders' (CSR 2011: 6). One of the unions had adopted this definition as its basic principle on CSR issues. Amongst the other unions it was commonly thought that, even though the ideas of CSR were important from their point of view, there was no accurate definition of what it meant to them. Some interviewees even stressed that no definition was necessary. One respondent drew attention to the vagueness surrounding the concept as follows:

> That's one of the problems. This is so new and strange that there's quite a lot of confusion over the concepts here and that definitely affects people's awareness too, when people perceive the same concept in so many different ways.
>
> (TEK)

Definitions of the concept, and how much people knew about CSR, varied among the respondents from a vague understanding to an accurate and complex grasp of the subject, with the majority somewhere in between. There was, however, a general tendency to understand the nature of CSR differently depending on whether it was a question of the national or the international context.

In the national context, formal regulations and collective agreements in society together with key Finnish social values such as keeping promises, accountability and trustworthiness were seen as providing the framework for social responsibility in companies. Voluntary CSR was understood as beneficial to employees but external social activities were not viewed as being so important. In the Finnish context topics like wellbeing at work, career prolongation, continuing professional development, employee participation, organizational downsizing and its consequent reductions in the workforce, the salaries and working conditions of foreign employees, and matters linked to the use of a flexible workforce, were all typically considered relevant to CSR.

In the international context, mention was made of the increasing importance of and need for agreements with global companies, and of the fact that the different standards and recommendations that were encountered meant that neither global legislation nor common values in employee–employer relationships could be relied on. Even if there were no clear agreement about any one dominant framework for standards, agreements and recommendations, the Conventions and Recommendations of the ILO were typically mentioned as forming important guidelines for CSR, although they were recognized as being difficult to monitor in the varying global environments.

Important topics in the international context were the effects of different cultural values on employee–employer relationships, challenges in global supply chains, problems in enforcing employees' rights to participate in unions, and compliance with international human rights regulations and local legislation. Mention was also made of the environmental problems that companies can cause to their surroundings, poor working conditions and occupational health and safety, long working hours, the use of child and forced labour, poor management and leadership practices, and poor wages. However, there was little discussion of charity and social involvement in the community. Although some interviewees considered that CSR was a way to solve social problems, particularly in less developed societies, only a few examples of this were mentioned and it was said that the issue was relatively new.

When the length of time of involvement in CSR was discussed, respondents commonly emphasized that social responsibility has always been a significant issue for trade unions even if the concept of CSR itself may be new. The following extract from the interview with the representative of the Finnish Electrical Workers' Union reinforces this opinion:

> These things aren't new by any means, this hasn't just been invented in the last ten years. These are certainly really old issues. The concept might be new, the terms in which we're discussing it nowadays, but these are old ideas.
>
> (Sähköliitto)

According to the interviewees, discussion of CSR as a concept and its recognition as a phenomenon have only just started to emerge in the trade unions. However, there was some variation in the respondents' opinions about this. Some claimed that CSR was already a topic in the 1990s while others, as the quotation above shows, said that it had become a significant topic only during the last few years. On the whole, union awareness of

CSR occurred during the early and mid-2000s, and it has now increased since then.

Attitudes towards CSR in the trade unions were clearly more positive than negative. This is illustrated in the following extract from the interview with SAK:

> Yes, for us this is definitely a tool. But I do understand those more critical attitudes towards this, especially in countries in which the trade union movement is weaker, in Europe and just about all the countries outside the Nordic area.
>
> (SAK)

CSR was often thought to be a potential contributor to the development of working life and to dialogue between management and employees. It was seen as aligned and supportive of the traditional aims of the union movement.

Interviewees often expressed the view that it was important for large companies to make CSR visible, particularly those companies that are operating in international markets. It was also important in this context for there to be respect for international agreements, standards and recommendations. There were clear signs of explicit CSR in the domestic environment too when the interviewees discussed the reporting of responsibility, particularly the Global Reporting Initiative (GRI) which contains a sustainability reporting framework to entitle transparence and clarity (GRI 2013). All the respondents except one were familiar with the GRI. Three interviewees had been members of the evaluation committee of the GRI competition in Finland and were therefore very familiar with it.

Several respondents thought that the trade unions should actively require CSR from firms. For example, the discussion with the interviewee of Trade Union Pro highlights the topic in the following way:

> There have been demands for corporate social responsibility from companies in general, even in the media, and our union has demanded it from firms.
>
> (Ammattiliitto Pro)

Although the general attitude towards CSR was positive, some scepticism was also expressed. All the interviewees agreed that when CSR is taken seriously by companies and genuinely applied in their practices it is a very positive thing. However, it was felt that CSR can sometimes be just a question of public relations, a way of polishing up or improving the corporate image without any real connection to company practices.

Interviewees were also sceptical about how far employees were really able to participate in CSR practices such as GRI reporting, since the reporting process is often undertaken by external consultants and/or management. However, they also mentioned that processes like the GRI can improve transparency and credibility in and around firms. It can also allow the verification of companies' CSR policies and act as a means of developing their responsibility practices. Consequently, the respondents sometimes had conflicting attitudes towards CSR. Mostly it was evaluated as positive, as being in line with the aims of the trade union movement, but sometimes it was seen as merely providing cover for unacceptable practices. The interviewees talked about white or green washing. According to them, some companies indicate their responsibility mainly by polishing their public image. Generally, the interviewees considered that CSR was not in competition with the trade unions but could support their goals. One reason given for this view was that the position and power of the trade unions and labour regulation in Finland were so strong; no voluntary activity such as CSR could really challenge the situation. However, all interviewees believed that there were likely to be more problems at the European level with employer–employee relationships, since CSR could reduce the value of formal mechanisms between employer and employee in countries where trade unions are not as strong.

Finally, there was the company perspective. Respondents often expressed the view that CSR is important since responsibility initiatives bring rewards to firms. Thus, the business case for CSR was typically adopted as an underlying rationale for business engagement with responsibility issues, although this line of thought could be criticized. Normative notions were also mentioned as being crucial in CSR; in other words, CSR should be expected from companies because it is ultimately the right thing to do.

Union policies on CSR

There is no formal collective policy towards CSR amongst Finnish unions. However, in December 2011, they issued a joint statement on the new CSR strategy of the European Commission. A comment from the interviewee at STTK highlights the importance they place on it, as follows:

> We've got a very recent joint statement from halfway through December from the central union organizations, in which we comment on just this new strategy from the Commission and explain a bit what we think it is. We are all – the employees' organizations and the employers too – involved in this consultative committee on social and business responsibility.
>
> (STTK)

The general idea in the statement is that the voluntary nature of CSR does not mean the replacement of legally codified employee rights. The respondents emphasized that the essential element in trade union policy should be that respecting laws and formal agreements is a precondition for CSR. Additionally, it was said that in the international arena an important guideline in union policy is to support and advance the conclusion of agreements with global companies and to control their activities. Within Finland they said that what was particularly important was to pay attention to employees' issues and public sector procurements from private companies, and that getting rid of the hidden economy should be an essential part of union CSR policies. A few interviewees believed that voluntary CSR was not needed at all, but rather that CSR should be developed as part of traditional collective bargaining.

A CSR policy document was explicitly included in one union's policy programme (SAK). Another union was planning to include a policy paper as part of its programme in the near future (Ammattiliitto Pro). Other unions did not explicitly cover CSR in their programmes and there was therefore no direct documentation on the issue. However, in some cases it was said that although the concept of CSR was not explicitly mentioned as such, the phenomenon in its various forms was subsumed in other union documents, such as their industrial policy programme, an action plan, meeting protocols or framework agreements.

Union engagement with CSR

None of the interviewees believed that the significance of CSR is decreasing. On the contrary, they thought that it was on the increase, and that union engagement in the issue was likely to be stronger in the future. This is exemplified by an interviewee (SAK), who said that 'the importance of responsibility issues is increasing all the time, the current government programme emphasizes it'. Some of the respondents emphasized that the trade unions should have an active and proactive engagement in CSR in addition to traditional collective bargaining and agreements.

Unions today are typically experiencing increasing pressure from members facing downsizing, dismissal and outsourcing, and so pay greater attention to company responsibility and adopt stronger stances on the issue. Younger members were mentioned as being particularly interested in this. An active role in CSR was understood by some respondents to offer the unions a new way of gaining legitimacy in the future. The comment from one interviewee sums up the pressures coming from union members:

> For instance, when factories are closed down or activities are shifted to other countries and as a consequence you get a lot of redundancies, well, in those circumstances especially these questions of responsibility arise and the idea that they should be considered more. The effect of this is, most of all, and it's somehow natural, that these questions come strongly to the fore and people want the issues to be considered more broadly.
>
> (Akava)

A few respondents, on the other hand, held the view that legislation and collective agreements form a strong enough basis for dealing with the issue. For example, the interviewee from JHL said that 'existing legislation and agreements are enough for our organization'. Even though the unions mostly considered that engagement in CSR was important, there was some disagreement among the respondents as to whether the unions should have an active role or should just leave it alone. The reason for leaving it alone, however, seemed to be ignorance about CSR rather than a positive desire to ignore the topic.

The interviewees said that active unions use companies' explicit CSR as a way of putting pressure on them, and often also on their subcontractors, to act responsibly in practice. When trade unions and multinational companies negotiate guidelines and framework agreements the unions pressurize the companies to follow their CSR declarations. An interviewee, for example, talked about the issue in the following way:

> The use of the companies' own ideas about social responsibility in our campaigns, it's a bit questionable. But then these international framework agreements, they are gentlemen's agreements and they're negotiated with these multinational corporations. We certainly do use them. We use them in connection with client companies. If you don't play by the rules, the generally accepted rules, then your contractor has these instructions and we will make it known to them and we often do that, too.
>
> (Metalliliitto)

Many companies are afraid of losing their reputation and are therefore co-operative with the unions. Other examples of engagement at an international level that were mentioned included launching a framework agreement system between the union and global companies, financing an NGO to investigate working conditions in supply chains and increasing networking with foreign trade unions.

In Finland itself some unions had fought against questionable business practices by participating actively in public discussion about procurements made by public sector organizations from the private sector. The unions have demanded more responsible supply-chain management from public organizations due to the fact that they are financed through taxation. In addition, the increasing privatization of health care services and their passing into the hands of foreign companies was criticized on the grounds that these companies are transferring their profits to tax havens and not making any substantial contribution to Finnish society.

The majority of respondents considered that the institutionalized forms of collective bargaining in Finland, as well as the co-operative tradition between employers' organizations and the unions, and the unions' participation in such institutions as the EU's Economic and Social Committee, the Roundtable Discussion Forum between the Finnish labour market organizations and the Finnish Committee on Social and Corporate Responsibility, all offer the unions important arenas in which they can influence issues related to CSR, even if the actual concept of CSR may not be used in all cases. The Finnish Committee on Social and Corporate Responsibility is a consultative body representing various authorities, trade and industry, and labour market and civic organizations.

The Committee acts as the national contact point for the implementation of the OECD Guidelines for Multinational Enterprises together with the Ministry of Employment and the Economy.

In addition, active co-operation with NGOs both in Finland and internationally was viewed as crucial in CSR practices. As examples of co-operation, several NGOs or other movements and campaigns were mentioned, such as Finnwatch, Fair Trade and the Clean Clothes Campaign. Two of the respondents had also participated in the ISO 26000 development process. ISO 26000 provides guidance on how businesses and organizations can operate in a socially responsible way. It helps businesses and organizations translate principles into effective actions and shares best practices relating to social responsibility, globally.

A sizeable minority of the interviewees said that their union aims to increase knowledge about CSR among its members and includes the topic in training programmes and seminars. CSR was said to be an integral and essential part of all training in SASK, described as follows: 'We organize training as a part of our trade union activities here in Finland. These themes are there in every training session that we organize'.

The interviewees did not, however, perceive the Finnish trade union movement as leading the way in CSR. It was specifically the consumer movement that was identified as being responsible for setting the pace here. For example, an interviewee explained matters as follows: 'The consumers' organizations have definitely kept these things in the public eye. And in some ways the need for drawing up norms has arisen out of that' (TEK). Even though the consumer movement was said to have acted as the impetus behind CSR and the unions did not perceive themselves as being in the vanguard, a large majority of the respondents emphasized the current active role of the unions and thought that it was likely to increase in the future.

Discussion

This chapter shows that there is no consensus over a coherent definition of CSR, no agreed framework for the concept and no specific CSR policies among the Finnish trade unions, but the unions each tend to articulate their own version of the phenomenon. However, the unions do seem to be able to agree to some extent on the terminology and the ways in which they understand CSR in the light of international CSR recommendations, initiatives and standards, which are growing in popularity both nationally and internationally. These include the European Commission's definition of CSR, CSR guidance document ISO 26000 and the CSR reporting framework by the Global Reporting Initiative (GRI). Additionally, some convergence is a result of the unions' collaboration with various CSR-related committees, movements and NGOs, as well as of the unions' own educational initiatives. It is commonly accepted in the Finnish unions that CSR is voluntary in nature and does not mean a replacement of formal agreements between employers and employees and legally codified employee rights.

The three pillar model of CSR consisting of social, environmental and economic responsibilities is mostly recognized among the Finnish unions. The social responsibility dimension is clearly emphasized as the most crucial pillar, and the 'company-internal' element dominates the 'external' dimension in both the national and international contexts. Finland's welfare state with its large public sector is likely to be a reason for the dominance of the company-internal interpretation in the domestic arena. Moreover, the mission of the trade union movement in general, with its emphasis on the protection of employees, may explain the unions' orientation in not only the Finnish but also the international context.

The Finnish trade unions have felt under significant pressure to engage in CSR as a result of the institutional changes in the business environment that have accompanied globalization. The unions are increasingly facing pressure from their members to defend their interests in this changing and challenging situation. CSR, which is increasingly popular not only in companies' strategies but also in public discourse (Panapanaan *et al.* 2003; Juholin 2004; Kourula 2010; Siltaoja 2010), may thus have instrumental value to the unions. Additionally, there are signs in the interview data that we obtained that union members, especially younger ones, are making moral demands on the unions to show responsibility not only as a means to achieve other targets, such as a good image in public and among potential and current members, but also as an end in itself.

Despite certain reservations, the Finnish trade unions mostly have a positive attitude towards CSR. CSR is not seen as contrary to the unions' aims but rather as being in alignment with them, and complementary to them. The unions do not appear to be experiencing any sense of threat from CSR. In addition, the importance of CSR is expected to grow in the future, and this again is not seen as a danger. The reason for this positive union orientation may well be the national institutional system, which provides a strong and powerful basis for the trade unions. The unions view themselves as having a legitimate status in the institutional system, since they are widely regarded as a necessary and established part of the system. Their position is not questioned.

However, in the international context, where the unions cannot rely on the same sort of institutional system as in Finland itself, the situation appears to be more demanding. Here the unions are increasingly networking, negotiating and acting in co-operation with foreign unions, NGOs and multinational corporations. The challenge to negotiate on working conditions and employee rights with multinational companies has increased. However, since trade union membership is in fact declining in Finland nowadays (Nergaard 2011), the unions may face more challenges in the long run also in the national arena: their status and power might weaken in the future.

The unions' positive orientation to CSR can also be explained through the lens of the Finnish value system. Since such values as trustworthiness, honesty and co-operation are regarded as crucial in Finnish society, and since the trade unions have traditionally had an interdependent and co-operative relationship with the employers' organizations and think they know them well, the unions are likely to trust CSR initiatives and not be inclined to consider them as hypocritical or misguided.

Conclusions

Despite some convergence in terminology and understanding of CSR, we conclude that in the Finnish trade unions CSR is more implicit than explicit in nature (Matten and Moon 2008). As shown in this chapter the unions have engaged in several responsibility initiatives in practice, but they have seldom defined the concept precisely, and they do not have coherent policies on the issue. For example, the trade unions have jointly organized media events on decent work. Akava, SAK and SASK together with Kesko (a Finnish trading sector conglomerate) have been implementing a joint project in Vietnam, where they trained companies importing their products to Finland to take the environmental, social and work safety norms into consideration. The unions seem now to tend towards taking the initiative to make CSR explicit, although the dominant feeling is vagueness about the concept of CSR. The unions seem to be considering how CSR, which was originally a business-driven initiative, could be applied to support their goals.

It is suggested here that CSR arose in discussions in the Finnish trade unions during the early and mid-2000s, largely in reaction to changes in the national business system in the 1990s when, as various researchers have found (Tainio and Lilja 2003; Moen and Lilja 2004; Oinas 2005; Skippari 2005; Lilja *et al.* 2009; Lilja *et al.* 2011), international companies became important players in the Finnish economy and Finnish companies started to become international. Since the unions were – and are – increasingly facing pressure from the globalized markets, they have begun to reflect upon their attitude to CSR.

There are differences between the orientations to CSR in the different unions we interviewed. In one of them CSR was ignored almost completely while another was very keen on the topic. In the majority of the unions CSR is recognized and the unions are engaged across a range of CSR practices, even though there is variation in their use of the terminology and their understanding of the phenomenon. We conclude that CSR seems to on its way to becoming institutionalized in Finland and more explicit in Finnish trade union thinking. Our conclusion must also be that the attitude of Finnish trade unions towards CSR is generally open and trusting, and definitely more positive than negative.

References

Akava (2011) *Framework Agreement (2011)*. Online. Available: www.akava.fi/files/5828/Framework_agreement_13102011.pdf (accessed 14 February 2013).

Böckerman, P. and Uusitalo, R. (2006) 'Erosion of the Ghent System and Union Membership Decline: Lessons from Finland', *British Journal of Industrial Relations*, 44(2): 283–303.

Chamber of Commerce (2009) *Yrityskulttuuriopas*, Helsinki.

CSR (2011) *Corporate Social Responsibility (CSR)*. Online. Available: http://ec.europa.eu/enterprise/policies/sustainable-business/corporate-social-responsibility (accessed 30 October 2013).

GRI (2013) *Global Reporting Inititiative*. Online. Available: www.globalreporting.org/information/about-gri/what-is-GRI/Pages/default.aspx (accessed 28 October 2013).

Hall, P. A. and Soskice, D. (eds) (2001) *Varieties of Capitalism: The Institutional Foundations of Competitive Advantage*, Oxford: Oxford University Press.

Helkama, K. and Seppälä, T. (2004) 'Arvojen Suomessa 1980–2000', in R. Heiskala and E. Raekallio (eds) *Uusi jako: Miten Suomesta tuli kilpailukykyinen yhteiskunta*, 131–155, Helsinki: Gaudeamus.

Ilmonen, K. and Jokinen, K. (2002) *Luottamus modernissa maailmassa*, Jyväskylä: Sophi.

Juholin, E. (2004) 'For business or the good of all? A Finnish approach to corporate social responsibility', *Corporate Governance*, 4(3): 20–31.

Koivuniemi, J. (2000) *Tehtaan pillin tahdissa: Nokian tehdasyhdyskunnan sosiaalinen järjestys 1870–1939*, Bibliotheca Historica 64, Helsinki: Suomalaisen kirjallisuuden seura.

Kourula, A. (2010) 'Finland', in W. Visser and N. Tolhurst (eds) *The World Guide to CSR: A Country-by-Country Analysis of Corporate Sustainability and Responsibility*, Sheffield: Greenleaf.

Kujala, J. (2004) 'Managers' moral perceptions: change in Finland during the 1990s', *Business Ethics: A European Review*, 13(2/3): 143–165.

Kujala, J. (2010) 'Corporate responsibility perceptions in change: Finnish managers' views on stakeholder issues from 1994 to 2004', *Business Ethics: A European Review*, 19(1): 14–34.

Kujala, J., Lämsä, A.-M. and Penttilä, K. (2011) 'Managers' moral decision-making patterns over time: a multidimensional approach', *Journal of Business Ethics*, 100(2): 191–207.

Labour Court Establishment (2013) Online. Available: www.oikeus.fi/tyotuomioistuin/2022.htm (accessed 16 February 2013).

Lähdesmäki, M. (2012) *Studies on Corporate Social Responsibility in the Finnish Small Business Context*, Seinäjoki: Ruralia Institute, University of Helsinki.

Lamberg, J.-A. and Laurila, J. (2005) 'Materializing the societal effect: organizational forms and changing patterns of dominance in the paper industry', *Organization Studies*, 26(12): 1809–1830.

Lämsä, A.-M. (2007) 'Yrityksen vastuullisuus – mitä ja miksi?', in Päivi Vauhkonen (ed.) *Liiketoiminnan vastuullisuus, minkä väristä se on?*, 42–52, Oitmäki: Johtamistaidon opisto.

Lämsä, A.-M., Vehkaperä, M., Puttonen, T. and Pesonen, H.-L. (2008) 'Effect of business education on women and men students' attitudes to responsible business in society', *Journal of Business Ethics*, 82(1): 45–58.

Lilja, K., Laurila, J. and Lovio, R. (2011) 'Finland: innovating the global positioning of flagship companies and foreign-owned subsidiaries', in Peer Hull Kristensen and Kari Lilja (eds) *Nordic Capitalisms and Globalization: New Forms of Economic Organization and Welfare Institutions*, 47–85, Oxford: Oxford University Press.

Lilja, K., Laurila, J., Lovio, R. and Jääskeläinen, J. (2009) 'Fighting for global mandates from peripheral regions of the Finnish innovation system', in Peer Hull Kristensen and Kari Lilja (eds) *New Modes of Globalizing: Experimentalist Forms of Economic Organization and Enabling Welfare Institutions. Lessons from the Nordic Countries and Slovenia*, 54–96, Helsinki: Helsinki School of Economics.

Matten, D. and Moon, J. (2008) '"Implicit" and "explicit" CSR: a conceptual framework for a comparative understanding of corporate social responsibility', *Academy of Management Review*, 33(2): 303–424.

Moen, E. and Lilja, K. (2004) *Change in Coordinated Market Economies: The Case of Nokia and Finland*, Helsinki: Helsinki School of Economics.

Nergaard, K. (2011) 'Fagorganisering in Norden: Status og utviklingstrekk', *Fafo-notat*, 2010: 25. Online. Available: www.fafo.no/pub/rapp/10121/10121.pdf (accessed 28 February 2013).

Oinas, P. (2005) 'Finland: a success story?', *European Planning Studies*, 13(8): 1227–1244.

Panapanaan, V. M., Linnanen, L., Karvonen, M.-M. and Phan, V.T. (2003) 'Roadmapping corporate social responsibility in Finnish companies', *Journal of Business Ethics*, 44: 133–148.

Pohjola, M. (2003) 'Olemmeko maailmassa parhaimmistoa? Kansallisen kilpailukykymme puntarointia', in K. Alho, J. Lassila and P. Ylä-Anttila (eds) *Talouden tutkimus ja päätöksenteko. Kirjoituksia rakennemuutoksesta, kasvusta ja talouspolitiikasta*, 163–181, Helsinki: Yliopistopaino.

Puohiniemi, M. (2006) *Täsmäelämän ja uusyhteisöllisyyden aika*, Limor Kustannus.

Sala-i-Martin, X., Bilbao-Osario, B., Blanke, J., Drzeniek Hanouz, M. and Geiger, T. (2011) 'The Global Competitiveness Index 2011–2012: setting the foundations for strong productivity', in K. Schwab (ed.) *The Global Competitiveness Report 2011–2012*, 3–50, Geneva: World Economic Forum. Online. Available: www3.weforum.org/docs/WEF_GCR_Report_2011-12.pdf (accessed 21 February 2013).

Siltaoja, M. (2010) *Discarding the Mirror: The Importance of Intangible Social Resources to Responsibility in Business in a Finnish Context*, Jyväskylä Studies in Business and Economics 86, Jyväskylä: University of Jyväskylä.

Skippari, M. (2005) *Evolutionary Patterns in Corporate Political Activity: Insights from a Historical Single Case Study*, Publication 522, Tampere University of Technology.

Tainio, R. and Lilja, K. (2003) 'The Finnish business system in transition: outcomes, actors and their influence', in B. Czarniawska and G. Sevon (eds) *National Capitalisms, Global Competition, and Economic Performance*, 69–87, Trelleborg: Liber/Abstrakt/Copenhagen Business School Press.

Takala, T. (1991) *Managerial beliefs concerning social responsibility of the firm*, Jyväskylä: University of Jyväskylä.

Takala, T. (2004) 'Yrityksen yhteiskuntavastuu globalisoituvassa maailmassa', in Ilkka Kauppinen (ed.) *Moraalitalous*, 212–232, Tampere: Vastapaino.

Vitols, S. (2010) *The European Participation Index (EPI): A Tool for Gross-national Quantitative Comparison*, Background paper, European Trade Union Institute. Online. Available: www.worker-participation.eu/About-WP/European-Participation-Index-EPI/%28language%29/eng-GB (accessed 28 February 2013).

4 France

State influence over union strategies on CSR

Christelle Havard and André Sobczak

> [The national stakeholder dialogue organized by the government and known as Environment Grenelle] has led us to define our position towards CSR, work on specific plans and analyse the strategies of the other unions. It was a moment that accelerated our thinking and activity in this field.
>
> (CGT, General Confederation of Labour)

Introduction

The aim of this chapter is to highlight the strong influence that the state has over the strategies and actions of French trade union representatives in the field of Corporate Social Responsibility (CSR), which we define as the implementation of sustainable development at the level of the company. While some French union representatives use the term 'sustainable development' rather than CSR, we shall retain the term CSR, which is more appropriate when dealing with strategies and activities taking place at the level of companies.

Two examples that we shall further develop below illustrate the influence of the state. A first example is the 2008 legislation on collective bargaining that reviews the rules on the representativeness of the unions and requires a certain percentage in professional elections to be able to negotiate collective agreements. By pressurizing the unions to seek new members and retain their current ones, this reform shapes the strategies of the various French unions towards CSR. Some unions consider that CSR issues provide an opportunity to gain new members, while others prefer to concentrate on more traditional issues to maintain existing members. A second example of state influence is the decision of the French government to involve unions and other stakeholders in the definition of the national strategy on sustainable development. Being regularly consulted by the government on economic, social and environmental issues, the major French unions have been encouraged to appoint experts, or at least to develop a coherent discourse, in this field and, to a certain extent, to develop proactive, reactive or critical strategies.

National business system

In Amable's (2003) typology of forms of capitalism, the French national business system is characterized as an example of the 'continental European model'. Other authors, by contrast, argue that the French system is rather specific and occupies an intermediate position between the American or British and the German or Rhineland model (Hall and Soskice 2001). To describe national business systems, Redding (2005) uses different elements that interact with each other: business systems (structures and systems for co-ordinating economic behaviour and exchange); institutions as 'forms of order' organizing physical capital as well as human and social capital; the role of the state and of civil society; and the cultural system specified through identity, authority and the use of rationales.

French companies are more often than elsewhere family owned and are small or medium-sized (SMEs) (Maclean *et al.* 2007). Furthermore, public ownership is still strong, even if it has decreased significantly over the last 20 years. These elements explain why corporate governance in France is more oriented to a long-term view than in the UK or USA, even if the influence of globalization tends to shorten strategic perspectives. The French education system and the training of managers are strongly influenced by the principle of meritocracy. Relationships at work are for the most part hierarchical and the labour force has become more highly skilled over the last 30 years. Finally, as in other countries, there is a trend towards deregulation of the labour market.

However, the main characteristic of the French national business system identified by many researchers is related to the strong influence of the state. The state plays an extended function beyond its regulatory role. The state is a principal investor, a significant owner of key industries and an influence over the development of individual companies through strong business legislation (Schlierer and Seidel 2009). According to Charkham (1995: 120), in France the 'government's right to influence and, where necessary, intervene quietly and effectively behind the scenes is expected, respected, and, it would seem, admired'.

Industrial relations system

French industrial relations are marked by a tradition of conflict rather than consensus and by the dominant role of the state, which regulates the relations between employers and employee representatives. Despite the importance of legislation in the field of employment and working conditions, social dialogue and collective bargaining have evolved strongly in France over the last 30 years (Ministry of Labour 2012).

Traditionally, according to the French favourability principle (*principe de faveur*), collective agreements had to improve and not reduce workers' rights defined by legislation or agreements negotiated at a higher level.

Over the last 15 years, however, the legislator has defined certain areas where the social partners have the opportunity to negotiate so-called 'derogatory' or exemption agreements (*accords dérogatoires*) that reduce workers' rights defined by legislation or agreements at a higher level. This opportunity has arisen because – to be valid – collective agreements are now submitted for signature by one or more unions that represent at least 30 per cent of the workers, provided too that there is no opposition voiced from those trade unions that represent at least 50 per cent of the workers. This new system, established by Law No. 2004–391 of 4 May 2004, reinforces the legitimacy of unions and collective bargaining, but threatens the existence of smaller unions.

As in other developed countries (Hayter *et al.* 2011), collective bargaining in France has developed significantly over the last 15 years at different levels (national, sector and company), but especially at the company level (European Employment Review 2006). More than 90 per cent of employees are covered by a collective agreement (EIRO 2008) compared with an average of 66 per cent in the rest of Europe (Ministry of Labour, 2012). This high level of coverage results historically from the extension by the Ministry of Labour of agreements at sector level to all companies belonging to the sector, but it is also more recently linked to the increase of bargaining at company level. As Andolfatto and Labbé (2012) point out, the number of agreements at company level increased from 6,479 to 33,869 between 1990 and 2011 (a 522 per cent rise).

The support of public policy and legislation played a significant role in this development. First, at national level since 2007, the government has been required to consult the trade unions' and employers' representatives (the social partners) before any reform of industrial relations, employment, vocational training or social welfare. Second, at company level, it is mandatory by law to negotiate on more and more topics (such as disability, older workers and diversity management). The economic crisis also played a significant role in the development of collective bargaining, since the social partners have met to adapt rules to the economic context, such as employment, training and retirement (Ministry of Labour 2012). During negotiations, employer representatives at national and sector levels, and employers at company level, have in most cases been the initiator and organizer of the bargaining process (Andolfatto and Labbé 2012), but the state also retains a significant role in stimulating collective bargaining.

Collective representation of employees in France is dual. On the one hand, the representation of *collective* interests is the preserve of the unions, which have represented the general interests of workers since the beginning of the twentieth century at national and sectoral levels. Each union considered 'representative' has the power to negotiate collective agreements at national, industry and company level.[1] On the other hand, the representation of *individual* interests is assigned to other actors, such as employee representatives (*délégués du personnel*) and works councils (*comités d'entreprise*), which defend individual rights at the workplace (Le Queux and Sainsaulieu 2010). This historical dichotomy is however difficult to capture: indeed the presence of union delegates at company level and, more importantly, the priority given to union candidates in the workplace elections of employee representatives and works councils[2] blurs the borders between union and non-union forms of representation (Gumbrell-McCormick and Hyman 2006). This explains why, despite a very low rate of unionization overall (7 or 8 per cent), unions are still well established in companies and in the public sector (more than 40 per cent of employees declared in 2005 that unions were present in their organization: Wolff 2008). Unions also sit on various joint bodies at local, regional or national levels according to the principle of parity (*paritarisme*) (Pernot 2005). Thus, French unions are institutionalized and considered legitimate by the state and employer organizations (Le Queux and Sainsaulieu 2010; Bevort and Jobert 2011).

This historically low rate of unionization is structurally due to the fact that a worker does not need to belong to a union to benefit from the advantages negotiated in collective agreements at company level or the extended sector agreements. As unions represent the general interest when they negotiate, the advantages of social dialogue benefit every employee. However, even if this institutionalized embeddedness of unions is not regarded as problematic, the low density of membership does raise a challenge. This challenge is not primarily financial because, over and above membership fees, unions receive financial resources from the state, while union delegates are paid by their employers to exercise their functions (Andolfatto and Labbé 2011). The challenge is, rather, more linked to their representativeness (Pernot 2005; Bevort 2012).

Since 1966, five trade unions had been recognized *de jure* as representative at national level by the public authorities: the *Confédération Générale du Travail* (CGT); the *Confédération Française Démocratique du Travail* (CFDT); *Force Ouvrière* (CGT-FO); the *Confédération Française des Travailleurs Chrétiens* (CFTC); and the *Confédération Générale des Cadres* (CFE-CGC). Other unions are recognized as representative at industry or company level. Law No. 2008–789 of 20 August 2008 made important changes to the representativeness rules: union representativeness is now based on the results of workplace elections and only representative unions have the right to sit at the negotiating table. However, the results of the last elections published in March 2013 for the national level did not change the ranking of the five trade unions, which keep their representativeness (see Table 4.1).

The French trade union landscape is therefore very fragmented, with a traditional division between the unions with a secular background (CGT, CGT-FO and CFE-CGC) and those with a Christian background (CFTC and CFDT) (Pernot 2005). Trade unions historically compete with each other for membership and to defend their own identity. Trade unions are mostly presented as 'conflict-ridden' and 'politicized' (Le Queux and

Table 4.1 Results of the most recent union elections in France

Results of the two last elections for the industrial courts in 2009 and in 2012				*Results for the public sector elections (state, hospitals, territorial authorities) in 2011*		
Lists	*Votes cast 2009*	*Percentage 2009*	*Percentage 2012*	*Lists*	*Votes cast*	*Percentage*
CGT	1,570,500	33.98	30.63	CGT	24 700	24.7
CFDT	1,007,985	21.81	29.74	CFDT	18,900	18.9
FO	730,855	15.81	18.23	CGT-FO	18,500	18.5
CFTC	401,494	8.69	10.63	UNSA[1]	9,200	9.2
CFE-CGC	379,027	8.20	10.78	FSU[2]	9,000	9
UNSA	288,924	6.25	6.3	USS[3]	6,600	6.6
USS	176,140	3.81	3.47	CFTC	4,000	4
Others	66,771	1.44	1.4	CFE-CGC	2,900	2.9
				Others	6,200	6.2

Source: Ministry of Labour, 2009 (www.fonction-publique.gouv.fr/statistiques-24).

Notes

1 Union Nationale des Syndicats Autonomes, the national association of autonomous unions, but not recognized by the state as representative.

2 Fédération Syndicale Unitaire, the largest union in the education sector.

3 Union Syndicale Solidaires, an association grouping unions unaffiliated to any of the other main French union confederations.

Sainsaulieu 2010), but these features have tended to fade over the last 20 years, mainly for the following reasons:

- unions' capacity to mobilize workers is weakening (Pernot 2005; Le Queux and Sainsaulieu 2010);
- unions are more and more engaged in collective bargaining and often sign agreements. According to the Ministry of Labour (2012) the propensity to sign for each trade union was: 93 per cent for CFDT; 91 per cent for CFE-CGC; 90 per cent for CGT-FO; 88 per cent for CFTC; and 84 per cent for CGT;
- unions have tended to become far more professional at bargaining (Andolfatto and Labbé 2012);
- the biggest union (CGT) has distanced itself from the Communist Party (Pernot 2005) and, during its 2009 Congress, declared its willingness to adopt a reformist agenda and become the 'privileged interlocutor' for the government, thus breaking with its radical past (Le Queux and Sainsaulieu 2010).

The evolution of the CSR debate

We have already highlighted the strong tradition in France of state intervention in the economy and the nature of the relationship between business and society. It is therefore not surprising that French public authorities at national and regional levels also play an important part in encouraging managers to integrate social and environmental factors into corporate strategies and practices and in offering platforms for stakeholder dialogue on CSR (Berthoin Antal and Sobczak 2007).

The most visible activity of the French public authorities in the field of CSR is related to the development of mandatory social and environmental reporting. Since the end of the 1970s, companies with more than 300 employees have been required to publish a social report containing a detailed list of social indicators and to discuss it with their works council (Rey 1980). Since 2001, companies listed on the French stock market have had to integrate a list of social and environmental indicators into their annual report to shareholders that is also generally available to internal stakeholders and the general public (Delbard, 2008). In 2012, the French government decided to extend this obligation progressively to companies that are not listed, but have a minimum of 500 employees. This legislation encourages managers to think about companies' social and environmental impacts and to develop performance indicators to monitor progress in these areas. For French unions and worker representatives, it guarantees extensive information about corporate social and environmental strategies, practices and performance, hence enabling the development of union activity in the field of CSR.

A second important feature of the French CSR context is the role played by public authorities in the organization of stakeholder dialogue on social and environmental issues, both at national and local levels. In 2007 the French government organized a national consultation process called 'Environment Grenelle' (*Grenelle de l'environnement*)[3] that brought together representatives from the national and regional governments, and from business, trade unions and non-governmental organizations (NGOs) to agree on a joint analysis of the major environmental challenges facing the country and to define future policies in this area (Stanziola Vieira and Bétaille 2008). For three months, these stakeholders met within six working groups on subjects such as climate change, biodiversity, sustainable production and consumption, green jobs and competitiveness. Each working group comprised 40 members, that is, eight for each stakeholder group. Their mission was to propose measures to support sustainable development and to identify obstacles to their implementation. Despite many criticisms highlighting an insufficient translation of the conclusions into legally binding regulations, there is a broad consensus among experts on the positive impact of this stakeholder dialogue on the levels of awareness regarding environmental challenges and the potential for innovation in this field. In a similar vein, at the regional level, some public authorities involve the various stakeholders, particularly the trade unions, in the development of innovative programmes encouraging local companies to develop and implement CSR strategies (Sobczak and Cam 2012). These initiatives contribute towards raising awareness among French unions of the CSR debate and promoting the clarification of policy or even the appointment of CSR experts within some unions.

Methods: unions interviewed

Our study is based on interviews carried out in 2012 with the five major trade unions currently recognized as representative (CFDT, CFE-CGC, CFTC, CGT and CGT-FO), which participated in the Environment Grenelle process in 2007. We supplemented this set of interviews with further ones carried out by the authors in 2006 (Havard and Sobczak 2006) with three unions in the chemical sector (CGT, CFDT, CGT-FO) (see Table 4.2.). Interviews lasted 1.5 hours and were generally face to face, though one was by phone.

Conducting interviews before and after the Environment Grenelle process helps to highlight the evolution of perceptions and activity with respect to CSR for CGT, CFDT and CGT-FO, even if the structure of the two samples was not exactly the same during the two data collection phases. The main questions that the interviewees were asked focused on their perception of sustainable development and CSR and the actors involved in these fields, the way CSR was covered by the union's strategy, the way unionists work with other stakeholders (for instance NGOs) on CSR, how unions are organized to support CSR activities, the provision of training programmes to support members, and the processes through which the union participates in negotiations on CSR.

Union understanding of CSR

French trade unions understand the link between sustainable development and CSR in different ways. CFDT clearly sees CSR as aiming at applying the concept of sustainable development to companies. The union is very

Table 4.2 Interviewed French unions

	2006		*2012*	
	National union	*Sector union*	*National union*	*Sector union*
CGT	1	2 (energy and metalworking)	1	0
CFDT	1	2 (chemicals and energy)	1	0
CGT-FO	1	1 (energy)	1	2 (energy)
CFTC	0	0	2	0
CFE-CGC	0	0	1	0
Total	8		8	

well informed about the debates in this area and tries to influence them. CFE-CGC considers that CSR corresponds to the social dimension within the concept of sustainable development, which also covers an economic and an environmental dimension. After Environment Grenelle, CFE-CGC developed its activities in the field of CSR to highlight the social aspect of sustainable development. CGT also underlines that many citizens tend to reduce sustainable development to simply environmental aspects. The union thus uses the term 'sustainable human development' to emphasize the social aspects of sustainable development.

A main contrast in approach sets those French unions that believe it is possible to defend social and environmental aims simultaneously, thereby creating win-win situations, against those that believe this to be impossible. CFDT and CGT are clearly in the former category, adopting an approach to CSR that aims at integrating the economic, social and environmental challenges. CGT affirms that social and environmental dimensions have to be and can be closely linked: creating a green economy with bad jobs would not be conforming with CSR. CGT considers that the integration of environmental challenges presupposes a better trained and more secure workforce. Hence they believe, like CFDT, in win–win situations.

For CFTC, a company is a community of interests. It is normal that the members of this community are treated with respect, but also that the community respects other communities. A company's success depends largely on its various stakeholders, and its managers therefore have the responsibility to share the benefits with them. These ideas have always been at the heart of the Christian tradition of CFTC. In other words, this union – like many companies – considers that they have always reflected the concept of CSR, even though they did not use the term in the past. They do not consider themselves as environmental experts and so focus more on the social dimension. However, they regard Nature as an important part of the divine creation that merits protection not only as an end in itself but also as the condition to secure the future of humanity. They therefore try to take into account environmental dimensions in their CSR strategy and activities.

CFE-CGC and CGT-FO, by contrast, are sceptical about the possibility of linking the social and environmental dimensions. CFE-CGC explains that their members have very different perceptions about where to set priorities according to the sector in which they work. For example, on energy issues, their members in the gas and petroleum sectors may combat stricter environmental norms in order to save their jobs, whereas those in the metalworking sector might hope that the development of new forms of energy will create jobs in their companies. In other words, the development of the green economy will create some jobs, but destroy others. As a union, CFE-CGC sees its main role as focusing on the social impact of this transition rather than taking positions on which kind of environmental norms it prefers. In a similar way, CFE-CGC concentrates in multi-stakeholder debates on the health of workers rather than on health issues for the general population. This choice is also linked to the union's limited resources.

CGT-FO remains the French union that is the most sceptical or even hostile to the concepts of sustainable development and CSR. The union considers that these concepts are used to weaken the interests of workers within a multi-stakeholder dialogue. Given limited economic means, any investment in improving the environmental performance of companies is seen as an effort that does not benefit the workers through wage increases or better working conditions. CGT-FO believes that the union has no expertise and legitimacy on environmental issues and – similarly – denies that other actors, such as NGOs, have expertise and legitimacy on social issues, which it believes are a union preserve. CGT-FO prefers clearly shared responsibilities among the actors rather than the development of multi-stakeholder dialogue where every actor gives his or her opinion on all subjects. This also means that CGT-FO does not want to participate in corporate governance, which is, according to this union, the aim of CFDT and CGT. For CGT-FO, unions should concentrate on defending workers' interests, and not try to play the role of the state, which is to ensure compliance with labour law. They even criticise the involvement of unions in initiatives aimed at promoting equal opportunities, since it is the task of the labour inspectorate to monitor compliance with legislation on non-discrimination; taking over this task gives the government an excuse to reduce its budget for labour inspection.

Union policies on CSR

For the Environment Grenelle process, unions had to appoint at least one representative for each of the six parallel working groups that held numerous meetings over a short time period. Absence from these consultations was not a real option for the unions, not even for those that were sceptical, since they wanted the government and the public to be aware of their opinions. This was a huge challenge for the smaller unions, since the number of personnel required to support multi-stakeholder dialogue on sustainable development and CSR risked limiting their capacity to make progress on other important projects.

The French unions used different strategies to take part in the various debates. CFDT developed a team dedicated to 'business and society' at the intersectoral level that included experts on subjects like biodiversity, water, energy, agriculture, industrial policies and governance. The team members had been identified for their expertise on specific subjects, but each team member is able to participate in conferences and roundtables aimed at informing union members or the broader public on the various aspects of CSR. By contrast, CGT decided not to dedicate anyone full-time to sustainable development and CSR, but rather to set up a network of about 15 individuals at intersectoral and sectoral level. This allowed the union to share representation within the different multi-stakeholder dialogues and promoted co-ordination between the intersectoral and sectoral levels. The three other unions appointed only one or two individuals to take charge of co-ordinating CSR-linked activities. They usually also have other duties within the union and need to rely on the support of other members, in particular when it comes to representing the union in multi-stakeholder dialogue.

The Environment Grenelle process led the unions to develop a clear perspective regarding the way in which they perceive CSR and their respective strategies inside and outside their organization. It has also led the unions to become particularly well acquainted with each other's positions. To date, all unions have developed a communications policy and a discourse on CSR at the intersectoral level mainly to allow their members to respond to potential requests for information from companies. But these policies depend on the importance the trade unions attach to CSR and the resources they are able to spend. For example, CFDT has been engaged for a long time in communicating its policies by means of its Congresses. Having adopted the first resolution on this subject at its 2002 Congress, entitled 'The World We Want', CFDT formulated a second resolution at its 2006 Congress, which demonstrated that the majority of its members who voted in favour were perfectly aware of the changes that were necessary to policy. Immediately after this Congress, the union's team in charge of CSR decided to prepare a summer university on sustainable development for 2007. This four-day event, which had been decided largely before the launch of the Environment Grenelle process, brought together 250 CFDT members and allowed them to discuss specific projects with representatives from employers' associations, NGOs and the state. When the Environment Grenelle process opened a few days later, the CFDT members were therefore particularly well prepared, which allowed them to play an important role during the debates as well as in the preparation of the legislation designed to implement the measures commonly agreed. CGT invested in its website to give information about its activity on CSR. CFTC communicated internally in 2010–2011 on social traceability (*traçabilité sociale*), a social monitoring of the supply chain (see below). CGT-FO formulated in 2012 a communication for its members presenting its critical position on CSR. CGT-FO and CFE-CGC have found it difficult to develop a common point of view on CSR through their different sector federations, which assert their independence over their degree of integration into the union.

The French unions' engagement in disseminating the principles of sustainable development and CSR among their members differs according to their strategies. As the union that aims to be the most proactive in this field, CFDT has developed a large number of initiatives together with actors at sector and regional levels. The intersectoral level organizes various training sessions in order to help members understand the challenges and possible activity in the area of sustainable development and CSR. The team created at intersectoral level sometimes takes part in seminars or debates at the sector or regional level, but in most cases these actors have set up their own dedicated teams. Since the 2010 Congress, CFDT has decided to organize monthly 'sustainable development afternoons' to co-ordinate strategies and activities at the different levels within the union. These meetings usually focus on specific subjects, such as water, transport or nanotechnologies. They bring together between 12 and 50 members.

In a similar way, CGT and CFTC also offer training sessions on sustainable development and CSR to their members (CFTC has trained its members since 2005–2006). Their intersectoral experts are regularly invited to intervene in debates or seminars at sector or regional level. CGT has proficient experts in some areas, for example on biodiversity. However, CGT has not yet created a real network on sustainable development and CSR. This may be a plan for the future, as it is for CFE-CGC, which would like to create such a network bringing together people in charge of sustainable development and CSR at sector and regional levels. However, it has not yet succeeded in doing so.

CGT-FO does not plan any kind of joint activity with the unions at regional level, since – it argues – it is facing so many other challenges with the economic crisis and is very resistant to the idea of sustainable development and CSR. Nevertheless, having noticed that its members at sector level are sometimes involved in the negotiation of agreements dealing with sustainable development or CSR, CGT-FO considered offering training sessions in 2012 on how to conduct such negotiations, but a follow-up interview in 2013 revealed that they did not take place.

Union engagement with CSR

At the beginning of the 2000s, several other initiatives at the intersectoral level revealed an increasing interest on the part of French unions in CSR. In 2000, CFDT, CFE-CGC and CGT joined several major companies in creating a joint think tank on CSR called the Observatory on Corporate Social Responsibility (*Observatoire de la Responsabilité Sociétale des Entreprises* – ORSE). In 2002, CFDT, CFE-CGC, CFTC and CGT created a joint committee on employees' savings in order to develop an endorsement for socially responsible savings funds and to encourage union members at company level to invest in them. Finally, in 2004, CFDT and CGT joined several NGOs and academics in creating the Citizens' Forum on CSR (*Forum Citoyen pour la Responsabilité Sociale des Entreprises*) whose aim was to develop and advance common positions on CSR in discussion with companies and policy makers. Among the major French unions, only CGT-FO decided not to take part in any of these initiatives.

All major French unions are involved in the negotiation of agreements at company level related to sustainable development or CSR, whether they are transnational company, national or site agreements. In general, these negotiations are conducted locally without any intervention from the national unions that are often not even aware of all initiatives. This means that even CGT-FO representatives take part in such negotiations and sign agreements. All unions are involved in negotiations on CSR at the sector level, in particular in chemicals, energy and the car industry.

French unions are also very active in the field of CSR reporting. Apart from CGT-FO, all unions emphasize the importance of the legislation on mandatory reporting of companies' social and environmental impacts in their annual reports, and aim at its improvement. First, they would like to broaden the scope of existing legislation that currently applies to companies with more than 2,000 employees to SMEs. They consider that the information available in the annual reports is very useful for worker representatives. Second, and more importantly, they would like worker representatives to be consulted before the publication of the reports. This would strengthen social dialogue on sustainable development and CSR. CFTC has developed a very interesting initiative which it calls 'social traceability', which consists in monitoring the supply chain to show the social and environmental impacts of the product to consumers. The union is building partnerships with certain companies to develop this concept further. Through this initiative CFTC wants to participate in the CSR debate in an innovative way and to improve its visibility with employers, consumers and employees.

The French unions have developed very different strategies towards NGOs. While CFDT, CGT and CFTC co-operate closely with NGOs, CFE-CGC and CGT-FO do not aim to develop particular relationships with them and criticize their growing role in relation to social regulation. In line with its proactive strategy towards sustainable development, CFDT has created a partnership with the environmental NGO, FNE (*France Nature Environnement*). For CFDT, this NGO has a reformist view that is similar to its own. Both organizations believe that it is useful to compromise and sign agreements allowing them to achieve a large proportion of their aims rather than expecting the other party to accept all their priorities. Moreover, FNE has a significant membership, which makes it different from other NGOs that are sustained mainly by donors. For the moment, the partnership focuses principally on the intersectoral level, but some projects also take shape at sectoral or regional level. Meanwhile, CGT does not want to conclude a partnership with a specific NGO. It prefers to hold discussions with all NGOs and then to launch specific projects with the ones that are interested. Most of these contacts emerge in the Citizens' Forum on CSR that CGT and CFDT created in 2004 with several French NGOs. In a similar way, CFTC co-operates with various NGOs, in particular on projects in emerging countries.

These three unions emphasize the common aims and objectives that exist between themselves and NGOs and the fact that many of their members are also involved in NGOs. They believe that co-operation with them is a way to access expertise, particularly on environmental issues, as well as an opportunity to renew their image or even to recruit new members. By contrast, CGT-FO and CFE-CGC underline the differences between unions and NGOs. CFE-CGC argues that NGOs aim at protecting the environment, whereas unions have a mandate to defend workers' interests. For this union, these two aims are not necessarily compatible, which makes co-operation difficult. CGT-FO also states that unions and NGOs have different priorities. The union insists moreover that NGOs lack legitimacy and representativeness. For CGT-FO, NGO leaders often represent only themselves, while unions communicate with their membership and have a transparent process of appointing or electing their leaders and defining their strategies. These major differences explain, according to CGT-FO, why traditional bilateral social dialogue between employers and unions should not be widened to NGOs.

Discussion

The institutionalist theoretical framework outlined in the introduction to this volume is particularly relevant for the analysis of the French situation: companies, but mainly government and regulation, have influenced the strategy of the 'reactive' trade unions. But in turn, the most pro-active unions have acted as real 'institutional entrepreneurs', that is, as organized actors with sufficient resources to contribute to changing institutions or to creating new institutions altogether (DiMaggio 1988; Battilana *et al.* 2009).

French unions have been influenced by the national institutional context. First, legislation on mandatory CSR reporting encourages companies to develop CSR policies and sometimes to negotiate agreements with unions on social and environmental issues. Second, recent developments in French industrial relations provide a favourable environment for unions to engage in CSR. For example, the development of collective bargaining, particularly at company level as promoted by legislation, offers new opportunities for unions to negotiate. Indeed, over recent years, French unions have shown a greater propensity to negotiate and to sign agreements. They have become increasingly professional when engaging in social dialogue. Moreover, new rules on union representativeness create a climate of enhanced competition between unions, especially for the less representative ones. CSR may be considered as a means by which unions participate in social dialogue and become more visible to employees and consumers, and thus increase their membership.

French unions have also been influenced by the negotiation of transnational company agreements on CSR between multinational companies and European or international workers' representatives (Schoemann *et al.* 2008). French union representatives have been at least informed about these negotiations and in some cases were members of the negotiating team or even signatories, thereby illustrating the role unions could play in the field of CSR. However, those agreements covered – and still cover – only a small number of multinational companies concentrated in certain sectors, while most worker representatives largely ignored CSR and its potential impact on union activities (Havard and Sobczak 2008).

At the same time, at sector level, some French union federations have also developed activities on CSR. For at least two reasons, these sectors were the same as those concentrating on transnational company agreements, that is, food, metal, energy, chemicals and construction. First, environmental risks were particularly important for companies in these sectors and threatened damaging consequences for the health and safety of their workers. Second, consequently these companies were likely to face stricter legislation, which might have had an impact on their economic situation and thus on employment levels. Finally, the Environment Grenelle process played a significant role in encouraging union engagement in CSR, especially for those unions which had not been involved in this area before 2007. The most committed unions (CFDT, CFTC and CGT) revealed their expertise during the dialogue with other stakeholders and the less involved ones (CFE-CGC and CGT-FO) had no choice but to be present at the multi-stakeholder dialogue, since their legitimacy was at stake. All the unions therefore mobilized resources to participate in this important event that was widely covered by the media.

Connected to this institutional context, the business context also played a role in stimulating union activity in the field of CSR. The development of international framework agreements initiated at the end of the 1990s by large French international companies (such as Danone and Rhodia) offered opportunities for unions to negotiate on CSR (Sobczak 2007). From this point of view, companies can be viewed as 'institutional entrepreneurs' (in DiMaggio's definition, 1988; Battilana *et al.* 2009) that have contributed a conducive dynamic to CSR, as indeed some unions have also done. This favourable national and business context has not produced homogenous union strategies. On the contrary, some unions engaged very early on CSR (at the beginning of the 2000s) and adopted a particularly proactive strategy in this field. They dedicated human and financial resources and developed communication and training activity and expertise in this area at intersectoral level. Other unions engaged later (during and after the Environment Grenelle process) and one union – CGT-FO – still maintains a critical attitude towards CSR. However, all unions have developed a position on CSR, whether favourable or critical, and actively communicate their approach to their members.

Today, some French unions play a significant role in promoting CSR at several levels: at the national level through lobbying conducted jointly with NGOs to influence public authorities; at the sectoral level in some industries through negotiating agreements on CSR; at the regional level through taking part in CSR projects initiated by local public authorities (Sobczak and Cam 2012); and at the company level through negotiating agreements, but also by trying to disseminate a CSR culture among employee representatives.

In 2003, the report published by Segal *et al.* (2003) revealed a strange paradox: although CSR deals with social topics traditionally handled by unions, this field has been primarily implemented by management. Today this paradox seems to be irrelevant for some French unions which can be considered as 'institutional entrepreneurs' in CSR (DiMaggio 1988). Their 'institutional work' (Lawrence *et al.* 2011) in promoting CSR is legitimate as a result of their status as trade unions that are considered legally representative of employees, even if their membership level is very low compared with other European countries. CSR might be an opportunity for unions to deepen their informal legitimacy not only in the eyes of employees, but also in the eyes of other stakeholders (managers, consumers, NGOs and civil society, amongst others). Like CGT, CFDT and CFTC, they could become 'societal stakeholders' (Delbard 2011).

Conclusions

This chapter has aimed to outline the strategies and activities of French trade unions in the field of CSR and highlight the role of the state in the development of these strategies. The study undertaken over several years among the five main French unions shows that, even placed in the same national context, trade unions adopt different strategies and actions. Some of them are proactive, others reactive and one is altogether resistant towards CSR.

To understand the differences in union strategies and activities, it is important to go beyond the role of the state and to understand the influence of other stakeholders, in particular NGOs, employers and other unions. It would be fruitful to build on research related to stakeholder theory for this purpose. The findings of this chapter could be supplemented by further research not only among NGOs and employer associations but also among union members to understand their perception of their unions' strategies and activities in the field of CSR and the ways in which they try to influence them. Finally, further research could focus on the influences of European and international unions on French unions in the field of CSR.

Notes

1 A trade union is considered as representative and is allowed to negotiate at national level if it obtains at least 8 per cent of the votes at the last professional elections. It is considered as representative at the sector and company level, if it obtains at least 10 per cent.

2 As Gumbrell-McCormick and Hyman (2006: 482) explain:

> 'Representative' unions have a privileged role in elections: they alone can nominate candidates in the first round, and only if these fail to attract half the available votes, is there a second round open to non-union candidates.

3 The name 'Grenelle' comes from a stakeholder dialogue organized by the French government after the protests in May 1968 at the Ministry of Social Affairs in the Rue de Grenelle, Paris.

References

Amable, B. (2003) *The Diversity of Modern Capitalism*, Oxford: Oxford University Press.

Andolfatto, D. and Labbé, D. (2011) *Sociologie des syndicats*, Paris: La découverte, 3rd edn.

Andolfatto, D. and Labbé, D. (2012) 'The future of the French trade unions', *Management revue*, 23(4): 341–352.

Battilana, J., Leca, B. and Boxenbaum, E. (2009) 'How actors change institutions: towards a theory of institutional entrepreneurship', *Academy of Management Annals*, 3(1): 65–107.

Berthoin Antal, A. and Sobczak, A. (2007) 'Corporate social responsibility in France: a mix of national traditions and international influences', *Business and Society*, 46(1): 9–32.

Bevort, A. (2012) 'Représentativité', in A. Bevort, A. Jobert, M. Lallement and A. Mias (eds) *Dictionnaire du travail*, Paris: Presses Universitaires de France, pp. 666–672.

Bevort, A. and Jobert, A. (2011) *Sociologie du travail: Les relations professionnelles*, Paris: Armand Colin, 2nd edn.

Charkham, J.P. (1995) *Keeping Good Company: A Study of Corporate Governance in Five Countries*, Oxford: Oxford University Press.

Delbard, O. (2008) 'CSR legislation in France and the European regulatory paradox: an analysis of EU CSR policy and sustainability reporting practice', *Corporate Governance*, 8(4): 397–405.

Delbard, O. (2011) 'Social partners or full-fledged stakeholders? Trade unions and CSR in Europe (France, Germany and the UK)', *Society and Business Review*, 6(3): 260–277.

DiMaggio, P.J. (1988) 'Interest and agency in institutional theory', in L. Zucker (ed.) *Institutional patterns and organizations*, Cambridge, MA: Ballinger, pp. 3–22.

EIRO (2008) *France: Industrial Relations Profile*, Eurofound. Available: www.eurofound.europa.eu/eiro/country/france.htm.

European Employment Review (2006) 'Enterprise-level social dialogue', *European Industrial Relations Review*, January.

Gumbrell-McCormick, R. and Hyman, R. (2006), 'Embedded collectivism? Workplace representation in France and Germany', *Industrial Relations Journal*, 37(5): 473–491.

Hall, P. and Soskice, D. (2001) *Varieties of Capitalism: The Institutional Foundations of Comparative Advantage*, Oxford: Oxford University Press.

Havard, C. and Sobczak, A. (2006) 'Corporate Social Responsibility: Threat or Opportunity for Labour Organisations in the Era of Globalization?', Communication to the 22nd Congress *EGOS*, Bergen, 6–8 July.

Havard, C. and Sobczak, A. (2008) 'Implementing International Framework Agreements on Corporate Social Responsibility within Multinational Companies: The Involvement of Local Actors Matters', Communication to the International Labour Process Conference 'Work Matters', Dublin, 18–20 March.

Hayter, S., Fashoyin, T. and Kochan, T.A. (2011) 'Review essay: collective bargaining for the 21st century', *Journal of Industrial Relations*, 53(2): 225–247.

Lawrence, T., Suddaby, R. and Leca, B. (2011) 'Institutional work: refocusing institutional studies of organization', *Journal of Management Inquiry*, 20(1): 52–58.

Le Queux, S. and Sainsaulieu, Y. (2010) 'Social movement and unionism in France: a case of revitalization?', *Labor Studies Journal*, 35(4): 503–519.

Maclean, M., Harvey, C. and Press, J. (2007) 'Managerialism and post-war evolution of the French national business system', *Business History*, 49(4): 531–551.

Ministry of Labour/Ministère du travail (2009) *Résultats des élections prud'homales de 2008 par collège*, 17 March. Available: www.travail-emploi-sante.gouv.fr/espaces,770/travail,771/dossiers,156/relations-professionnelles,308/les-elections-prud-homales,1376/resultats-des-elections-prud,1380/resultats-des-elections-prud,9502.html.

Ministry of Labour/Ministère du travail (2012) *La négociation collective en 2011*, Paris: Ministère du travail.

Pernot, J.-M. (2005) *Syndicats: lendemain de crise?*, Paris: Editions Gallimard.

Redding, G. (2005) 'The thick description and comparison of societal systems of capitalism', *Journal of International Business Studies*, March, 36: 123–155.

Rey, F. (1980) 'Corporate social performance and reporting in France', in L.E. Preston (ed.) *Research in Corporate Social Performance and Policy*, Vol. 2, Greenwich: JAI, 291–325.

Schlierer, H.-J. and Seidel, F. (2009) 'Corporate social responsibility: the French way. A longitudinal study of corporate annual reports', *EBEN Annual Conference*, Athens, 10–12 September.

Schoemann, I., Sobczak, A., Voss, E. and Wilke, P. (2008) *Codes of Conduct and International Framework Agreements: New Forms of Governance at Company Level*, Report to the European Foundation for the Improvement of Living and Working Conditions, Dublin.

Segal, J.-P., Sobczak, A. and Triomphe, C.-E. (2003) *Corporate Social Responsibility and Working Conditions*, Dublin: European Foundation for the Improvement of Living and Working Conditions.

Sobczak, A. (2007) 'Legal dimensions of international framework agreements in the field of corporate social responsibility', *Relations Industrielles–Industrial Relations*, 62(3): 466–491.

Sobczak, A. and Cam, C. (2012) 'The role of local public authorities in inter-organizational learning for corporate responsibility. The example of a local charter for corporate responsibility in Western France', *Academy of Management Annual Meeting*, 3–7 August, Boston.

Stanziola Vieira, R. and Bétaille, J. (2008) 'Grenelle de l'environnement: is France making up for lost time?', in K. Bosselmann, R. Engel and P. Taylor (eds) *Governance for Sustainability. Issues, Challenges, Successes*, IUCN Environmental Policy and Law Paper, No. 70, 201–204.

Wolff, L. (2008) 'Le paradoxe du syndicalisme français: un faible nombre d'adhérents, mais des syndicats bien implantés', *Premières informations Premières synthèses*, DARES, 16.1.

5 Germany

Binding agreements preferable to voluntary CSR

Axel Haunschild and Florian Krause

> If CSR is voluntary but not arbitrary, it might be useful. [...] However, it should not undermine German labour standards. We as unions advocate respected laws, whereas CSR promotes voluntary duties.
>
> (IG BCE, Mining, Chemical and Energy Workers' Union)

Introduction

Germany is often described as an archetypal co-ordinated market economy (CME). Key features of the system are close relationships between companies, their suppliers and customers, internal decision-making structures and processes that are strongly consensus-based as well as a longer-term orientation towards company finance. The country's industrial relations system is furthermore characterized by a high degree of institutionalization and legal codification of union rights, both at company and industry levels. Germany's social market economy can be described as a business system in which the creation and maintenance of consensus on a wide range of issues is important. Companies and their fields of activities are thus strongly influenced by society in general and by established networks of societal actors in particular.

This chapter presents results from interviews with corporate social responsibility (CSR) experts of major German trade unions, together with a supplementary analysis of relevant documents. In general, all German trade unions see a danger in the rise of CSR, namely that voluntary agreements could undermine obligatory standards or lead to deregulation. Their main claim is that companies should implement the international labour standards and the additional standards agreed by the International Labour Organization (ILO) before they engage in voluntary CSR initiatives. At the same time, unions also see CSR as a vehicle for protecting human rights abroad through voluntary agreements. The general scepticism among German trade unions towards CSR is a result of negative experiences they have had with voluntary agreements on improving working conditions abroad. The unions hence share a critical position towards enforcing international labour standards through such agreements.

National business system

According to Hall and Soskice (2001), Germany is a typical representative of a co-ordinated market economy (CME), in contrast, for example, to the UK as a liberal market economy (LME). CMEs can be roughly defined by reference to close relationships between companies, their major suppliers and customers, by cross-shareholding between companies and by joint memberships of companies and other actors in societal institutions. Also, the internal structure of firms and their decision-making processes are, in comparison with LMEs, much more based on consensus and less centred on management. Collective bargaining remains comparatively strong and takes place mainly at the industry level (Hall and Soskice 2001). The German business system can be characterized further as having a comparably well regulated labour market, as applying a long-term approach towards company finance, and as benefiting from a dual education system that combines practical training with class room instruction (Whitley 1992). Overall, these specific features lead to a collaborative or even highly co-ordinated business system (Whitley 2000).

Within Germany, the country's business system is referred to as 'social market economy' (*soziale Marktwirtschaft*) or as 'Rhenish capitalism' (*rheinischer Kapitalismus*) (Windolf 2002). The social market economy is distinguished by a high degree of market regulation, a high level of income redistribution and a highly skilled labour force (Dörrenbächer 2002). Education is provided mainly through a dual training system, which combines on-the-job training and class-room instruction. Besides its well-known large MNCs, for example in the chemical and car industries, Germany is also home to highly specialized and globally operating small and medium-sized enterprises (SMEs). At the core of the social partnership model is the system of co-determination, which gives employees a say in certain fields of a company's decision making. Legislation prescribes co-determination for specific types of companies, chiefly those with more than 2,000 employees. Although only 10 per cent of German companies have co-determination institutions, these cover 45 per cent of all employees (Ellguth and Kohaut 2010).

It has been argued that globalization and a higher degree of interdependence between markets would force the German system to converge on the US model. However, it has also been argued this might not necessarily be the case for the whole national business system and that certain German institutions would persist, such as co-determination (Windolf 2002). Indeed, during the economic crisis that started in 2008, the German system revealed its strengths: based on the country's corporatist structure, the social partnership model and support from the state, firms were able to react flexibly to decreasing demand. They did so in co-operation with their workforce, for example with employees avoiding severe salary cuts by working reduced hours. As a result, Germany has performed comparably well in many indicators, such as employment and consumer spending (Ebert 2012). In contrast for example to the UK, Germany has maintained a comparatively large manufacturing sector contributing about 30 per cent to total GDP (Statista 2012).

Industrial relations system

The system of industrial relations in Germany reflects a 'high degree of institutionalization and juridification' (Jacobi 2003: 19). An important feature is its corporatist structure (Windolf 2002), which provides a framework for collective bargaining between trade unions and employers' associations. Corporatist countries can furthermore be characterized by 'consensus-based decision-making, governance in partnership with different interests in society and policies that result in obligations for all actors' (Preuss *et al.* 2006: 264). The strong position of trade unions in Germany derives primarily from Article 9 of the German Constitution, which guarantees freedom of association and declares that all 'agreements that restrict or seek to impair this right shall be null and void'.

A second mainstay of Germany's corporatist system is the Works Constitution Act (1952), which stipulates that works councils are to be elected by the entire work force. These councils are legally independent from both the employers and the unions (Jacobi 2003). They should 'work together (with the employer) in a spirit of mutual trust and in co-operation with the trade unions and employers' associations for the good of the employees as well as of the enterprise' (Jacobi 2003: 19). Third, there is free collective bargaining according to the Act on Collective Agreements (1949), which grants exclusive rights to unions and employers' associations to bargain and settle agreements on a variety of issues. Moreover, only the social partners (employers' associations and trade unions) have the right to conduct industrial disputes, that is, strikes and lockouts, if they are unable to reach a compromise in their negotiations and subsequent arbitration procedures (Jacobi 2003). In addition, the German government can declare a collective agreement to be generally binding for a sector provided the represented employers employ more than 50 per cent of the sector's workforce and if such a move seems to be in the public interest.

A further characteristic of German industrial relations is its two-tier system. Workers are represented at both company and multi-employer level, although the powers of the two levels of representation remain separated (Marsden 2000; Jacobi *et al.* 1998; Silvia 1999; Zimmer 2002). Trade unions have the exclusive right to negotiate collective agreements and call for a strike, whereas works councils have a right to information, consultation and co-determination at the company level. This separation of powers has to be put into perspective, though, since works council members can at the same time be leading union officials. Furthermore, where a collective agreement contains an opening clause that allows deviation from agreed terms under specified circumstances (*Öffnungsklausel*), the works council becomes authorized to undertake the respective negotiations at the company level. The rising number of such agreements is seen by many protagonists as both a threat to the system and a move towards a liberal market economy (Hall and Soskice 2001). At the same time, the resulting company-level negotiations between works councils and employers are still embedded in a corporatist structure and continue to reflect the fundamental consensus of social partnership. Besides, many employers base employment contracts on the terms negotiated in collective agreements even if they are not members of an employer's association. For our purposes, it can be concluded that, due to the corporatist system and their legal privileges, the importance of trade unions for Germany's national business system remains strong.

German trade unions mostly follow the principle of 'one industry – one union', which means that they represent the employees of an entire sector, no matter what kind of work they do (Segal *et al.* 2003). While this principle has prevented inter-union competition in the industrial relations system, it is still subject to debate. Indeed, there are some powerful groups of workers who try to pursue their own interests and thus to fragment unions. However, it is a different question altogether whether such changes already constitute an erosion of the system (Hassel 1999; Klikauer 2002).

Trade unions in Germany are organized in three umbrella organizations:

- DGB, *Deutscher Gewerkschaftsbund* (Confederation of German Trade Unions), represents eight unions with 6,155,899 members in 2011, about three-quarters of all union members in Germany (Dribbusch and Birke 2012). All DGB unions follow the principle of 'one industry – one union'.
- DBB, *Deutscher Beamtenbund* (German Civil Service Federation), represents a number of small unions and associations within the public sector. Some 908,000 of a total of 1,265,720 union members worked in the civil service in 2011. Unions representing employees in the civil service cannot be actively involved in collective bargaining or call a strike (Dribbusch and Birke 2012). Compared with DGB unions, their influence is therefore limited. In parts of the public sector, DBB unions compete with unions of the DGB, but their members do not usually get elected to works councils.
- CGB, *Christlicher Gewerkschaftsbund Deutschland* (Christian Trade Union Federation of Germany), with 283,000 members in 16 unions and associations in 2011. Some of these organizations recently lost their status as authorized unions and so cannot represent workers in collective agreements anymore.

There are also small, independent unions that altogether represent approximately 270,000 members. One example is the *Marburger Bund* which represents workers in medical professions. According to OECD data, union density in Germany was about 18.5 per cent in 2010 (OECD 2013). However, this figure does not adequately reflect actual union power. Although not all firms are members of employers' associations, many of them accept the employment terms negotiated in collective agreements. Hence about 43 per cent of German companies base most of their contracts on the conditions negotiated in collective agreements while another 18 per cent accept just some of their terms (Ellguth and Kohaut 2005; Artus 2005).

The evolution of CSR

Describing the evolution of CSR in Germany is not an easy task since the explicit use of the term is a rather recent phenomenon. Compared with other European countries, Germany still seems to be uncharted territory in terms of CSR (Habisch and Wegner 2005). To explain this situation, Matten and Moon introduced the term 'implicit CSR'. Implicit CSR 'refers to a country's formal and informal institutions through which the corporations' responsibility for society's interests are agreed and assigned to corporations' (Matten and Moon 2008: 324).

Germany's situation can be explained by its corporatist structure and the idea of social partnership. Many of the institutions shaping the social partnership model and the role of the state as 'problem solver' or 'enforcer of accepted reasonable ideas' have their roots in the period of industrialization. In the 1880s, Germany became the first country in the world to provide state-financed welfare benefits, such as old age pensions, medical care and unemployment insurance. Designed at the time to take the wind out of the socialist movement's sails, the state implemented social security systems top-down and over time Germans got used to the state as a 'perfectly functioning agency for the provision of public goods' (Habisch and Wegner 2005: 112). As part of Rhenish capitalism, the idea of integrating private commitment into the state system developed and led, for example, to the dual system of industrial training. Thus German firms do demonstrate certain types of engagement that can be described as CSR (Matten and Moon 2008), but the areas firms should become engaged in, as well as the frameworks for such corporate engagement, are determined by society and enforced by the state. Given the German legal and cultural context, the very idea that firms *should* develop their *own* standards of responsibilities and demonstrate engagement in fields that society has not earmarked for them has not really taken hold.

Therefore, (explicit) CSR (Matten and Moon 2008) was not an issue in Germany until the European Commission published its Green Paper in 2001. In national strategy papers on sustainability (Bundesregierung 2002 and 2004), the German government explicitly pointed out that firms have responsibilities for the development of society in national and international frameworks (Hansen and Schrader 2005). Various forums have been established by societal actors like NGOs, companies or the government to discuss CSR issues, for example econsense, a forum for sustainable development of the German economy, or the CSR Forum. The CSR Forum was set up by the Federal Ministry of Labour and Social Affairs in 2009 and includes 44 CSR experts from the corporate, union, NGO and political sectors (German Federal Government 2010). The forum supported the government in developing a 'National Strategy for Corporate Social Responsibility – Action Plan for CSR – of the German Federal Government', which was published in 2010. Although pointing out that 'corporate social responsibility is a fundamental element in the country's social market economy system', the paper stresses that CSR 'is not however a substitute for political action' (German Federal Government 2010: 7).

Some initiatives like the CSR Forum award prizes for CSR projects. A CSR Award of the German Federal Government has even been established. Despite its promotion, CSR is not explicitly used by all multinational companies, let alone SMEs. If they do use it, typical CSR initiatives involve co-operation with NGOs, reduction of emissions and corporate donations especially to social or cultural projects. One reason for the comparably rare use of the term 'CSR' seems to be its interchangeability with other, more common terms, such as sustainability (*Nachhaltigkeit*) or social responsibility (*soziale Verantwortung*).

Methods: unions interviewed

Semi-structured face-to-face interviews with CSR experts from the following unions were conducted between January and March 2012:

- DGB, the main national union federation, representing eight unions with 6,155,899 members. Interview with a member of the department of co-determination policy;
- IG BCE, active in mining, chemicals and energy, 672,195 members. Interview with a member of the steering committee;
- IG Metall, covering the engineering and textile sectors, 2,245,760 members. Interview with members of the department of international union co-operation;
- ver.di, organizing in the service sector, 2,070,990 members. Interview with a member of the federal administration, department of politics and planning.

The interview respondents were chosen by the unions themselves. The DGB is the biggest and most influential organization. Its member unions represent the majority of employees in the manufacturing and service sectors. IG Metall and ver.di are the biggest unions both within the DGB and in Germany. The selected unions also play the roles of 'pace-setters in collective bargaining and of social pioneers' (Jacobi 2003: 21). Notably, IG BCE has been involved in a number of CSR projects. Furthermore, we analysed documents pertaining to CSR provided by the unions. Since the experts interviewed had often been involved in the development of these documents, many positions expressed in the interviews are also reflected in the documents.

Union understanding of CSR

The DGB sees the CSR debate mainly as 'a response to worldwide criticism of socially and environmentally irresponsible corporate behaviour' (DGB 2009a: 1). At a first glance, German trade unions have a unified understanding of CSR, codified in the DGB's Ten Points Paper (DGB 2009a), to which all interviewees referred. The Ten Points Paper defines CSR as a binding commitment of companies 'to improve working and living conditions, to do their bit in caring sustainably for the environment and to protect consumers'. In other documents, the European Commission's definition is used, including its distinction between an external and an internal dimension of CSR (DGB 2009b). The external dimension of CSR refers to companies' activity in countries without labour and environmental standards or where governments fail to enforce them. In such an environment, unions, consumers and NGOs confront firms with their demands. By contrast, the internal dimension focuses on companies' social and ecological responsibilities towards their workers (such as health and safety issues and socially responsible reorganization).

The interviewees argued that CSR arose in an Anglo-Saxon environment of industrial relations, where codified co-determination does not exist and where statutory provisions for social and environmental issues are low compared with Germany (see also Preuss *et al.* 2009). Against this background, it seems understandable that for them the concept stresses the voluntary engagement of companies with these issues. This, however, would contrast with the North and Central European systems of co-determination, which have their roots in laws and collective agreements.

> Through international union cooperation, we have received evidence that CSR is used in Anglo-Saxon and Latin American economies as an instrument for the suppression of union and worker rights.
>
> (DGB 2009b: 3)

Unions stress the importance of working conditions and a commitment to the German co-determination system as the basic responsibility of a firm. From this starting point, they are open to CSR engagement in social and environmental fields – as long as these are not arbitrary, which means that they should not be determined only by management. All interviewees pointed out that, on the one hand, there are many companies that want to account for the social and ecological consequences of their actions in Germany and abroad. However, all interviewees also mentioned that, on the other hand, many companies use CSR as window-dressing. They boast of their ability to ensure the quality of their products throughout their entire supply chains without being able to make binding statements about compliance with employee rights. Unions complain, in particular, that the verification of companies' compliance with voluntary agreements or social or environmental labels is practically impossible.

Union policies on CSR

Our interviewees see trade unions as active in supporting many of the issues addressed by CSR, because in the long history of industrial disputes they initiated the implementation of many of the laws on employee rights, whereas CSR centres on voluntary commitments.

> CSR must not be used by companies to redefine or reinterpret their responsibilities. Protection and support for working men and women should not be founded purely on management concepts. [...] Nationally and internationally, the same principle applies: corporate commitment will only be acknowledged by the trade unions united in the DGB if it extends beyond existing and agreed standards. We rest our case: companies have no political right to define their social responsibility themselves.
>
> (DGB 2009a: 5)

Despite this critical position, unions have to deal with the subject, because workers' representatives are confronted with CSR at many levels. Also, while companies are dealing with CSR issues, they do not usually consider the workers' perspective. However, getting involved in CSR 'harbours both opportunities and risks' (DGB 2009a: 2; see also Mutz and Ebringhoff 2006). Key union policies on CSR are codified by the DGB in the above mentioned Ten Points Paper, which has become a guideline for all the unions interviewed. In this paper, CSR is seen as 'not sufficient in itself to ensure the required level of protection for worker and trade union rights'; however, it can provide 'additional protection [...] beyond these statutory rules' (DGB 2009a: 1). Hence trade unions call for 'binding intergovernmental modes of operation to assert the core labour standards' at the national as much as at the international level. They demand a greater degree of company liability for the social, environmental and humanitarian effects of their actions. 'Governments and parties concerned must have an opportunity to sue them in court' (DGB 2009a: 4).

The OECD Guidelines, 'in spite of their weaknesses', are seen as 'the most comprehensive instrument available today for asserting internationally valid environmental, labour and social standards' (DGB 2009a: 3). By contrast, ISO 26000 'needs clear objective criteria, a review of compliance with these objectives and criteria and, in the event of failure to observe requirements, an initial chance to remedy the situation' (DGB 2009a: 5). The DGB also called for mandatory corporate reporting, since 'transparency, verifiability, comparability and participation are indispensable CSR criteria' (DGB 2009a: 4). For unions, CSR reporting has to include specifically working and employment conditions throughout the entire company, co-operation with workers' representatives, support for disadvantaged groups and work-life balance. Trade unions see a responsibility for governmental institutions here as well. Public contracts should be awarded only if a firm demonstrates compliance with collective bargaining agreements: 'There must be an end to wage dumping in public contracts' (DGB 2009a: 4).

Nevertheless, CSR is also seen as a chance for unions to promote their own issues. Moreover, unions stressed that CSR often reveals regulation gaps that should be closed by the government. In contrast to many other European countries, the German government is actively involved in the CSR debate. A Sustainability Council was set up to discuss a German understanding of CSR, an 'Action-Plan CSR' was passed in 2010 and a label 'CSR – Made in Germany' created. In addition, the CSR Forum was established in 2005 to enable stakeholders to debate CSR. Despite their involvement in the CSR Forum, unions interpret this forum mainly as proof that politicians seek to avoid regulation by promoting CSR. In the words of one union CSR expert: 'Politicians try to get around closing regulation gaps'. Furthermore, politicians themselves selected the stakeholders involved in the CSR Forum. There is also a perception that in cases where stakeholders have called, for example, for further regulation, politicians adopt a veto role and, by referring to the forum's consensus principle, block such moves.

Another position towards CSR is that works councils could enlarge their area of influence to include issues that traditionally were not covered by codetermination (see also Feuchte 2009), such as strategic business decision making and the conditions of workers abroad. As best practice, unions consequently advocate Global Framework Agreements, binding und traceable agreements between companies and global union federations, unions or European works councils. The advantages and disadvantages of the involvement of works councils in CSR are discussed in the DGB's document 'Theses on the Relationship between Co-determination and CSR' (DGB 2009b). Workers' representatives should handle CSR with caution and their involvement in CSR activities should be based on binding agreements. Voluntary agreements could be used to undermine or replace collective bargaining agreements. Furthermore, workers' representatives might not have sufficient influence over CSR activities, since CSR is usually driven by management. Management might, for example, implement a CSR strategy without giving workers' representatives a chance to shape this strategy. In this case, an involvement could create an 'illusion of social and ecological sustainability' (DGB 2009b: 4). In addition, the inclusion of works councils in the process of designing a firm's CSR strategy might consume much of the time that works councils need to fulfil their legal obligations. Last but not least, unions are sceptical about CSR consulting firms. If companies co-operate with such a firm, works councils should scrutinize its attitudes towards the role of workers, co-determination and the internal dimension of CSR in general.

Unions differ in their assessment of the danger that the concept of CSR might constitute for them, especially in the light of Germany's clear legal constraints. Voluntary agreements might be useful to complement national, European and international laws and binding agreements, but they should never substitute for them. In addition, CSR should not hinder the further enhancement of legal and collective agreements. 'Initiatives that aim to replace the legal framework for co-determination with a framework for negotiated solutions or agreements are to be refused' (DGB 2009b: 3). There is some empirical evidence for the position that CSR could strengthen co-determination rather than weaken it; but unions see a need for more research to be done here (Hauser-Ditz and Wilke 2005). Since the system of co-determination is continuously under attack, especially from overseas companies, all unions see the necessity to protect it, which further explains unions' scepticism towards CSR.

Union engagement with CSR

In general, German unions remain reluctant to engage in CSR. One root for this scepticism can be found in the experiences they had with voluntary agreements, for example in the textile industry. Unions criticized working conditions in the industry abroad, and this criticism was accepted by the companies involved. It led, not least, to the negotiation of a code of conduct, which was supposed to improve the workers' situation. However, this code did not improve their conditions and unions now interpret this code as corporate window-dressing. Another example mentioned in the interviews was the union experience with combating child labour. The ILO Minimum Age Convention came into force in 1976, but it did not solve the problem of child labour. Hence in 2000 the ILO Convention Concerning the Prohibition and Immediate Action for the Elimination of the Worst Forms or Child Labour was passed, but child labour is still a problem today. The experience that even the most basic commitments to employee protection seem to have no more than a marginal effect increased the unions' scepticism of voluntary agreements. The economic crisis is seen as additional proof that voluntary commitments do not lead firms to sustainable forms of responsible behaviour.

Our interviewees generally stated that CSR could be useful if it is 'voluntary, but not arbitrary'. To ensure meaningful CSR activities, the democratically elected workers' representatives should, according to the DGB, be involved in designing and executing CSR strategies (DGB 2009a). Unions believe that companies have an interest in establishing standards and verification in order to prevent illegitimate competitive advantage. One interviewee (IG BCE) saw a chance for unions here, since CSR strategies often lack the internal dimension, that is, attention to workers' positions and demands. Unions could fill this gap through employing and training their own CSR experts and then helping firms to develop a credible CSR strategy. To support this, IG BCE is working on training programmes on CSR, developed to train works council members. The DGB (2009b), too, wants to train workers' representatives in the requirements for a genuine CSR concept. Its main focus is the evaluation of CSR strategies both on the internal and external dimension. Workers' representatives should be involved in CSR strategies at an early stage and make sure that these are designed in a way that does not conflict with collective agreements and the evolution of co-determination.

In line with their own policies, unions demand that CSR strategies should be laid down in binding agreements between companies and unions. There is an example of a CSR initiative in the former DaimlerChrysler company, where an international agreement on 'Fundamental Social Rights' was negotiated between DaimlerChrysler representatives and the DaimlerChrysler World Employee Committee in 2002. Such agreements are legally binding in Germany. Regardless of such examples, empirical studies have shown that works councils in approximately two-thirds of all German firms – albeit increasingly facing CSR as a field of their company's activity – are not or do not want to be involved in CSR projects (Mutz and Ebringhoff 2006).

Despite a willingness to train works council members in CSR, the topic is addressed in very few seminars arranged by unions, let alone in training programmes for union officers. Still, CSR has become a topic in educational programmes closely related to unions. For example, there is an annual symposium for worker representatives on company supervisory boards organized by the Hans-Böckler Foundation, the DGB's research foundation, which also has funded research on CSR. CSR is also taught at a seminar series for works council members, which is run by a further education college in Springe, Lower Saxony, in collaboration with the University of Hannover. So far, there have been only a few explicitly CSR related projects with unions as partners. Recently, the IG BCE has started a larger project, called CaeSaR, which aims to support CSR in SMEs by developing tailor-made strategies at firm level. The project is funded by the Federal Ministry of Labour and Social Affairs and the European Social Fund. Although engagement with CSR is still only a minor aspect of union activity, the number and impact of trade unions' CSR activities is likely to go up in the near future.

Discussion

In order to understand the position German trade unions have adopted towards CSR, it is worth mentioning that consideration of companies' social responsibilities was an important reason for the union-driven implementation of co-determination after the Second World War (Feuchte 2009). The DGB states that in a democratic society companies should not be allowed to define responsible behaviour themselves. It refers to article 14(2) of the German Constitution, which stipulates: 'Property entails obligations. Its use shall also serve the public good'. In the unions' interpretation, it is the duty of companies to improve working and living conditions and also to contribute to environmental protection (DGB 2009a). Against this background, the largely sceptical views among German unions of the more management-centred aspects of CSR become understandable. Unions usually interpret the whole CSR debate in a broader political sense. For example, they align it with a position expressed at the Conference of G8 Labour Ministers in 2007: 'First of all, it is the state's duty to accomplish and advance human rights and labour standards', otherwise social rights will become privatized (Priegnitz 2011: 10). This can be seen as a typical attitude for Germany, where the debate over frameworks and conditions that promote a certain type of behaviour is usually more dominant than discussions of individual decisions and activities.

Although all CSR experts referred to their shared definition of CSR as codified in the DGB's Ten Points Paper, they also mentioned that individual unions could have somewhat different views. In fact, the personal opinions on CSR of the individual interviewees were quite heterogeneous. They went from 'unholy stuff' or 'some label, people want to show off with' to 'a field we can use for our own interests'. The drivers of these differences might be variations in past experiences with voluntary agreements or co-operation with management. However, it generally came across that CSR itself is seen as being unable to protect employee rights either in Germany or abroad, or to guarantee the continued existence of unions as social actors. For unions, international labour standards and the additional standards of the International Labour Organization have to be adhered to first. Once these are fully observed and enforced, voluntary commitments by companies can make an additional contribution (see also Priegnitz 2011: 10). Since we interviewed only unions associated with the DGB, it is worth mentioning that, alongside the DGB, the DBB as the second largest union association also referred to CSR in a statement made in 2011. The DBB writes that CSR should be fostered through a duty to report continuously on social and environmental issues. The DBB (2011) emphasises that social activities by the firm can be complementary only to state-funded welfare services and legal duties of the employer. Even though this view is not as explicit as the DGB's position, the two perspectives are compatible.

Trade unions or works councils can address violations of international labour standards and repressions against unionized workers, for example, by demanding company adherence to international labour standards, but within the German system they also might have direct influence over the people in charge of determining working conditions abroad. From a CSR logic, a company's compliance with international standards like the UN Global Compact or ISO 26000 would be a substitute for this influence. Trade unions are very critical of such initiatives. Their main concern is that there are few sanctions against a company that does not comply with the respective document. Unions also reported that codes of conduct are sometimes used for anti-union behaviour or to provide legitimization for workers' committees implemented by the management itself (Singh 2011).

Unions seem to have had mainly negative experiences with CSR. One result of the rise of CSR has been the disappearance of the Round Tables. These forums were a favourite place for unions to deal with international labour rights and to discuss violations of labour standards since they included managers directly involved in international operations. Today these topics get more and more discussed under the concept of CSR, and unions now usually discuss them with managers of corporate strategy, who are mostly not involved in the labour issues themselves. Another critical point for trade unions is that, from a CSR perspective, they are just one stakeholder amongst others, which conflicts with their understanding of themselves as unique stakeholders *sui generis*. This status is derived from the legal foundations of the industrial relations system in Germany as well as from their ability to act inside the company through unionized works councils. When looking at possible ways to enforce CSR issues, collaborating with NGOs can therefore entail conflicts for unions. Whereas NGOs usually put pressure on a company by disseminating negative information about it, unions are not interested in harming a company through negative publicity as doing so could endanger jobs in Germany and abroad.

The preferred way for unions to deal with violations of labour standards is the 'internal way'. Typically for the German social partnership model, it entails influencing company policies through co-determination of management strategies as well as through the negotiation of plant-level and industry-level agreements. Conflicts with other stakeholders, like NGOs, thus do exist, but they are not seen as crucial overall. For example, sometimes compromises have to be found between an environmental NGO and a union that represents workers in a resource-intensive business. In general, NGOs are seen as partners, especially concerning their ability to monitor companies' activities abroad and in the environmental field. However, unions stress their unique role in improving working conditions, and they try to improve their competencies regarding environmental issues by increasingly promoting an environmental dimension of their work (DGB 2011; IG BCE 2012). CSR seems to have introduced some innovatory practices into the unions too, since they have started to approach environmental issues more explicitly. This can be seen as a more recent development, since, as Delbard (2011: 269) stated, '[t]he German DGB does not consider environmental issues to be part of their agenda, nor to be part of CSR'. Today, unions do consider environmental issues, and even by 2009 the Ten Points Paper stated that '[c]ompanies must be held liable to a greater degree for the social, environmental and humanitarian effects of their activities' (DGB 2009b: 4).

Conclusions

Our findings reveal a sceptical position of German unions towards CSR. In the interviews, a general scepticism towards voluntary agreements to ensure workers' rights became visible. The unions' critical views are a likely result both of their strong position embedded in the institutional context in Germany and of their negative experiences with voluntary agreements. The latter applies in particular to the textile industry with its high degree of internationalization and its often opaque supply chains. Consequently, the scepticism towards CSR labels or standards is quite strong, mainly because companies' compliance with these standards is not verifiable. Another explanation for the mostly reserved attitude can be found in the two-tier system of industrial relations where works councils, and not unions, are actively involved in many company strategies. At this level, several CSR projects in co-operation with works councils can indeed be found (Preuss *et al.* 2009).

Union views on whether or how to get involved in CSR activities are quite heterogeneous. On the one hand, there are unions that consider using CSR to promote their own agendas; on the other hand, unions see a danger in supporting voluntary agreements since they could potentially undermine legislation. Under the CSR concept, unions find themselves as one stakeholder among many, which is at odds with their self-perception and legal status. Also, their ability to act inside a company through unionized works council members seems to separate them from other stakeholders, like NGOs. However, despite occasional conflicts due to incompatible aims or varying approaches to solving conflicts, unions see NGOs in general as partners.

Within the German system of social partnership, unions have actively and self-confidently addressed their agendas through many projects of their own, like the DGB's project 'Decent Work' (*Gute Arbeit*). Unions also offer advice to companies on many topics, including CSR-related ones. However, besides highly active individual CSR experts within the unions, CSR has remained a minor issue for unions as a whole. Other and currently more important matters for unions are normally not regarded as typical CSR issues. Work-life balance and concerns about declining membership figures can be mentioned as examples here. A major exception in terms of union engagement with CSR is the project run by IG BCE to support CSR in SMEs. With this project, the union seeks to act as a partner for credible CSR commitments and to provide training for the actors involved.

Most unions nonetheless state that CSR can be an appropriate vehicle to transmit their own views and issues to works councils and company employees. CSR is seen as potentially useful if it is ‘voluntary, but not arbitrary’. This reflects the German system of a social market economy in which social dialogue largely determines the framework within which firms act. However, corporate responsibility itself is seen as being unable to guarantee labour rights in Germany and abroad. In general, unions still lack a consistent strategy for using CSR, which could be a consequence of the sceptical view discussed above. Rather, they have adopted a position that involves actively addressing CSR *issues* without explicitly relating them to the *concept* of CSR.

References

Artus, I. (2005) ‘Betriebe ohne Betriebsrat: Gelände jenseits des Tarifsystems?’, *WSI Mitteilungen*, 7, 2005: 392–397.

Bundesregierung (2002) *Perspektiven für Deutschland: Unsere Strategie für eine nachhaltige Entwicklung*, Berlin: Bundesregierung der Bundesrepublik Deutschland.

Bundesregierung (2004) *Perspektiven für Deutschland: Unsere Strategie für eine nachhaltige Entwicklung, Fortschrittsbericht 2004*, Berlin: Bundesregierung der Bundesrepublik Deutschland.

Burckhardt, G. (2011) ‘Zusammenfassung der Beiträge und Fazit: Freiwillige CSR Initiativen zur Umsetzung von Unternehmensverantwortung’, in G. Burckhardt (ed.) *Mythos CSR – Unternehmensverantwortung und Regulierungslücken*, Bonn: Horlemann, 111–112.

DBB (2011) ‘Stellungnahme zur Mitteilung Binnenmärkte: Zwölf Hebel zur Förderung von Wachstum und Vertrauen “Gemeinsam für neues Wachstum” ’, Berlin: Deutscher Beamtenbund. Online. Available: www.dbb.de/fileadmin/pdfs/stellungnahmen/110413_binnenmarktakte.pdf (accessed 20 February 2013).

Delbard, O. (2011) ‘Social partners or full-fledged stakeholders? Trade unions and CSR in Europe (France, Germany and the UK)’, *Society and Business Review*, 6(3): 260–277.

DGB (2009a) *10-Point Paper on Corporate Social Responsibility (CSR) Adopted by the German Confederation of Trade Unions (DGB) and its Affiliates – Binding Rules for One and All!*, Berlin: Deutscher Gewerkschaftsbund. Online. Available: www.dgb.de/search/++co++mediapool-d53cc7ab420124dd635aa3dc03429f87 (accessed 19 April 2012).

DGB (2009b) *Thesen zum Verhältnis von Mitbestimmung und CSR*, Berlin: Deutscher Gewerkschaftsbund. Online. Available: www.dgb.de/themen/++co++mediapool-0e5430849aa5ba6e283ce3d3df99bdca (accessed 19 April 2012).

DGB (2011) *Energieumstieg – Position des Deutschen Gewerkschaftsbundes (DGB) zur Energiepolitik*, Berlin: Deutscher Gewerkschaftsbund. Online. Available: www.dgb.de/themen/++co++f1d58ae0–9730–11e0–6e8a-00188b4dc422 (accessed 20 April 2012).

Dörrenbächer, C. (2002) 'National business systems and the international transfer of industrial models in multinational corporations: some remarks on heterogeneity', *WZB Discussion Paper*, FS02–102, Berlin: Wissenschaftszentrum Berlin für Sozialforschung.

Dribusch, H. and Birke, P. (2012) *Die Gewerkschaften in der Bundesrepublik Deutschland: Organisation, Rahmenbedingungen, Herausforderungen.* Berlin: Friedrich Ebert Stiftung. Online. Available: http://library.fes.de/pdf-files/id-moe/08986.pdf (accessed 20 February 2013).

Ebert, M. (2012) *Flexicurity auf dem Prüfstand – Welches Modell hält der Wirtschaftskrise stand?*, Berlin: Sigma.

Ellguth, P. and Kohaut, S. (2005) 'Tarifbindung und betriebliche Interessenvertretung: Aktuelle Ergebnisse aus dem IAB-Betriebspanel', *WSI Mitteilungen*, 7(2005): 398–403.

Ellguth, P. and Kohaut, S. (2010) 'Tarifbindung und betriebliche Interessenvertretung: Aktuelle Ergebnisse aus dem IAB-Betriebspanel 2009', *WSI-Mitteilungen*, 4(2010): 204–209.

European Commission (2001) *Green Paper – Promoting a European Framework for Corporate Social Responsibility*, Brussels: European Commission. Online. Available: http://eur-lex.europa.eu/LexUriServ/site/en/com/2001/com2001_0366en01.pdf (accessed 20 February 2013).

Feuchte, B. (2009) *Positionspapier der Hans-Böckler-Stiftung (HBS) zu Corporate Social Responsibility (CSR)*, Berlin: Hans Böckler Stiftung. Online. Available: www.boeckler.de/pdf/mbf_csr_positionspapier_hbs.pdf (accessed 20 February 2013).

German Federal Government (2010) *National Strategy for Corporate Social Responsibility – Action Plan for CSR*, Berlin: Bundesregierung der Bundesrepublik Deutschland. Online. Available: www.bmas.de/SharedDocs/Downloads/EN/PDF-Publikationen/a398-csr-action-plan-englisch.pdf?__blob=publicationFile (accessed 20 February 2013).

Habisch, A. and Wegner, M. (2005) 'Germany – overcoming the heritage of corporatism', in A. Habisch, J. Jonker, M. Wegner and R. Schmidpeter (eds) *Corporate Social Responsibility across Europe*, Berlin: Springer.

Hall, P.A. and Soskice D. (2001) *Varieties of Capitalism: The Institutional Foundations of Comparative Advantage*, Oxford: Oxford University Press.

Hansen, U. and Schrader, U. (2005) 'Corporate social responsibility als aktuelles Thema der Betriebswirtschaftslehre', in *Die Betriebswirtschaftslehre*, 65(4): 373–395.

Hassel, A. (1999) 'The erosion of industrial relations in Germany', *British Journal of Industrial Relations*, 37(3): 483–505.

Hauser-Ditz, A. and Wilke, P. (2005) 'Handlungsfelder für Arbeitnehmervertretungen – Ergebnisse einer Betriebsbefragung', in DGB (ed.) *Corporate Social Responsibility: Neue Handlungsfelder für Arbeitnehmervertretungen*, Berlin: Deutscher Gewerkschaftsbund, 6–11.

Hoffmann, M and Maaß, F. (2009) 'Corporate Social Responsibility als Erfolgsfaktor einer stakeholderbezogenen Führungsstrategie? Ergebnisse einer empirischen Untersuchung', in Institut für Mittelstandsforschung Bonn (ed.) *Schriften zur Mittelstandsforschung*, 116, Wiesbaden: Springer, 1–52.

IG BCE (2012) 'CaeSaR-Projekt', Hannover: Industriegewerkschaft Bergbau, Chemie, Energie. Online. Available: http://qfc.de/qfc.de/projekte/aktuelle-projekte/caesar (accessed 12 December 2012).

Jacobi, O. (2003) 'Renewal of the collective bargaining system?', in W. Mueller-Jentsch and H. Weitbrecht (eds) *The Changing Contours of German Industrial Relations*, Munich and Mehring: Rainer Hampp, 15–39.

Jacobi, O., Keller, B. and Müller-Jentsch, W. (1998) 'Germany: Facing new challenges', in A. Ferner and R. Hyman (eds) *Changing Industrial Relations in Europe*, Oxford: Blackwell, 190–238.

Klikauer, T. (2002) 'Stability in Germany's industrial relations: a critique on Hassel's erosion thesis', *British Journal of Industrial Relations*, 40(2): 295–308.

Marsden, D. (2000) 'A theory of job regulation, the employment relationship, and the organization of labour institutions', *Industrielle Beziehungen* (German Industrial Relations Journal), 7(4): 320–347.

Matten, D. and Moon, J. (2008) '"Implicit" and "explicit" CSR: a conceptual framework for a comparative understanding of corporate social responsibility', *Academy of Management Review*, 33(2): 404–424.

Mutz, G. and Ebringhoff, J. (2006) 'Das ist immer eine Gratwanderung', *Mitbestimmung*, 10, 2006: 27–29.

OECD (2013) 'OECD.StatExtracts', Paris: Organisation for Economic Co-operation and Development. Online. Available: http://stats.oecd.org/Index.aspx?QueryId=20167 (accessed 13 June 2013).

Preuss, L., Haunschild, A. and Matten, D. (2006) 'Trade unions and CSR: a European research agenda', *Journal of Public Affairs*, 6(3/4): 256–268.

Preuss, L., Haunschild, A. and Matten, D. (2009) 'The rise of CSR: implications for HRM and employee representation', *International Journal of Human Resource Management*, 20(4): 953–973.

Priegnitz, K. (2011) 'Vorwort', in G. Burckhardt (ed.) *Mythos CSR – Unternehmensverantwortung und Regulierungslücken*, Bonn: Horlemann.

Segal, J.P., Sobczak, A. and Triomphe, C. E. (2003) *CSR and Working Conditions*, Dublin: European Foundation for the Improvement of Living and Working Conditions. Online. Available: http://edz.bib.uni-mannheim.de/www-edz/pdf/ef/03/ef0328en.pdf (accessed 12 February 2013).

Silvia, S. (1999) 'Every which way but loose: German industrial relations since 1980', in A. Marin and G. Ross (ed.) *The Brave New World of European Labor – European Trade Unions at the Millenium*, New York: Berghan Books, 75–124.

Singh, S. (2011) 'Verhaltenskodex: Ein echtes Anliegen oder bloß Augenwischerei?', in G. Burckhardt (ed.) *Mythos CSR – Unternehmensverantwortung und Regulierungslücken*, Bonn: Horlemann, 114–118.

Statista (2012) 'Anteil der Wirtschaftsbereiche am Bruttoinlandsprodukt (BIP) in Deutschland im Jahr 2012', Hamburg: Statista GmbH Online. Available: http://de.statista.com/statistik/daten/studie/36846/umfrage/anteil-der-wirtschaftsbereiche-am-bruttoinlandsprodukt (accessed 13 June 2013).

Whitley, R. (1992) *European Business Systems: Firms and Markets in their National Contexts*, London: Sage.

Whitley, R. (2000) 'The institutional structuring of innovation strategies: business systems, firm types and patterns of technical change in different market economies', *Organization Studies*, 21(5): 855–886.

Windolf, P. (2002) 'Die Zukunft des rheinischen Kapitalismus', *Kölner Zeitschrift für Soziologie und Sozialpsychologie*, 42 (special issue): 414–442.

Zimmer, S. (2002) *Jenseits von Arbeit und Kapital? Unternehmerverbände und Gewerkschaften im Zeitalter der Globalisierung*, Opladen: Leske & Budrich.

6 Hungary

CSR between socialism and export-oriented MNCs

Matthew Lloyd-Cape

> Corporate strategy determines which MNCs act responsibly. An Audi or Mercedes comes to Hungary not only to employ people but also to invest in some R&D.... In the case of Suzuki, there are no such initiatives. They only want to employ people at [the] lowest cost.
>
> (VASAS, Hungarian Union of Ironworkers)

Introduction

Hungarian trade unions have an ambivalent and somewhat paradoxical attitude towards corporate social responsibility (CSR). While most respondents considered it as 'window dressing' for foreign MNCs, interviewees often referred to socially responsible behaviour as something more closely related to the social role that enterprises played in workers' lives before the end of socialism. CSR is thus linked to both a history of state control over aspects of social life through the workplace and to foreign MNCs as the new dominant actors in the Hungarian economy. Regardless of how CSR is perceived, however, there is very little action taken by unions, or other civil society organizations, to engage with CSR. No union has a specific policy on CSR, and neither is there much of a domestic debate over the term more generally. CSR is most evident at the enterprise level, specifically within large foreign MNCs, but practices there are considered to be externally imposed rather than negotiated with domestic stakeholders. In contrast to previous research (FIDH 2006), very little adaptation of CSR to the local context was identified.

In this chapter the development of a national business system dependent on foreign direct investment (FDI) post-1989, as well as socialist legacies prior to this period, are shown to present limitations for union engagement with CSR. Prior to 1989, enterprises controlled a significant proportion of workers' social as well as economic lives, such as organizing housing, holidays and leisure activities. This legacy strongly influences Hungarian unionists' conception of what social 'responsibilities' firms should engage in, and to a certain degree this defines the parameters of social responsibility quite differently from the Western European understanding of CSR. Domestic channels for engaging with the CSR debate are extremely limited, and so these views are hardly ever expressed. After 1989 a major part of the planning for the transition to a capitalist economy was to attract FDI, with exports realigning from eastern to western European markets. Consequently the Hungarian economy is highly reliant on FDI. The majority of FDI comes from co-ordinated market economies (CMEs), such as Austria, Germany and the Netherlands, followed by France, the United States and Japan. This pattern provides an interesting opportunity to assess whether home country CSR practices are transmitted to host country subsidiaries.

This chapter shows, first, that the concept of social responsibility holds different meanings within and between unions. Few NGOs or other societal organizations actively engage with CSR campaigns or policies, which has led to CSR discourse and practice being largely an internal discussion of the business elite with little engagement of wider society. No clear 'Hungarian' conception (or even translation) of CSR exists. Where CSR debate and practice do manifest themselves, they remain mostly at the enterprise level and emerge in an ad hoc manner only. While one union federation experimented with using breaches of company CSR policy as a campaign tool to 'name and shame' companies, in general unions do not engage with CSR through policy, training or discussion with other societal actors. Civil society and unions do not act as societal watchdogs for CSR; hence CSR is top down, discretionary and paternalistic, and mainly conducted by large foreign MNCs.

National business system

Central and eastern Europe have received a relatively high degree of attention from scholars of national business systems (NBS) and varieties of capitalism (Cernat 2007; Dörrenbächer 2002, 2004; Feldman 2006, 2007; Greskovits 2005; King 2007; Lane and Myant 2007; Mykhnenko 2007; Nölke and Vliegenthart 2009; Whitley 1999; Whitley and Czabán 1998). This attention is due to: (1) the 'natural experiment' in political-economic terms that the collapse of the Soviet Union brought to central and eastern Europe; (2) an effort to evaluate the impact of Europeanization as the European Union (EU) and the Eurozone have spread east; and (3) a desire to understand the effects of home and host country institutions on MNCs as they entered these new markets. Several typologies have been applied to Hungary in the national business systems literature. Despite slight differences in name and detail between the typologies, there is general agreement on many significant features of Hungary's business system, particularly a dependence on export-oriented FDI for investment and innovation, liberalized education and industrial relations institutions, but a commitment to a hugely popular and politically inviolable benefits and pension system.

These features, which will be discussed below in greater detail, are evident in the typifying of Hungary as a 'liberal dependent economy' (King 2007), a 'dependent market economy' (Vliegenthart and Nölke 2009), or an 'embedded neoliberal political economy' (Bohle and Greskovits 2012).

The literature suggests that countries in the central and eastern European region followed significantly different paths after 1989, rather than conform to an ideal type category. Despite their broad diversity there is a tendency towards viewing the Visegrád countries – the Czech Republic, Hungary, Poland and Slovakia – as something close to a 'type' due to their similar political and economic post-socialist transitions. They all show a heavy reliance on foreign capital in the financial, manufacturing as well as service sectors, unions are fragmented with little in the way of effective tripartism, yet comparatively strong levels of compensation of workers have been maintained through relatively generous pension and disability schemes (Adam *et al.* 2009; Birch and Mykhnenko 2009; Bohle and Greskovits 2007a, 2007b; Vanhuysse 2007). However, differences in the business systems of these countries should not be ignored. Research and development (R&D) spending for example differs significantly, with 60 per cent of total R&D spending being provided by foreign firms in Hungary, compared with only 18 per cent in Poland in 2007 (King 2007).

Historically, Hungary was a major manufacturing centre in the eastern bloc and thus in a relatively favourable position to enter the capitalist system, with levels of infrastructure development, technology and workforce skills that were high for the region. Hungary was the regional first mover in terms of offering attractive packages to encourage MNCs to make pioneering investments in the uncertain period following the fall of communism (Bohle and Greskovits 2012: 31). Inward FDI stocks rose quickly from roughly 24 per cent of GDP in 1995 (UNCTAD 2012), to over 80 per cent in 2012 (UNCTAD 2014). While this had the effect of turning the country into a major export centre, especially in the electronics and automotive sectors, relatively little investment in R&D by domestic firms has taken place, with foreign subsidiaries accounting for 72 per cent of total R&D in the mid-2000s (King 2007). At present, foreign firms own more than half of all corporate capital and employ more than 20 per cent of the workforce. FDI from Germany, the Netherlands, Austria, Luxemburg and France dominates in Hungary, followed by the US and Japan (Sass and Kalotay 2012). This situation is exacerbated by a lack of government support for SMEs (Greskovits 2010), making the country increasingly dependent on FDI for technological transfer (King 2007).

The effect of this reliance on external capital on the wider business system should be treated as significant for the analysis in this chapter. Whitley (1998) suggests that where multinational companies have generated a significant stake in vital sectors the strategies of these firms may influence institutional forms, particularly in the labour market, interfirm relations and corporate financing. These theoretical conjectures are borne out to a certain extent by empirical research. Mosley (2003) finds 'strong and broad' effects of foreign capital on the policy choices available for emerging economies. These can significantly shape political choices which, in turn, affect the business system. For example, the choice of the Hungarian government in the mid-1990s to carry out major austerity programmes was most likely due to external pressure from economic actors. FDI reliance has also contributed to a degree of 'regime competition' with neighbouring countries to attract FDI in key sectors, especially the auto industry. This is seen as putting downward pressure on industrial relations institutions and reducing the firm-level negotiation position for workers (Vliegenthart and Nölke 2009).

These factors contribute to an 'incomplete social pact' in Hungarian industrial relations, with skilled labour appeased through individual or company-level agreements, while the majority of workers have little formal protection from international market forces, nor the institutional means to voice their concerns (Vliegenthart and Nölke 2009). Attempts at building neo-corporatist institutions have failed or atrophied, and union interests are overlooked, while workers are pacified through unsustainably large welfare payouts (Bohle and Greskovits 2012). While in the early transition era policy-makers did attempt to build a national model of capitalism based on social partnership, Hungary ultimately abandoned these goals and 'instead embarked on a path of embedded neoliberal and transnational capitalism' (Bohle and Greskovits 2012: 140).

Industrial relations system

In 1988 the National Interest Reconciliation Council (OÉT) was established in Hungary, a comparatively early experiment with tripartite governance structures for an eastern bloc country. Rather than operate as a truly corporatist institution, the primary purpose of this institution was to maintain social stability. Over time, the tripartite board went through several incarnations, generally acting as a consultation body for the government, making annual recommendations on minimum wage setting and commenting on labour legislation. However, in 2012 the tripartite board was replaced by the National Economic and Social Council (NGTT), which has much weaker powers than its predecessor.

Attempts to evaluate the level of employment protection in eastern European countries place Hungary on the more flexible end for both permanent and atypical forms of employment (Boudier-Bensebaa 2008). Union density, at 11 per cent in 2011 (EIRO 2011), is low, and fragmentation is high, both within and between unions (Visser 2011). Confederations vie for overlapping membership, and unions often have explicit ties to either the reformed Hungarian Socialist Party (MSzP), or to the right-wing populist Fidesz party. There are six competing union confederations in Hungary: MSzOSz, ASzSz, SzEF, ÉSzT, LIGA and MOSz, as well as many independent unions, a very high number for a country with population and union density rates as low as Hungary. The National Council of Trade Unions (MOSz) and the Democratic Confederation of Free Trade Unions (LIGA) emerged from anti-communist movements while the remaining four are all reformed elements of the socialist era SzOT confederation.

Politically, LIGA is linked to the right-wing Fidesz party, the governing party at the time of writing, while MSzOSz is linked to the socialist party MSzP, having signed an electoral agreement with it in 2005. Generally speaking, the confederations preside over different parts of the economy, although demarcations between these areas are not clear and competition for members exists between the confederations. In broad terms, MSzOSz represents workers in manufacturing and some private sector services, such as retailing. ASzSz represents workers in the utilities and transport, as well as the chemical industry. SzEF and ÉSzT both cover public sector services, with ÉSzT organizing employees in higher education and research institutes only. SzEF organizes public sector employees in health, social services, primary and secondary education as well as local and central government. LIGA and MOSz both represent workers across the whole economy.

Recent years have seen a dizzying array of reforms to the constitution as well as to labour legislation. The supermajority attained by the Fidesz government in the landslide 2010 election, and a lack of effective opposition, have allowed the government to rewrite the constitution, revoke the powers of the constitutional court and limit the freedom of the press, thus reducing many civil and labour rights. Most significantly for this chapter, the labour code of 1992 was replaced. The new code limits effective union organization and worker freedoms through a variety of mechanisms, including an emphasis on individual rather than group contracts, the possibility to negotiate conditions in individual and group contracts at a level below the standards of the labour law and a removal of union privileges, such as an exemption of union organizers from work duties (Tóth 2012).

In January 2012, the Fidesz government replaced the tripartite body OÉT with the National Economic and Social Council (NGTT). The NGTT includes representatives from a broader set of social actors, including employers, workers, the chambers of commerce and the church, but it can only propose changes and no longer acts as the de facto setter of the minimum wage. All six union confederations criticized this transition from the OÉT to the NGTT as a backward step in industrial relations, which reduces the institutional space for the reconciliation of interests. While the weakening of worker protection has been particularly intense under the Fidesz government, the decline in institutional importance has been ongoing since the mid-2000s, even under 'friendly' political conditions when the socialist party was in government (Neumann 2012).

Overall, the characteristics of neither liberal nor corporatist models of employment relations systems were closely reproduced in Hungary

(Aguilera and Dabu 2005), despite original attempts to set up German-style works councils and tripartite national institutions. The transformation experienced by the formerly socialist country resulted in a hybrid type of industrial relations system. There are (now weakened) tripartite systems at the national level and decentralized workplace representation and relations at the workplace level, with enterprise unions having their own legal status (Pollert 2000). However, very little effective sectoral or regional level industrial relations developed in between (Neumann 2012). Notwithstanding EU efforts to strengthen sectoral bargaining in eastern Europe, industry-level negotiations and agreements are very underdeveloped. In a nutshell, the import of institutions from CMEs has not been a success, due to their mismatch with economic circumstances, a minimal role of unions and the underdevelopment of civil society more generally.

The evolution of CSR

The history of the social responsibilities of enterprises (and trade unions) in pre-1989 Hungary is complex (see Ferge 1999; Müller 2002; Nelson 2001), and shapes Hungarian attitudes to the contemporary CSR debate in distinct ways. Prior to 1989, enterprises collectively had a legal duty to provide full employment and carried out a great many other social roles, including providing day-care nurseries, libraries, holiday resorts, healthcare, sports teams, cafeterias, pensions and housing. Companies contributed to social funds to finance these social duties, and often ran the distribution and management of these jointly with trade unions. During the early transition in the 1990s corporations were released from their legally enforced social obligations and many dropped their social welfare commitments. However, privatization deals often included the phasing out of some aspects of these social duties. Companies that have upheld these higher than legal standards and obligations are often referred to as being socially responsible by workers and unions, although such activities do not necessarily conform to the contemporary discourse on CSR.

CSR as it is contemporarily understood by the literature is not much discussed in Hungary. Primarily such conversations occur within the business community rather than as a result of interaction between civil society and business. Civil society is relatively weak and the public relatively sceptical about the concept of CSR. While MNCs dominate the discourse, the concept has spread to a certain degree in the domestic business community too. Reportedly, 60 per cent of Hungarian firms had drafted a code of conduct by 2006 (FIDH 2006), however none of the interviewees could name a domestic firm with a CSR policy. In the same year, a code of ethics was developed by the retail sector, signed by large MNCs such as Auchan and Tesco, which conforms to classic CSR standards in terms of scope, stakeholders and practices. However, the sector offers infamously high levels of flexibilization and low wages and it appears that this code has had little effect on the ground. Since 2006 an industry body, CSR Hungary, has awarded annual prizes for CSR initiatives and good practices, yet as of early 2013 only 80 companies have applied for consideration, reinforcing the view that CSR does not have a strong ground presence in Hungary. A 2006 report by the human rights NGO, FIDH, found that civil society bodies, including NGOs and trade unions, do not act as a watchdog over the CSR commitments of companies, leaving the field of CSR largely to MNCs and large domestic companies (FIDH 2006).

International and supranational organizations have also attempted to encourage CSR in Hungary. An EU project in 2004 and a United Nations Development Programme (UNDP) regional project in 2007 aimed to accelerate the development of CSR forums and practices in the new EU member states. Business networks from Spain, the United Kingdom and Germany took part in the EU project, which attempted to contribute to the exchange of experience and spread of good practices in the field of CSR (European Commission 2007). More recently efforts have been made to develop domestic CSR initiatives. For example, KÖVET, the Hungarian Association of Environmentally Aware Management, developed training materials in Hungarian for MNCs and SMEs in 2008. Nevertheless, CSR is still largely considered to be an external concept. Where there is a recognition of company-level social responsibility, it is in the continuation or re-institution of hugely popular socialist-era programmes, such as generous pension or health care schemes (European Monitoring Centre on Change 2003a, 2003b). As such, there is a developed sense among workers of what the 'social responsibilities' of firms should be, based on pre-1989 paternalistic company policies. CSR in Hungary is thus largely driven by external factors. Limited domestic discourse, weak unions and a sparse NGO presence, as well as a pre-established discourse in MNC subsidiaries, limits the domestic uptake of 'Western'-style CSR, as does the heritage of enterprise-level social practices prior to transition.

Methods: unions interviewed

The selection of unions to be interviewed was based on four criteria: sectoral coverage, links to political parties, size and the degree of dependence on FDI of their sectors. Interviewees cross the political spectrum as they include the two largest national confederations which are aligned with opposing right- and left-wing political parties. At sector-level, representatives from the automotive and building materials sectors were chosen, both important sectors for the national economy. The auto industry ranks higher in most economic indicators, such as exports and value added, though construction is the larger employer. They represent quintessentially high-skill and low-skill types of employment. In the automotive sector, VASAS, the Hungarian Union of Ironworkers, were interviewed, as well as two enterprise level unions, one at an MNC and the other at a domestic firm, to explore differences between union experiences. ÉFÉDOSzSz, the Building Materials Industry Workers' Union, were chosen to represent the construction sector, and workers' representatives from a large CME-based furniture manufacturing MNC and a large building materials manufacturer were also selected. In the furniture manufacturing case interviewees asked for anonymity and so the name of the MNC is excluded. The following trade unions were interviewed:

Confederations

- LIGA, Democratic Confederation of Free Trade Unions – 110,000 members, linked to the governing right-wing Fidesz party. LIGA covers workers across the entire economy but recently the balance of membership shifted after a merger with the union organizing the police and the military. Interview conducted with the LIGA President in February 2012.
- MSzOSz, National Confederation of Hungarian Trade Unions – 205,000 members, aligned with the Hungarian Socialist Party. MSzOSz also covers workers from across the economy. Interview conducted with the Chairman of the Pensioners' Association in March 2012.

National Sectoral Unions

- ÉFÉDOSzSz, Building Materials Industry Workers' Union – part of the MSzOSz confederation. 6,000 members representing roughly 4 to 5 per cent of the sectoral workforce. However, over the past 15 years large-scale outsourcing of jobs to agencies has hugely affected sectoral density rates. Interview conducted with the President of the union in March 2013.
- VASAS, Hungarian Union of Ironworkers – 31,000 members in total. 3,000 active members, 5,000 pensioners, approximately 3,000 students. Interview conducted with a sectoral organizer of the auto and engine sector in May 2012.

Company Level Unions

- AHFSz, Audi Hungary Independent Union – organizes roughly 4,300 members of the approximately 7,000 strong workforce at Europe's largest engine factory, which produces many complete Audi sports cars as well as engines for many of the Volkswagen group's brands. Interview conducted with a shop steward in April 2012.
- Raba-Holding Employee Union – this union incorporates roughly 300 out of the 835 employees at this previously state-owned automobile and components manufacturer. The company is reliant on government orders for military and emergency vehicles and received a government rescue package in order to stay afloat. Interview conducted with the leader of the company union in April 2012.

- A large furniture manufacturing MNC from a CME – this furniture manufacturer is one of the largest in the world, with interests in most eastern European countries. In Hungary it employs roughly 450 workers, none of whom is unionized. Interviews were carried out with a works council representative and former union leader, as well as various staff members between July 2012 and March 2013.
- Strabag Independent Workers' Union – the Austrian Strabag Group is one of Europe's largest construction materials companies. In Hungary it employs roughly 2,800 workers at previously state-run enterprises. After the initial privatization contract expired the company went through an intensive process to outsource unskilled jobs, which significantly reduced the size of the workforce. Interview conducted with a shop steward in March 2013.

Union understanding of CSR

Broadly speaking, there was consensus at the national and sectoral levels that CSR refers to a new, relatively unknown and 'nondomestic' concept and set of practices. The term CSR has no accepted Hungarian translation and it was suggested by several interviewees that society at large does not fully understand the term, not even HR managers in many firms or union staff who make policy on it (ÉFÉDOSzSz, VASAS, LIGA). Of the eight interviews with unionists, the LIGA president and the Audi shop steward offered clear definitions which correlated with definitions in the literature. The president of LIGA defined CSR as 'worker-friendly arrangements going beyond legal requirements and other actions and programmes that promote the wellbeing of communities'. The MSzOSz interviewee referred to stakeholder involvement, stating that companies should try to maintain employment during an economic downturn, sign collective agreements with unions and involve associations representing women, pensioners and young people in decision making. However, most respondents saw CSR as a marketing tool for MNCs or equated it with philanthropic activities.

One striking aspect of the responses was the conceptualization of CSR, not as a system by which civil society can hold companies to account, nor as a management system that allows auditing of social and environmental commitments, but as a continuation or reinstatement of socialist-era policies, such as contributing to full employment, providing housing assistance and organizing social activities. When asked for their own definition of CSR, the respondents from ÉFÉDOSzSz and the Strabag company union both referred to pre-reform enterprise-level policies, such as mortgage assistance, full employment and social funds for disadvantaged workers, as examples of practices that MNCs should replicate in order to be socially responsible. Adherence to these clauses was relatively strong during the early years of independence, but as the initial contracts ran out these social commitments were often not sustained (Strabag union, Raba-Holding Union, ÉFÉDOSzSz).

In general, unions expressed mixed reactions to the emergence of CSR. Our interviewees were generally sceptical about how seriously businesses take corporate responsibility. At the time of writing, their primary concern was actually governmental irresponsibility, given the changes in labour legislation, the weakening of the tripartite institutions and a lack of adequate engagement with unions. Tellingly, the newly formed Union for Multinational Enterprise Workers declined to participate in this research. They voiced strong scepticism over the efficacy of CSR, saw it as nothing but marketing for the company and refused to have anything to do with CSR research. CSR is generally seen as a 'foreign concept' by Hungarian unions, coming through EU structures and individual enterprises (Raba-Holding Union, LIGA).

Union policies on CSR

None of the unions interviewed had explicit policies or formalized stances toward CSR. CSR was not discussed as a topic or used as a reference point internally, other than in one example at the confederation level where LIGA briefly engaged with an EU project on CSR in the new EU member states. Discussions were held over how to utilize the concept, and the confederation leaders proposed making use of CSR as a leverage tool over bad company practices by publishing a blacklist of companies with poor records on employment relations. Three of the eight interviewees had some experience of engagement in writing codes of conduct or participating in multi-stakeholder CSR activities, but only the Audi representative felt positive about the experience. However, even here the union was not involved in enforcing these efforts as CSR at the plant is top down and paternalistic. Nonetheless, another union reported having used Audi's good track record of community involvement and human resources practices as a campaign strategy with poorer performing companies nearby (VASAS).

When discussing the business case for CSR, interviewees suggested that this might relate to some large MNCs, such as those which offer mutually beneficial internal training to their staff which also boosts innovation and productivity, but not to subcontracted workers or those in domestic SMEs. Interviewees reacted to the questions about a 'market for virtue' by saying that it does not exist in Hungary since the activities associated with CSR add local costs which are hard to recoup from export markets (ÉFÉDOSzSz, LIGA). Significantly, the firm with the most image-sensitive brand, the furniture manufacturer, also had the worst CSR track record. Respondents alleged that it fails to respect basic union rights and engages in illegal holiday and shift rostering without workers' consent, contributing to a high staff turnover at 30 per cent per annum.

Union engagement with CSR

The EU and MNCs were seen as the main promoters of CSR and, although all the respondents from the sectoral and confederation levels considered CSR to be of growing importance, none expected to be significantly more involved with CSR in the near future. As one respondent put it, making firms more socially responsible requires 'a change in the value system in which economic activities are embedded' (LIGA) and went on to say that such a shift would require systemic changes to capitalism at the regional or global levels. Unions took little ownership of CSR policies or practices in all but one interview (Audi). In the context of weakening institutional protection, low union density and little cohesion, most interviewees put CSR low on their list of ways to improve working conditions. Instead, they prefer to focus their efforts at reinstating legal standards and finding ways to protect jobs.

A telling example was the reaction of the chemical workers' union (not interviewed) to the 'red sludge' spill at an alumina plant in Veszprém County, western Hungary, in October 2010, which flooded nearby towns and water systems with approximately one million cubic metres of toxic effluent. This was clearly a breach of social responsibility which led to nine deaths and millions of Euros in damaged property, as well as severe environmental damage. However, the plant union's main concern was to ensure that the factory remained open to protect local jobs (ÉFÉDOSzSz, Strabag). This highlighted somewhat graphically the often expressed belief that a bad job is better than no job at all. CSR is thus something a firm can 'do' should it choose, rather than something socially negotiated or enforced, and unions are mainly concerned with defensive measures to protect members' interests. As such it appears that the downward shift of industrial relations from national and sectoral levels to the enterprise-level seems to have carried over into the CSR debate. For nearly all of our interviewees CSR was seen as something individual enterprises engaged in as and when it suited their purposes.

Discussion

As this chapter was written, Hungarian trade unions found themselves in a perilous position. On current trends, union density will be in single figures in the next few years. In early 2013 Hungary slipped back into recession (IMF 2013) while unemployment has remained at or above 10 per cent since late 2009 (Hungarian Central Statistical Agency 2013). In addition to these economic problems the labour code has been rewritten, further undermining the structural power of unions. These issues somewhat overshadowed our discussions with unionists regarding CSR. However, several significant trends are highlighted in the following discussion. Overall, it suggests some explanatory power of the national business system approach for the way in which CSR is understood and acted out by unions and businesses in Hungary.

MNCs dominate the Hungarian economy and, as such, the debate over home country effects on MNC behaviour is particularly relevant. Whitley (1998) suggests that where host country institutions are weak, MNCs are more able to introduce selectively home country practices. Similarly, Matten and Moon argue for such an agency-influenced institutional approach to understanding MNC CSR strategies, in which interactions between stakeholders are shaped by 'multiple and complex institutional arrays' (Matten and Moon 2008:14). Corroborating this home country institutional effect thesis to a certain extent, unions often identified country of origin as a major contributing factor to the level of social responsibility of a company. As one respondent said, there were major differences between the corporate cultures of western and eastern companies, particularly differences between corporations from western European countries such as Germany or Sweden on the one hand, and eastern companies, such as Korean, Japanese or Chinese companies on the other, where workers have to 'fight for bare subsistence' (VASAS). Another interviewee described this as a 'bad fit' between 'eastern' corporate cultures which were considered to be top down, with limited involvement of workers in decision making, and that found in Hungary (ÉFÉDOSzSz). Audi and Suzuki were the archetypal best and worst examples, respectively. Audi, on the one hand, provided good in-house training, career development, stable pay and conditions, strong worker representation through the works council and the company union, and a proactive management who, for example, automatically increase wages to inflation levels. The company had contributed to numerous social projects, such as environmental and local infrastructure projects (Audi, Raba-Holding Union). Suzuki, on the other hand, refused to recognize legal union representation at their plant. It engaged in a long legal battle over fundamental union rights and illegal dismissals, which it eventually lost (FIDH 2006).

However, country of origin alone does not account for all divergence. Among the counter-examples in our research are Bosch and Electrolux in the electrical goods sector, which were both considered to have poor human resource management and CSR reputations (MSzOSz). Company profitability was also forwarded as a reason for such differences. However, the furniture manufacturer, which is CME-based and enjoys high profits, counters both these explanations again. Other respondents suggested that the MNCs which moved to Hungary immediately after the transformation of the early 1990s tend to have better social practices than the newer MNCs which 'come and go as they please' without consideration for social responsibilities (Raba-Holding Union). This also suggests that companies with long-term investment strategies are more likely to be socially responsible. Investment scale is another feasible explanation. Here Audi claims to account for 9 per cent of Hungary's exports and to employ 7,000 people directly, with another 10,000 workers downstream in its Hungarian supply chains. However, Suzuki has also invested significantly since establishing a plant in 1991 and today employs nearly as many workers as Audi.

For our interviewees, CSR is correlated with micro-corporatist industrial relations practices, rather than impacting sectoral or national industrial relations. Good employers tended to be more socially responsible and vice versa. Rather than identify country of origin as the sole explanatory variable for CSR practices, it is more feasible that industrial relations and CSR practices of MNCs in eastern Europe are multi-faceted; 'instead of simply transferring practices, companies must then scrutinize their original, richer, and varied spectrum of options, beneath the surface of idealized national models' (Meardi *et al.* 2009: 509). For Hungarian unions, defining which social responsibilities firms should hold is furthermore influenced by the country's socialist past. Due to the country's export-driven national business system, Hungarian workers have been exposed to the vicissitudes of global markets, so it is not surprising that the social protection which enterprises took responsibility for prior to privatization is seen as a yardstick to measure CSR. Since this approach does not fit the CSR definitions used by MNCs, current and future union engagement with CSR may be limited.

Overall CSR has remained decidedly undeveloped in Hungary. Civil society organizations have limited engagement with business initiatives, the state has not been involved in any major CSR project, such as the Ethical Trading Initiative in the UK, and unions have not developed strategies for the application of CSR tools, like codes of conduct. Furthermore the business community has not fully embraced the discourse either. More fundamentally, there is very little public awareness of the concept of CSR, which does not have a domestic translation or commonly understood definition. Together these factors add up to an infrequently applied, paternalistic and externally driven type of CSR in Hungary. The example of Audi provides a best case scenario of this paternalistic CSR model. The involvement of trade unions, community groups and NGOs was limited and generally followed company schemes rather than initiating schemes for themselves. While interviewees at the confederation and sectoral levels thought that CSR would over the coming years grow in importance for unions, none had explicit plans to engage with CSR in the short term. For them, measures to protect legal rights and social dialogue institutions at the national level are currently of greater priority.

Conclusions

The national business system approach utilizes path dependency to explain the divergence of national socio-economic types and critical junctures to explain changes to business system characteristics. In this chapter an attempt has been made to show how both path dependency and critical junctures have played a role in determining trade union attitudes to CSR. First, due to the social roles that employers had prior to 1989, definitions of 'good CSR' among unionists are often quite different from the 'western' CSR discourse. Second, the heavy reliance on FDI in the transition to capitalism led to a reliance on export-oriented production by foreign MNCs which in turn contributed to enterprise-level industrial relations and social policies becoming far more important than national-level ones. These two features have produced a mismatch between employers' and unions' understanding of CSR.

Union attitudes towards CSR in Hungary can be summed up as indifferent, suspicious or non-existent. CSR as a concept covers a broad array of norms and practices, and in Hungary definitions varied greatly, with many being strongly coloured by the social welfare schemes that enterprises carried out during the socialist period. Firm-level responsibility for job protection, leisure activities and housing assistance were areas which interviewees saw as the most socially responsible. Regardless of policy specifics, CSR in general does not play a significant role in union thinking or strategy. No unions had developed explicit CSR policies or included CSR as a topic in their training. Unions do not engage in a broader conversation over CSR with other societal actors, since civil society organizations are relatively uninterested in CSR. The CSR discourse is therefore limited to a business community dominated by foreign MNCs and to projects run by supranational and intergovernmental organizations. This is perhaps best summed up by the lack of an adequate translation of the term into Hungarian. However, union strategy may change. One union confederation had expressed an interest in using CSR strategically, in a 'naming and shaming' campaign, although at the time of writing this plan was yet to be implemented. Unions in Hungary do maintain contact with foreign unions through European works councils, sectoral groups and global union federations. Should unions in other countries have success in utilizing CSR, this may influence future attitudes of Hungarian unions too.

Note

With many thanks to Dr Timea Pal, Jean Monnet Fellow at the Global Governance Programme of the European University Institute, without whose kind help this chapter could not have been written.

References

Adam, F., Kristan, P. and Tomšič, M. (2009) 'Varieties of capitalism in Eastern Europe (with special emphasis on Estonia and Slovenia)', *Communist and Post-Communist Studies*, 42(1): 65–81.

Aguilera, R. V. and Dabu, A. (2005) 'Transformation of employment relations systems in Central and Eastern Europe', *Journal of Industrial Relations*, 47(1): 16–42.

Birch, K. and Mykhnenko, V. (2009) 'Varieties of neoliberalism? Restructuring in large industrially dependent regions across Western and Eastern Europe', *Journal of Economic Geography*, 9(3): 355–380.

Bohle, D. and Greskovits, B. (2007a) 'The state, internationalization, and capitalist diversity in Eastern Europe', *Competition and Change*, 11(2): 89–115.

Bohle, D. and Greskovits, B. (2007b) 'Neoliberalism, embedded neoliberalism and neocorporatism: Towards transnational capitalism in Central-Eastern Europe', *West European Politics*, 30(3): 443–466.

Bohle, D. and Greskovits, B. (2012) *Capitalist Diversity on Europe's Periphery*, Ithaca and London: Cornell University Press.

Boudier-Bensebaa, F. (2008) 'FDI-assisted development in the light of the investment development path paradigm: evidence from Central and Eastern European Countries', *Transnational Corporations*, 17(1): 37.

Cernat, L. (2007) 'Europeanization, varieties of capitalism and economic performance in Central and Eastern Europe', *Socio-Economic Review*, 5(1): 149–179.

Dörrenbächer, C. (2002) *National Business Systems and the International Transfer of Industrial Models in Multinational Corporations: Some Remarks on Heterogeneity. Working Paper No. FS I 02–102*, Berlin: Social Science Research Center Berlin (WZB).

Dörrenbächer, C. (2004) 'Fleeing or exporting the German model? The internationalization of German multinationals in the 1990s', *Competition and Change*, 8(4): 443–456.

EIRO (2011) *Hungary Industrial Relations Profile*, Dublin: European Foundation for the Improvement of Living and Working Conditions. Available: www.eurofound.europa.eu/eiro/country/hungary.pdf.

European Commission (2007) *Corporate Social Responsibility National Public Policies in the European Union*, Brussels: Commisioner for Employment, Social Affairs and Equal Opportunities.

European Monitoring Centre on Change (2003a) *EMCC Case Studies: Corporate Social Responsibility in Matáv*, Dublin: European Foundation for the Improvement of Living and Working Conditions.

European Monitoring Centre on Change (2003b) *EMCC Case Studies: Corporate Social Responsibility in Mol*, Dublin: European Foundation for the Improvement of Living and Working Conditions.

Feldmann, M. (2006) 'Emerging varieties of capitalism in transition countries: industrial relations and wage bargaining in Estonia and Slovenia', *Comparative Political Studies*, 39(7): 829–854.

Feldman, M. (2007) 'The origin of varieties of capitalism: lessons from post-socialist transition in Estonia and Slovenia', in B. Hancké, M. Rhodes and M. Thatcher (eds) *Beyond Varieties of Capitalism: Conflict, Contradictions, and Complementarities in the European Economy*, Oxford and New York: Oxford University Press, pp. 328–351.

Ferge, Z. (1999) 'The politics of the Hungarian pension reform', in K. Müller, A. Ryll and H.-J. Wagener (eds) *Transformation of Social Security: Pensions in Central-Eastern Europe*, Heidelberg: Physica Verlag, pp. 231–246.

FIDH (2006) *International Fact-Finding Mission: An Overview of Corporate Social Responsibility in Hungary*, Paris: International Federation for Human Rights.

Greskovits, B. (2005) 'Leading sectors and the varieties of capitalism in Eastern Europe', *Actes de Gerpisa*, 39: 113–128.

Greskovits, B. (2010) 'Central Europe', in K. Dyson and A. Sepos (eds) *Which Europe? The Politics of Differentiated Integration*, Basingstoke: Palgrave Macmillan, pp. 142–155.

Hancké, B., Rhodes, M. and Thatcher, M. (2007) *Beyond Varieties of Capitalism: Conflict, Contradiction, and Complementarities in the European Economy*, Oxford: Oxford University Press.

Hungarian Central Statistical Agency (2013) *Key Figures*, Budapest: Hungarian Central Statistical Agency. Avalable: www.ksh.hu/?lang=en.

IMF (2013) *Hungary: 2013 Article IV Consultation and Third Post Program Monitoring Discussions. IMF Country Report No. 13/85*, Washington, DC: International Monetary Fund.

King, L.P. (2007) 'Central European capitalism in comparative perspective', in B. Hancké, M. Rhodes and M. Thatcher (eds) *Beyond Varieties of Capitalism: Conflict, Contradiction, and Complementarities in the European Economy*, Oxford: Oxford University Press.

Lane, D. and Myant, M. (2007) *Varieties of Capitalism in Post-Communist Countries*, Basingstoke: Palgrave Macmillan.

Matten, D. and Moon, J. (2008) '"Implicit" and "explicit" CSR: a conceptual framework for a comparative understanding of corporate social responsibility', *Academy of Management Review*, 33(2): 404–424.

Meardi, G., Marginson, P., Fichter, M., Frybes, M., Stanojević, M. and Tóth, A. (2009) 'Varieties of multinationals: adapting employment practices in Central Eastern Europe', *Industrial Relations: A Journal of Economy and Society*, 48: 489–511.

Mosley, L. (2003) *Global Capital and National Governments*, Cambridge: Cambridge University Press.

Müller, K. (2002) 'From the state to the market? Pension reform paths in Central–Eastern Europe and the former Soviet Union', *Social Policy and Administration*, 36(2): 142–155.

Mykhnenko, V. (2007) 'Strengths and weaknesses of "weak" coordination: Economic institutions, revealed comparative advantages, and socio-economic performance of mixed market economies in Poland and Ukraine', in B. Hancké, M. Rhodes and M. Thatcher (eds) *Beyond Varieties of Capitalism: Conflict, Contradictions, and Complementarities in the European Economy*, Oxford: Oxford University Press, pp. 351–379.

Nelson, J. (2001) 'The politics of pension and health-care reforms in Hungary and Poland', in J. Kornai, S. Haggard and R. Kaufman (eds) *Reforming the State: Fiscal and Welfare Reform in Post-Socialist Countries*, Cambridge: Cambridge University Press, pp. 235–266.

Neumann, L. (2012) 'Hungarian unions: responses to political challenges', *Management Revue*, 23(4): 369–385.

Nölke, A. and Vliegenthart, A. (2009) 'Enlarging the varieties of capitalism: the emergence of dependent market economies in East Central Europe', *World Politics*, 61(4): 670–702.

Pollert, A. (2000) 'Ten years of post-communist central Eastern Europe: Labour's tenuous foothold in the regulation of the employment relationship', *Economic and Industrial Democracy*, 21(2): 183–210.

Sass, M. and Kalotay, K. (2012) *Inward FDI in Hungary and its Policy Context*, New York: Vale Columbia Center on Sustainable International Investment, Columbia University.

Tóth, A. (2012) *The New Hungarian Labour Code: Background, Conflicts, Compromises*, Working Paper, Budapest: Friedrich Ebert Foundation.

UNCTAD (2012) *World Development Report 2012*, Geneva: United Nations Conference on Trade and Development.

UNCTAD (2014) *UNCTADstat*, Geneva: United Nations Conference on Trade and Development. Available: http://unctadstat.unctad.org/ReportFolders/reportFolders.aspx?sCS_referer=&sCS_ChosenLang=en.

Vanhuysse, P. (2007) 'Workers without power: agency, legacies, and labour decline in East European varieties of capitalism', *Czech Sociological Review*, 43(3): 495–522.

Visser, J. (2011) *Industrial Relations in Europe 2010*, Brussels: Directorate-General for Employment, Social Affairs and Inclusion.

Vliegenthart, A. and Nölke, A. (2009) 'Enlarging the varieties of capitalism: the emergence of dependent market economies in East Central Europe', *World Politics*, 61(4): 670–702.

Whitley, R. (1998) 'Internationalization and varieties of capitalism: the limited effects of cross-national coordination of economic activities on the nature of business systems', *Review of International Political Economy*, 5(3): 445–481.

Whitley, R. (1999) *Divergent Capitalisms: The Social Structuring and Change of Business Systems*, Oxford: Oxford University Press.

Whitley, R. and Czabán, L. (1998) 'Institutional transformation and enterprise change in an emergent capitalist economy: the case of Hungary', *Organization Studies*, 19(2): 259–280.

7 Lithuania

CSR on a wish list

Raminta Pučėtaitė, Virginija Jurėnienė and Aurelija Novelskaitė

> The concept of CSR is positive, but in practice we have not grown into it yet. We are growing.
>
> (MPF, Lithuanian Federation of Forest and Forest Industry Workers' Trade Unions)

Introduction

Corporate social responsibility (CSR) is not unknown territory to the Lithuanian trade unions, as the notion of putting people and, indeed, the planet before profits has long been an essential feature of their outlook. On a practical level this has translated into efforts to foster social dialogue, which have now almost completely erased the Marxist vocabulary of class conflict and building barricades from trade union terminology. However, perceptions of unions as an impediment to progress, or as structures that claim to defend workers' interests but in fact serve employers' interests, persist in business and society, making it difficult for them to engage in productive negotiations with employers and government. Furthermore, trade unions also lack understanding of CSR as a set of tools that they can use to help the employer improve business performance and therefore argue for the benefits of unionizing potential members and strengthening their position in social dialogue. Accordingly, they tend to view foreign companies and the processes of social and environmental harmonization in the European Union (EU) as the most likely drivers of change in the current situation.

The weakness of trade unions and the association of CSR almost completely with foreign companies in Lithuania can be explained by reference to the country's political-economic system and socio-cultural context. As a post-communist economy with some typical features of liberal market capitalism (such as a flexible labour market and liberal social protection) and some features that are untypical (such as an underdeveloped capital market and concentrated ownership of capital), Lithuania faces the following deficiencies: sustainability-based thinking and long-term investment; transparency in its business operations; integrity of its social institutions; respect for the rule of law; and, consequently, a weak civil society and system of industrial relations. These deficiencies have led Lithuanian society to regard notions of social welfare and well-being as mere rhetoric and to trivialize violations of the public interest, or to view them rather as the norm, all of which significantly undermines the development of CSR and demands a concerted approach to promote it.

National business system

Following the collapse of the iron curtain and the accession of new member states into the EU in 2004, numerous attempts have been made to locate post-communist economies within the typology of 'varieties of capitalism' proposed by Hall and Soskice (2001) and Amable (2003). These have resulted in categorizing post-communist countries as closer to liberal market economies (Knell and Srholec 2007), with some of their features ascribed to the Mediterranean model of capitalism (McMenamin 2004). Moreover, the Baltic states have been differentiated from other post-communist economies, such as the Visegrád countries, as being economically more liberal, less strongly dependent on transnational corporations and foreign direct investment and liable to apply 'shock therapy' when initiating and carrying out changes during the transition period (Bohle and Greskovits 2007; Nölke and Vliegenthart 2009). Some scholars go further by pinpointing considerable differences between Estonia, Latvia and Lithuania, characterizing in particular Estonia as a much more distinct version of neo-liberalism (Kuokštis 2011; Norkus 2008b).

Lithuania is often labelled as a liberal market economy (LME), based on the criteria of a high degree of labour market flexibility, a lack of collective bargaining and agreements, a business attitude towards human resources as a cost rather than an asset and hence the dominance of a generalist system of education, short-term investment (Bohle and Greskovits 2009; Kuokštis 2011; Norkus 2008a), high job mobility (Coppin and Vandenbrande 2006) and weak employee commitment (Gruževskis *et al.* 2006).

However, Lithuania's business system differs from the LME model in several respects too. First, in the early years following regained independence in 1990, national businesses did not invest in research and development, but relied rather on unskilled labour-intensive export goods (Bohle and Greskovits 2009). The issue was addressed by government and foreign telecommunication companies' investment in developing broadband internet since 2000, which has improved the country's potential for innovation and has resulted in a high rate of ICT-based businesses since 2009. As a result, Lithuania's position in the Global Innovation Index stands at 40 out of 142 states (Dutta 2012).

Second, capital markets, in particular the stock market, are significantly underdeveloped and the financial system is dominated by foreign commercial banks (Kuokštis 2011: 7). The perceived limitation of capital availability to small and medium-sized enterprises (SMEs) has been addressed by the government since 2009 by engaging in an EU-co-ordinated programme, Joint European Resources for Micro to Medium Enterprises (JEREMIE), and developing hybrid venture capital markets (Snieška and Venckuvienė 2011). Nevertheless, doing business in Lithuania is more complex than in other EU member states (World Bank 2013). In particular, long bureaucratic procedures when establishing and liquidating businesses are noted as barriers to development, although some advances were made by 2012, such as digitalizing the land registry, electronic tax administration and a new law on resolving the insolvency of private individuals (World Bank 2013: 140).

Third, the national economy is dominated by SMEs which often have limited liability and do not publicly trade their stocks. The owner of a company is usually the general manager, hence shareholders' control over professional managers is not the norm (Norkus 2008b: 70). On the one hand, this practice reduces the risk of hostile takeover and leads to high flexibility in decision-making and exit from the market (Kuokštis 2011). On the other hand, it impedes business development as the owners may lack professional and management skills. Overall, these arrangements hinder the development of mutually respectful and partnership-based relationships between employers and employees (Blaziene 2006).

There are other peculiarities of the Lithuanian model of capitalism that are typical of other post-communist societies as well, such as low trust in public institutions (Aidukaite 2009; Pučėtaitė *et al.* 2010; Sztompka 1999; Ungvari-Zrinyi 2001) and patronage networks which distort competition (Norkus 2008a: 569; Rehn and Taalas 2004). A final observation is that the country's accession to the EU in 2004 provided easier access to financial capital and opened opportunities for improving production facilities and reaching new markets with advanced technologies (in particular, electronics and laser products). Agricultural products are largely exported to the countries of the former Soviet Union, capitalizing on social connections from the Soviet times. In 2011, Russia remained Lithuania's single most important trading partner although more than half of its national trade is dependent on the EU (Statistics Lithuania 2012: 373).

Industrial relations system

Due to the country's slow industrialization, workers in Lithuania started unionizing rather late compared with other European societies – the first trade union was established by shoemakers in 1892 (Motiejūnaitė-Pekkinen 2012) when Lithuania still belonged to the Russian Empire. Lithuanian trade unions did not gain power during the First Republic (1918–1940) because of the country's strategic focus on agriculture and its authoritarian regime from the mid-1920s. It was only in the Soviet period that they became numerous and powerful. In 1980 over 1.7 million workers and public servants (the population at the time being 3.4 million) were 100 per cent unionized, the only employer being the State. Membership density was total, not because of a sense of solidarity but because of pressure from the Communist Party and due to social benefits available through membership of the unions (Ost 2009). Like elsewhere in the Soviet Union, Lithuanian unions distributed social benefits to the workforce, such as vouchers for cars, flats, trips to other Soviet republics, health and summer resorts and sports centres, but did not engage in 'real' labour issues through collective bargaining (Aidukaite 2009: 28). Union leaders enjoyed privileges similar to those of the nomenclature.

Following the reestablishment of independence in 1990, privatization created many social problems, with many workers becoming unemployed, emigrating or starting their own business. Nevertheless, the structure and density of unions had already been changing before 1990, owing to market liberalization and developments in employment relations resulting from *perestroika*. Members could voluntarily leave a union without fear of persecution afterwards. This change established unions as independent players in industrial relations but significantly diminished their membership. During the following decade unions were actively involved in dividing the assets of the former Soviet trade unions, in particular real estate (Aidukaite 2009). They were also active in legislation, particularly in establishing the Lithuanian Tripartite Council (1995) and the Labour Code (2003). However, unions did not manage to capitalize on these processes and to date their influence has been generally regarded as insignificant (Glinskienė and Krašenkienė 2010: 78).

Union density is 9 per cent, and collective agreements cover 15 per cent of the working population (Lithuanian Department of Statistics 2011; Fulton 2011), which count among the lowest in the EU (Pedersini 2010). The majority of union members (60–70 per cent) work in the state sector (Blaziene 2006). Most collective agreements are bilateral at company level and rarely improve on the conditions laid down under labour legislation (Ost 2009). However, two collective agreements that are broader in scope stand as exceptions: a sectoral agreement in the newspaper industry, signed in 2007, and a regional collective agreement covering constructors and designers in Western Lithuania. This was signed in autumn 2012 and was the first of its kind in the country. It resulted from the attempts made by Lithuania's Ministry of Social Security and Labour since the beginning of 2012 to improve the skills of unions and employers' associations in social dialogue and to increase the number of collective agreements in the country through financial and administrative measures using European structural funds (Blaziene 2012).

Several factors explain low union density and coverage of collective agreements. First, unions are viewed with distrust by employers as a leftover from Soviet times (Blaziene 2006; BNS 2013; Woolfson *et al.* 2008). Second, as civic society remains immature, employees prefer negotiating with the employer individually rather than engaging in acts of solidarity and collective bargaining. Third, the national economy is dominated by SMEs which employees rarely manage to unionize. Finally, 10 per cent of the working population are self-employed (Statistics Lithuania 2012: 127), which reduces the working population eligible for union membership.

The Tripartite Council of the Republic of Lithuania was founded in 1995 to improve the industrial relations system, though its activities have been criticized as insufficient and their decisions biased towards employers and not based on consensus. Unions on the Council are represented by three national-level umbrella confederations with a membership of about 110,000. These confederations are:

- LPSK, *Lietuvos profesinių sąjungų konfederacija* (Lithuanian Trade Union Confederation), established in 2002;
- LDF, *Lietuvos darbo federacija* (Lithuanian Labour Federation), established in 1919, active until 1940 and recreated in 1991; and
- Solidarumas, *Lietuvos profesinė sąjunga 'Solidarumas'* (Lithuanian Trade Union 'Solidarity'), established in 1989 as part of the national movement *Sąjūdis* and later becoming an independent institution in 1990.

Employers on the Council are represented by two major umbrella organizations:

- *Lietuvos verslo darbdavių konfederacija* (Lithuanian Business Employers' Confederation), founded in 1999 and uniting around 1,800 companies as well as regional and sectoral business associations; and
- *Lietuvos pramonininkų konfederacija* (Lithuanian Confederation of Industrialists), established in 1989 and consisting of up to 2,700 companies from nine regional and 42 sectoral associations.

Union influence on the Council is limited by several factors. The union confederations are partially financed from the national budget (Glinskienė and Krašenskienė 2010), which contributes to popular scepticism towards their activity. Friction between the unions in Lithuania also makes it difficult to lobby and represent employees' interests on a co-ordinated basis. Furthermore, until 2012 when the Social Democrats came to power, the number of union representatives on the Council was smaller than the number of employer and government representatives.

The evolution of CSR

The origins of interest in CSR in Lithuania can be traced back to 2003, when the National Sustainable Development Strategy was adopted by the government. The term 'CSR' came into use around 2004 when the National Network of Responsible Enterprises (NAVĮT; since July 2013 – Lithuanian

Association of Responsible Business) was established at the first conference on CSR, entitled 'Responsible Business in Society'. It had been patronized by the president of the Republic of Lithuania, promoted by the national office of the United Nations Development Programme (UNDP), and also responded to pressure for sustainable development from the EU (Vasiljeviene and Vasiljevas 2005). The conference examined the opportunities for Lithuanian enterprises to join the Global Compact – the following year, 39 companies joined, mostly subsidiaries of transnational corporations, since when the number has exceeded 80 (which was, however, just 0.1 per cent of all active companies in Lithuania in 2012).

Most of these companies were active in the NAVĮT, the presidency of which rotates amongst member companies every six months. However, the majority of the members of the Global Compact and the NAVĮT in Lithuania are large foreign companies. SMEs still lack the resources and capacity to engage in CSR. This factor, along with the lack of any supportive framework for interinstitutional and intersectoral co-operation, was found to be a major hindrance in an empirical study *Baseline Study on CSR Practices in Lithuania* carried out by the UNDP and the Public Policy and Management Institute in Lithuania in 2007. Several initiatives, in particular educational ones, were therefore organized to increase knowledge and skills in the field. However, their effect has not yet been measured.

The UNDP office in Lithuania and the Ministry of Social Security and Labour have been the most important players promoting CSR at national level (the UNDP office closed in 2013, but its responsibilities were taken over by the Lithuanian Association of Responsible Business). In 2006, the Ministry created the Standing Commission for the Co-ordination of Corporate Social Responsibility Development which is responsible for co-ordinating measures promoting CSR in Lithuania. In joint efforts in 2007, UNDP and three Ministries – Social Security and Labour, Economy, and Environment – established an Award for National Responsible Business which drew the attention of foreign and domestic companies of all sizes. The award is considered as an indicator of business progressiveness, and the number of companies submitting an entry has grown from 22 in 2008 to 51 in 2011 (Įmonių socialinės atsakomybės pažangos, 2012).

Another national initiative, *Baltoji banga* (The White Wave), was created in 2007 by the leaders of the national chapters of UNDP and Transparency International, the Institute of Civic Society, the Investors' Forum, the Business Support Agency of Lithuania and some other public figures to fight corruption, promote transparent and fair business practices and deepen social awareness of the issues related to tax avoidance in employment relations. It consists of a special emblem which is awarded to companies that comply with the law and encourage others to behave responsibly. This initiative could be regarded as a peculiarity of the country where the hidden economy comprises around a third of GDP (Žukauskas 2012), and the population regards the payment of taxes, in particular employment taxes, as a sign of social responsibility (TNS LT 2012).

In 2010 the Lithuanian government approved the *National Programme for the Development of Social Responsibility of Enterprises for 2009–2013* and the *Plan of Measures for its Implementation for 2009–2011* which focused on developing favourable conditions for CSR practices, deepening companies' awareness of CSR and increasing companies' and stakeholders' competence to handle CSR issues. The planned measures have been implemented, though the Programme has been criticized for omitting public organizations from its scope (Vilke 2011), and the results are still awaited.

Methods: unions interviewed

Eight interviews with one of the leaders (president or vice president) of the following Lithuanian trade unions were carried out between February and August 2012.

Union confederations:

- LPSK, Lithuanian Trade Union Confederation – around 90,000 members, comprising 26 industry federations, and the largest union confederation in Lithuania;
- LDF, Lithuanian Labour Federation – around 13,000 members, comprising eight industry federations with a representative on the Standing Commission for Co-ordination of Corporate Social Responsibility Development in Lithuania;
- Solidarumas, Lithuanian Trade Union 'Solidarity' – around 8,000 members, comprising 12 industry federations and 24 regional trade unions.

Sectoral unions:

- LMP, Lithuanian Food Industry Trade Union – the largest sectoral union;
- LCPDPSF, Lithuanian Chemical Industrial Workers' Trade Union Federation – one of the largest sectoral federations, most of its members work in factories built in Soviet times with union traditions. In May 2012 LCPDPSF merged with LEDPSF, *Lietuvos energetikos darbuotojų profesinių sąjungų federacija* (Lithuanian Federation of Energy and Electrical Workers' Trade Unions), a sectoral union, to form the Lithuanian Federation of Industrial Trade Unions;
- MPF, Lithuanian Federation of Forest and Forest Industry Workers' Trade Unions – a union representing workers in the furniture industry, the country's export leader;

- LPSDPS, Lithuanian Trade Union of Service Workers – selected as representing workers in the services sector, a priority for Lithuania's national strategy of economic development.

Company-level union:

- The union of the textile company, Utenos trikotažas (UT) – one of the largest exporting companies in Lithuania's textile industry, with around 700 members. The interview was carried out with the company's union leader instead of the leader of Lithuanian textile union, who at the time of the interviews had been recently elected to the position and, based on the communication with other leaders, was still new to the issues. The leader of the Utenos trikotažas union is one of the most experienced in the sector and is financially independent from the unionized company, which is a rare case at organizational level.

The latter five unions listed are affiliated to LPSK (though at the time of the interviews LCPDPSF had not yet merged with LEDPSF, so there were then six).

Union understanding of CSR

Some interviewees gave somewhat vague answers to the question about the meaning of CSR, such as 'the concept is not widely used although we are doing something in the field' (LEDPSF). A couple of union representatives reported that they do not have much knowledge about CSR, for example, 'I asked our administrator to search for some information on the internet before the interview' (LEDPSF). However, the majority could provide a definition of CSR which they tended to formulate in normative terms, ranging from personal obligation to enterprise responsibility:

> [It is] consciously striving to do good not only for myself, but for the entire environment, for every employee – this means, I have to be an example both for myself and for others, the example showing how one has to treat everything around us: the material and immaterial world, employees, everything.
>
> (Solidarumas)

> [F]irst, it is [...] showing consideration for the environment; second, it is an attitude towards an employee, meaning that he or she has to be respected, considered, protected and his or her health has to be considered; and, in general, [it means] an enterprise has to contribute to strengthening the country's welfare and donating towards some civil, social activity.
>
> (LDF)

Another representative was even more specific about the normative requirements placed on companies that want to be called socially responsible:

> [A] socially responsible enterprise must match three essential criteria. These are [...] ecology, transparent accountancy and normal social dialogue. In simple terms, ecology involves uncontaminated and progressive manufacturing, which does not pollute nature or produce toxic materials. Second, absolutely transparent accountancy is where everyone knows for what they are working and a tax inspector can understand where money is kept, where it comes from and where it goes. The third thing concerns representatives of employees [...]. Now we can say that there are works councils, not only trade unions.
>
> (LPSDPS)

This interviewee was rather confident that his understanding of CSR was directly related to a definition proposed by the International Labour Organization and was resolute in making efforts to realize it in practice. He noted societal benefits of the three pillars he quoted, such as increasing transparency and reducing the hidden economy, and pointed out the importance of an integrative approach to CSR: 'a socially responsible enterprise must definitely match all these three criteria. If any of the criteria are missing, I would not consider [the enterprise] as socially responsible' (LPSDPS). He criticized the government which, in his opinion, erroneously eliminates the dimension of social dialogue from CSR-related policy or 'thinks that a socially responsible enterprise is the one which employs disabled people' (LPSDPS). The idea of the government showing little interest in discussing CSR and consulting the unions on its development was expressed in a rather outspoken way by other unions as well. In this respect, the mass media are seen as being at the forefront of awareness-raising on CSR (LMP).

One of the major obstacles facing some unions in forming a particular understanding of CSR is the lack of factual examples, in particular during the economic crisis:

> There were more [discussions concerning CSR], [...] but the crisis impeded all these good wishes and the good work that was started; and it cast the enterprises in terms of CSR [...] five years backwards.
>
> (MPF)

Over this period, only the awards for National Responsible Business brought CSR into public attention (LMP). In this respect, the incentives to be acknowledged for CSR were enhanced: 'there is prestige to be awarded, to be noticed; [...] in educational terms, a compliment motivates better than a reproach' (LDF). However, the reported changes have taken place mostly in large, foreign enterprises, regretfully leaving smaller domestic companies to one side.

Union policies on CSR

When asked about the prevailing understanding of CSR amongst the unions, interviewees emphasized the 'people' dimension: 'we [the unions] understand CSR in the sense that manufacturing and the economy should serve the people, should improve working conditions so that people would respect the enterprise' (MPF). Others mentioned the environment as well: 'first of all we think about an employee, which means that we think how much an enterprise can care about its employees; second, we think about the effect on the environment in general' (LDF). A general attitude towards CSR amongst the unions was that it results from dialogue (MPF, LPSDPS, LDF, LMP, LEDPSF) which is carried out 'through collective agreements'.

Some respondents were aware of the growing importance of CSR in society and believed that their engagement in CSR gave an incentive to its institutional development: 'we want to be involved [...] as we want the changes to be on the positive side [...] this is a thing of progress' (MPF). Moreover, the interview at LEDPSF revealed that the union regarded CSR as an opportunity to attract more members in the future.

Union leaders had a clear notion of the benefits that CSR could provide to business. It was described as an efficient means for solving social and ecological problems (MPF, LDF, LPSK, LPSDPS) and as a more efficient alternative to economic and financial measures to mould corporate behaviour (LDF). The view that CSR can achieve positive change on a global scale was expressed forcibly in those sectoral unions which were particularly exposed to environmental issues and, therefore, more sensitive to them (such as in the forestry industry). Some interviewees saw CSR as a platform for international networking. For example, LDF located contacts in other retail networks who helped them attend Carlsberg's European works council. Specific examples of how CSR could benefit a company included employee loyalty (LPSDPS), enhanced qualifications and a positive culture (MPF) and corporate reputation (MPF). Several interviewees (LPSDPS, MPF, LMP) noticed that CSR has already changed the behaviour of some Lithuanian enterprises, for example in terms of tax payments and improved employee welfare programmes.

Speaking about perceived obstacles to CSR development, interviewees referred to economic slow-down and the scarcity of resources available for CSR (LDF) and to sympathizers with the former Soviet regime who disapproved of private business. They also explained the rise in illegal, 'hidden' businesses by reference to the unwillingness of those individuals with capital obtained by shady means to become transparent:

> Since traditions of business are absent [...] because of Soviet rule [...], politicians and lobbyists do not want [to promote CSR] because they understand perfectly well that transparency [which CSR rests on] would diminish the competitiveness of many Lithuanian enterprises.
> (LPSDPS)

The limitations of business managers and their short-term orientation in decision making were also seen as an obstacle to the development of CSR. Overcoming this requires macroeconomic stability as well as a general level of education and social maturity (MPF).

Some interviewees regretted that even companies which are publicly known for CSR activities ignore requests to initiate collective bargaining between sectoral unions and employers' associations (LPSK). The unions in such companies end up telling the employees 'not to sign employment contracts or any changes without having read them' (LMP) and distributing leaflets with basic information about employees' rights. Besides communications and dissemination of information to their members, most unions saw their role as engaging in a constructive social dialogue with employers as their main activity in the field of CSR: 'we try to have minimum conflict because the trade union is not an axe with which we come to fight an employer: we understand our work as a dialogue – striving to find a solution which is suitable for everyone' (LDF). Reaching an agreement depends on the goodwill of both sides (LMP).

When asked about their attitudes to companies' obligation to publish social and environmental reports, some union representatives expressed strong support: it 'must indeed be compulsory' according to LPSDPS, though others were more moderate and even a little sceptical: 'some reporting should exist, but this is just the formal side' (LMP). An opinion was also expressed that, although reports are compulsory, they are too numerous: 'there are so many reports now that the number should be halved' (MPF).

Union engagement with CSR

According to the unions interviewed, conscious discussions on CSR-related issues in Lithuania started around the year 2000, 'approximately 10–15 years ago' (LPSDPS, MPF). Some union representatives specified the year in which CSR entered public discourse: 'it was 2006 when we started discussing CSR questions seriously' (LDF). Involvement was sparked by events in the EU, such as 'European-level seminars' (MPF) and dissemination of good practice from other European countries (LPSDPS), followed by initiatives undertaken by Lithuanian employers, including seminars and conferences (MPF) and CSR-targeted legislation (LDF).

Other events which triggered sectoral union engagement in CSR were social and/or environmental standardization processes, such as the standard for decent working conditions SA8000 (UT) or the environmental management standard ISO 14001 (MPF), which were initiated in companies to meet foreign market requirements or in response to pressure from international organizations such as Greenpeace. UT, the textile company, was the first to receive SA8000 certification in the country in 2006, and is continually renewing it. UT's union representatives are therefore regularly interviewed by auditors about employee participation and social dialogue, and feel that standardization is the strongest argument for management to consult the union. However, when speaking about other CSR-related standards, such as CSR guidance document ISO 26000, interviewees were not so explicit as they knew too little. For example, one respondent said: 'I know it exists, but don't know exactly what it means' (LDF). In general, the dominant answer was vague: '[CSR standards] are known only in theory' (Solidarumas, LMP) or they 'have not been studied in-depth' (LMP) or they are too detached from what union representatives consider their direct duties: 'the specifics of our activities are slightly different' (Solidarumas).

With respect to the integration of CSR into their structures, none of the unions interviewed had a CSR-related policy or any other institutional tool, such as a code of conduct, a CSR officer or CSR auditing. Yet certain existing features of the union landscape could be developed into a CSR management system. For example, the leader of LPSK referred to the leader of LMP as a person knowledgeable on CSR issues who educates others in the Confederation. Indeed, the knowledge gained in externally organized events has proved useful for training other union members. There is a tendency to integrate CSR issues into existing topics, like collective bargaining, health and safety, industrial relations, remuneration, training and development and so on.

All the interviewees noted that their unions closely co-operate with others to implement CSR-related policy (LDF, LPSDPS). Forms of co-operation range from lectures and presentations for members of other unions (LPSDPS), seminars (MPF) and discussions of the main problems in the co-ordination centres of LDF, LPSK and Solidarumas, to joint projects (Solidarumas). Some leaders were rather open to co-operation: 'unions cannot be a closed caste' (LPSDPS), while others noted hidden pragmatism in the intention to co-operate and implied the existence of a more altruistic character and ease of co-operation with foreign parties (LMP).

The interviewees did not have much experience in co-operating with non-governmental organizations (NGOs), for two reasons. On the one hand, although NGOs were considered important for their contribution, the focus of their activities was regarded as different: 'if the third sector gets involved, then the dialogue becomes civil, and we are pro-*social* dialogue' (LDF). On the other hand, a large number of NGOs was considered an obstacle to engaging in productive partnership with them: 'there are plenty of NGOs – we are simply not able to keep up' (MPF, LPSDPS).

In general, the extent of union engagement with CSR depends on the sector, as observed by the interviewees (such as LPSDPS, MPF and LDF), which could be explained in several ways. First, co-ordination and agreement on certain issues, including CSR, between sectors is weak or non-existent, and so formal structures and organization cannot be achieved

(LPSDPS). Second, unions in manufacturing are much 'more concentrated' and powerful compared with the service sector (LPSDPS). Third, the private sector is much less well organized than the public sector:

> We can count on our fingers how many unions or organisations representing employees operate in the [private] sector [...] The most complicated cases are small enterprises based on private domestic capital because there an employer thinks that 'this is my money – I can do what I want'.
>
> (LDF)

Unions can therefore reach the employees and exercise their rights only in the most important sectors, such as food, education or medical care (LDF). Additionally, the power of a union depends on the territory in which it operates: unions in cities are more active compared with those in rural districts. Yet the factors union activity depends upon most are its leaders (Solidarumas, LEDPSF) and the goodwill of employers (LEDPSF), particularly when unions confront employee representation issues, which usually arise in the process of negotiation. Otherwise, an 'appeal to a higher state level is needed: to the labour inspectorate, environmental protection, or some other agency' (LPSDPS). The idea of dispute was clearly expressed when describing the measures required to deal with an employer, which included the publication of violations of agreements and norms in the mass media (LDF, LPSDPS) as well as appeals to EU level organizations (LPSDPS, LEDPSF). Such measures were regarded as sources of power in the fight to implement CSR at the national level.

Discussion

Our findings concerning unions' understanding of CSR, as well as their engagement with it, indicate that unions in Lithuania associate CSR either with personal duty and exemplary role-model behaviour towards human actors and the environment, or with a company's approach towards employee representation, the environment and sound accounting principles, which is a peculiarity of Lithuania as a post-communist society. Lithuanian unions perceive CSR predominantly as a tool that could lead to social dialogue and collective agreements rather than as an element in civil education. Such attitudes run the risk that unions will remain focused exclusively on social and employment-related issues.

The tendency of the unions to speak about CSR from a normative perspective should also be noted. Most definitions of the concept were infused with morally-laden vocabulary denoting obligation, which implies that few definite actions have been taken from a CSR perspective by union representatives. This may mean that deeper knowledge about how to turn CSR definitions into actual practice is a real need.

Increasing the scope and depth of CSR training within the unions is important considering the enthusiasm with which some of them spoke about CSR and its significance. All of them had participated in international events relating to CSR as well as in awareness-raising activities. However, these events had showed them what corporate practices were needed to implement CSR, rather than what they themselves could do to help companies become more responsible. Moreover, it seems that the educational events on CSR in which the interviewees participated had taken place some time ago as none of them could explain ISO 26000. This is particularly important in light of the dependence of union power on standardization processes and global initiatives.

Union policies with respect to CSR promotion still seem to be lacking. CSR remains a genuine challenge when bearing in mind the small size of companies that dominate the national business system. Furthermore, these still tend to act as the 'unacceptable face of capitalism', competing among themselves, and with large companies, by hiding their real income. However, survival in a domestic market of limited growth where 'proper' networks and acquaintances, or even politics (in the case of companies oriented towards exporting to Russia), may leave little room for manoeuvre regarding sustainability issues, and hence strengthen the short-term orientation that is generally a characteristic of the LME model.

Although Western markets, ILO conventions, EU directives and standardization processes may help to strengthen the role of the unions in establishing CSR-related practices, these factors affect mainly large companies. Yet a challenge for CSR comes from large companies as well. Union interviewees referred to several situations in which CSR could be regarded merely as a public relations exercise. Union scepticism in such instances could be understood given the socio-cultural context of a post-communist society where there is a gap between values voiced in public and reality (Ryan 2006; Vasiljevienė and Freitakienė 2002).

Although unions claim that they network, their low density and the small number of collective agreements imply the opposite. Union willingness to co-operate with NGOs could also be considered as an opportunity for gaining more public trust and support, which could eventually lead to an increase of power. However, they are perceived as partners in the process of social dialogue only because, according to the unions, their focus does not directly match NGO activities. A lack of recognition among employers of the role of the unions is also implied in those cases in which agreement (or rather compromise) between unions and employers was reached following a dispute rather than through social dialogue. The notions of 'conflict', 'fight' or 'war' occur when trade unions speak of the contexts where collective action is unavoidable, such as discussing company-level collective agreements, bills and participating in legislation. Given the fact that Lithuania is a young democracy and unions are still struggling to be de facto acknowledged as independent players by employers, the discourse of 'war' implies that rational, argument-based agreement-making processes and attitudes of both parties to each other as partners still have to be learnt. Otherwise, the possibility of a social contract as the basis for the promotion of the diverse meanings and practices of CSR is undermined. However, when it comes to specific relationships between employees and employers, particularly at company level, the unions try rather to find a mutually beneficial solution which, in many cases, may demand greater compromise on the part of employees than employers. Therefore, the need for Lithuanian unions to associate and act in solidarity together remains acute.

Conclusions

CSR is a very recent phenomenon in Lithuania that has so far gained most attention and engagement from large foreign companies which are more experienced players in the global market and possess greater resources to implement CSR strategies. Union engagement with CSR is, not surprisingly, weak, in line with their overall level of activity in the country. Negative attitudes from employers and the wider society towards unions persist from the Soviet past when they gained a reputation as ineffective pseudo-representative bodies. Such attitudes hinder the unions from gaining wider support for their activities over and above attempts to sign collective agreements. Unions are therefore currently struggling to be acknowledged, listened to and consulted by employers when making decisions that affect employees and their communities. This, however, means turning away from a business focus on shareholders, or the single owner's interests, to other stakeholders whose interests are also important from a long-term business perspective. Although this is not typical for the LME model that the country has turned into, it does not mean that such an approach would not create added value for the national economy.

A number of activities currently carried out by the unions and the extent of the power they wield may be associated with the sector they represent. Textiles, furniture and timber, as well as the public sectors of education and medical care, are much more unionized and union voices are more widely heard by media, society and government. This relative power is inherited from Soviet times. Hence, capitalizing on the past, these unions could become beacons for others. Moreover, union engagement in CSR could be increased through their presence on the boards of the bodies giving responsible business awards as well as involvement in social and eco-certification processes. The 'knowledge gaps' on how to implement CSR in practice that were implied during the interviews could be filled through networking, not only with other (including foreign) unions or participating in EU-funded projects, but also with NGOs concerned with CSR and the Lithuanian Association of Responsible Business.

However, the unions need to assume the role not only of a watchdog but also of an actor who drives business innovation forward. They have to translate their usual language about representing employees and social dialogue into a business discourse of caring about employees and enhancing their commitment and productivity to achieve their own and their business's goals. Speaking the language of partnership with employers, exchanging ideas about attracting and retaining talent in the domestic labour market, and engaging and empowering employees to make better decisions and ensure business growth, could be a strategy for the unions to promote CSR in a post-communist LME and to gain the recognition from employers that is required for collective agreements. Otherwise, just blaming government or 'big business' for being indifferent to union demands and CSR will most likely leave the situation unchanged and lead to a narrow approach focusing purely on possible amendments to the Labour Code.

Acknowledgements

The authors are grateful to Nida Šereikaitė and Gintaras Martinaitis, students at, respectively, Vilnius University Kaunas Faculty of Humanities and Vytautas Magnus University, for their help in collecting and processing the empirical data.

References

Aidukaite, J. (2009) 'Old welfare state theories and new welfare regimes in Eastern Europe: challenges and implications', *Communist and Post-Communist Studies*, 42: 23–39.

Amable, B. (2003) *The Diversity of Modern Capitalism*, Oxford: Oxford University Press.

Blaziene, I. (2006) *Capacity Building for Social Dialogue in Lithuania*, EF/06/51/EN – 5, Dublin: European Foundation for the Improvement of Living and Working Conditions. Online. Available: www.pedz.uni-mannheim.de/daten/edz-ma/esl/06/ef06515_en.pdf (accessed 12 December 2012).

Blaziene, I. (2012) 'Pioneering territorial collective agreement', *EIROnline,* 13 December. Online. Available: www.eurofound.europa.eu/eiro/index.htm (accessed 8 February 2013).

BNS (2013) 'Ekspertai: profsąjungų nepopuliarumą Lietuvoje lemia sovietmečio palikimas'. Online. Available: www.delfi.lt/news/daily/lithuania/ekspertai-profsajungu-nepopuliaruma-lietuvoje-lemia-sovietmecio-palikimas.d?id=61032559 (accessed 4 November 2013).

Bohle, D. and Greskovits, B. (2007) 'Neoliberalism, embedded neoliberalism and neocorporatism: towards transnational capitalism in Central-Eastern Europe', *West European Politics*, 30(3): 443–466.

Coppin, L. and Vandenbrande, T. (2006) 'Job mobility in the career of European workers', *Overwerk*, 3: 15–21.

Dutta, S. (ed.) (2012) *The Global Innovation Index 2012: Stronger Innovation Linkages for Global Growth*, Fontainebleau: INSEAD and WIPO.

Fulton, L. (2011) *Worker Representation in Europe*, Labour Research Department and ETUI. Online. Available: www.worker-participation.eu/National-Industrial-Relations/Countries/Lithuania (accessed 8 March 2013).

Glinskienė R. and Krašenkienė, A. (2010) 'Profesinės sąjungos, jų vaidmuo ir poveikis ekonomikai', *Taikomoji ekonomika: sisteminiai tyrimai*, 4(2): 65–82.

Gruževskis, B., Vasiljevienė, N., Moskvina, J. and Kleinaitė, I. (2006) *Įmonių socialinė atsakomybė: aktualūs socialinėės politikos klausimai*, 2006/7, Vilnius: Lietuvos Respublikos trišalė taryba.

Hall, P. and Soskice, D. (eds) (2001) *Varieties of Capitalism: The Institutional Foundations of Comparative Advantage*, New York: Oxford University Press.

Įmonių socialinės atsakomybės pažangos Lietuvoje šalies lygmeniu 2008–2011 m. vertinimo ataskaita (2012) Vilnius. Online. Available: www.undp.lt/uploads/Publications%20LT/ISA%20pazangos%20vertinimo%202011%20m.%20ataskaita.pdf (accessed 8 October 2012).

Knell, M. and Srholec, M. (2007) 'Diverging pathways in Central and Eastern Europe', in D. Lane and M. Myant (eds) *Varieties of Capitalism in Post-Communist Countries*, Basingstoke: Palgrave, pp. 40–62.

Kuokštis, V. (2011) 'What type of capitalism do the Baltic countries belong to?', *Emecon*, 1. Online. Available: www.emecon.eu (accessed 31 May 2013).

Lithuanian Department of Statistics (2011) 'Politinių partijų narių skaičius išaugo 1,6 tūkstančio', *Narystės organizacijos 2011 m.* Press release. Online. Available: www.stat.gov.lt/lt/news/view/?id=10175 (accessed 8 October 2012).

McMenamin, I. (2004) 'Varieties of capitalist democracy: what difference does East-Central Europe make?', *Journal of Public Policy*, 24(3): 259–274.

Motiejūnaitė-Pekkinen, R. (2012) 'Profesinė sąjunga – kolektyvinio veikimo įrankis', *Profsąjungų naujienos*, 31 December. Online. Available: www.lprofsajungos.lt/?lang=lt&mID=3&id=124 (accessed 8 October 2012).

Nölke, A. and Vliegenthart, A. (2009) 'Enlarging the varieties of capitalism: the emergence of dependent market economies in East Central Europe', *World Politics*, 61(4): 670–702.

Norkus, Z. (2008a) *Kokia demokratija, koks kapitalizmas? Pokomunistinė transformacija Lietuvoje lyginamosios istorinės sociologijos požiūriu*, Vilnius: Vilniaus universiteto leidykla.

Norkus, Z. (2008b) 'Lietuva tarp Estijos ir Slovėnijos: dėl pokomunistinio kapitalizmo tipologinės diferenciacijos', *Politologija*, 49(1): 42–84.

Ost, D. (2009) 'The end of postcommunism: trade unions in Eastern Europe's future', *East European Politics and Societies*, 23(1): 13–33.

Pedersini, R. (2010) *Trade Union Strategies to Recruit New Groups of Workers*, EIRO Comparative Report. Online. Available: www.eurofound.europa.eu/eiro/studies/tn0901028s/tn0901028s.htm (accessed 8 October 2012).

Pučėtaitė, R., Lämsä, A.-M. and Novelskaitė, A. (2010) 'Organizations which have the strongest potential for high-level organizational trust in a low-trust societal context', *Transformations in Business and Economics*, 9(2): 318–334.

Rehn, A. and Taalas, S. (2004) ' "Znakomstva i svyazi" (Acquaintances and connections): blat, the Soviet Union, and mundane entrepreneurship', *Entrepreneurship and Regional Development*, 16: 235–250.

Ryan, L.V. (2006) 'Current ethical issues in Polish HRM', *Journal of Business Ethics*, 66: 273–290.

Snieška, V. and Venckuvienė, V. (2011) 'Hybrid venture capital funds in Lithuania: motives, factors and present state of development', *Inzinerine Ekonomika–Engineering Economics*, 22(2): 157–164.

Statistics Lithuania (2012) *Statistical Yearbook of Lithuania 2012*, Vilnius.

Sztompka, P. (1999) *Trust: A Sociological Theory*, Cambridge: Cambridge University Press.

TNS LT (2012) 'Lietuviai socialiai atsakingą verslą su labdaringa veikla sieja rečiausiai'. Online. Available: www.tns.lt/lt/news/tns-lt-lietuviai-socialiai-atsakinga-versla-su-labdaringa-veikla-sieja-reciausiai (accessed 8 October 2012).

Ungvari-Zrinyi, I. (2001) 'Moralinės kultūros tendencijos postkomunistinėse visuomenėse', in N. Vasiljevienė (ed.) *Dalykinė etika*, Kaunas: Vilnius University, pp. 229–247.

United Nations Development Programme and Public Policy and Management Institute (2007) *Baseline Study on Corporate Social Responsibility Practices in Lithuania*, Vilnius: United Nations Development Programme and Public Policy and Management Institute.

Vasiljevienė, N. and Freitakienė, R. (2002) 'Are we ready to accept European standards?', in N. Vasiljevienė and R.J.M. Jeurissen (eds) *Business Ethics: From Theory to Practice*, Vilnius: Vilnius University, pp. 172–195.

Vasiljeviene, N. and Vasiljevas, A. (2005) 'The roadmap: from confrontation to consensus', in A. Habisch, J. Jonker, M. Wegner and R. Schmidpeter (eds) *Corporate Social Responsibility across Europe*, Berlin: Springer, pp. 183–193.

Vilke, R. (2011) 'CSR development problems in Lithuania: evaluation of promoting and hindering factors', *Social Responsibility Journal*, 7(4): 604–621.

Woolfson, C., Calite, D. and Kallaste, E. (2008) 'Employee "voice" and working environment in post-communist New Member States: an empirical analysis of Estonia, Latvia and Lithuania', *Industrial Relations Journal*, 39(4): 314–334.

World Bank (2013) *Doing Business 2013: Smarter Regulations for Small and Medium-Size Enterprises*, Washington, DC: World Bank Group.

Žukauskas, V. (2012) *Lietuvos šešėlinė ekonomika*, Vilnius: Laivosios rinkos institutas.

8 Poland

Much risk, little benefit in CSR

Jan Czarzasty

> CSR is not seen as a particularly important field of activity. There is some concern, though, that CSR may become a substitute for social dialogue, and some employers may even use it to justify and legitimize the absence of such dialogue.
>
> (Budowlani)

Introduction

Polish capitalism hardly fits into any specific type of market economy distinguished in the international literature. In line with the varieties of capitalism (VoC) approach, Poland is situated in between the co-ordinated market economy (CME) and the liberal market economy (LME), although it leans more towards the latter. The industrial relations system is pluralistic, with low trade union and employers' organization density, as well as moderate collective agreement coverage.

Corporate social responsibility (CSR) is a relatively new concept in the public discourse in Poland. Furthermore, it could be said that there are several parallel, sub-discourses on CSR: within academia, within the business community (which is deeply divided as far as CSR is concerned), and among other stakeholders, where one can find organized forms of employee interest representation, first and foremost trade unions. Trade unions began to fully explore the field of CSR only after the enlargement of the European Union (EU) in 2004 and, although they have advanced considerably in their quest, they are still at the early stage of the process. The concept itself is not well known among rank-and-file members, and union leaders – whose knowledge is more developed – often treat CSR with caution, seeing it as a long-term threat rather than an opportunity for organized labour. Considering the essentially adversarial nature of Polish industrial relations, this reluctance to embrace CSR is hardly surprising, as trade unions often suspect there is a hidden agenda on the part of employers engaging in CSR activities.

National business system

Poland, along with the other new EU member states from central and eastern Europe (CEE) with a post-socialist background, is usually treated with caution when it comes to defining its national model of capitalist development. In line with the varieties of capitalism (VoC) approach, Poland is often portrayed as an example of a mixed market economy (MME) marked by 'weak co-ordination', whilst bearing the qualities of both a liberal market economy (LME) and a co-ordinated market economy (CME). On the one hand, there is a moderate degree of regulation of the labour market, trade unions are relatively weak and defensive, foreign direct investment (FDI) plays an important role in the national economy, the welfare state is under continuous market pressure and shrinking, and the education system is oriented towards general skills – all typical features of an LME. On the other hand, the government is still a key actor in the national economy, the public sector retains a substantial position, the financial system relies on banks (not the stock market) as the main source of capital, and tripartism is present – all elements of a CME (Mykhnenko 2007).

Noelke and Vliegenthart (2009) coined the term 'dependent market economy' (DME) to describe the nature of capitalism in the Visegrád countries of central and eastern Europe (namely Poland, the Czech Republic, Hungary and Slovakia). In the DME dependence on intra-firm hierarchies within transnational enterprises is a distinctive co-ordination mechanism; foreign direct investments and foreign-owned banks are the primary means of raising investment; corporate governance is exercised by the headquarters of transnational enterprises; industrial relations rely on the appeasement of skilled labour and company-level collective agreements; education and training systems limit firms' expenditure on further qualifications; intra-firm transfers within transnational enterprises are the main platform for innovation; and assembly platforms for semi-standardized industrial goods in global value chains are the main source of comparative competitive advantage (Noelke and Vliegenthart 2009: 680).

Nevertheless, the most comprehensive analysis of Poland's contemporary capitalism is provided by Bohle and Greskovits (2012). According to these authors, Poland (as well as the other Visegrád countries) is a case of 'embedded neoliberalism', where a struggle between marketization and social protection takes place. 'Embedded neoliberalism' bears the following traits: marketization (understood as the advancement of liberalization, privatization and market-oriented institution-building processes) is moderate; industrial transformation has taken a direction which enables exports of relatively well-processed products; FDI is concentrated in the complex manufacturing industries, and state policies aim at alleviating the impact of market shocks on industry; social inclusion is restrained, yet the process of dismantling the welfare state has not advanced as much as in the case of the Baltic states; and the position of labour in the industrial relations system is not particularly strong. The countries identified as cases of 'embedded neoliberalism' are situated somewhere between the 'neoliberal' (the Baltic states) and 'neo-corporatist' (Slovenia) models (Bohle and Greskovits 2012: 138–181).

Industrial relations system

A variety of labels has been applied to Polish industrial relations, which are variously depicted as 'corporatism in the public sector, pluralism in the private sector' (Morawski 1995), 'illusory corporatism' (Ost 2000), 'pluralism' (Meardi 2002) or 'fake corporatism' (King 2007). Poland is an atypical case in terms of trade union structures, with unions highly decentralized and fragmented, reliant upon enterprise-level union organizations, and with the upper-level organizational units (federations at branch levels and confederations at the central level) being relatively weak.

Collective bargaining is very decentralized, with single-employer agreements dominating over multi-employer ones. Collective bargaining coverage is quite low at 38 per cent (European Commission 2010). In 2011, there were roughly 2,500 company-level collective agreements and additional protocols amending existing agreements, whilst in 2000 there were 4,144 (Towalski 2011). As of 2012, only about 3 per cent of the national workforce (390,000 people) is covered by multi-employer collective agreements, the vast majority of which have been concluded in the public sector. Social dialogue has been to some extent balanced by the development of tripartite social dialogue, which is pursued at three levels: national (Tripartite Commission for Social and Economic Affairs, *Trójstronna Komisja do spraw Społeczno-Gospodarczych*), sectoral (tripartite sectoral committees), and regional (regional social dialogue commissions).

By virtue of the Trade Unions Act of 1991, a threshold of 10 eligible employees within a workplace (a legal business entity) is required to establish a basic trade union organization (company-level union), which must be subsequently registered with the court of law. Liberal criteria for starting up a new company-level union, combined with political cleavages splitting the union movement in the 1990s, created fertile ground for the rise of 'competitive pluralism', a key factor behind the difficulty in developing sectoral and national social dialogue (Gardawski 2003). At one point the number of trade unions active in Poland reached 24,000 (Sroka 2000: 169). Although political tensions within the labour movement have lost their intensity, interunion co-operation at the supra-enterprise level is still hampered by advanced pluralization. In 2001 a new nationwide confederation Trade Unions Forum (*Forum Związków Zawodowych*, FZZ) was established, attracting independent unions, as well as some formerly associated with the All-Poland Alliance of Trade Unions (OPZZ). The new confederation is now well embedded in the public sector.

Since the early years of transformation, trade unions in Poland have experienced a rapid loss in membership. Whereas in 1990 union density was 36 per cent, by 2012 it had fallen to 17 per cent (Gardawski *et al.* 2012). There were a number of reasons behind the de-unionization process. Certainly, universal forces responsible for de-unionization worldwide apply, but country-specific factors have also contributed to the decline in density and the subsequent loss of influence of trade unions. These include: the phenomenon of 'labour quiescence' (Crowley and Ost 2001); the political involvement of major trade unions, resulting in a 'divided identity' of the unions (torn between direct political engagement and employee interest representation); ongoing privatization and industrial restructuring; and the inability of trade unions to break into the private sector effectively or challenge the dominant role of the state in industrial relations and social dialogue.

In 2013 there were three nationwide trade union organizations deemed representative at the central level:

- NSZZ Solidarność, Independent Self-Governing Trade Union 'Solidarność' (*Niezależny Samorządny Związek Zawodowy Solidarność*);
- OPZZ, All-Poland Alliance of Trade Unions (*Ogólnopolskie Porozumienie Związków Zawodowych*);
- FZZ, Trade Unions Forum (*Forum Związków Zawodowych*).

NSZZ Solidarność was established in 1980 (registered officially in 1981). Following the declaration of martial law in December 1981, Solidarność was outlawed, and then officially reinstated in 1989. Solidarność is not a confederation but a general workers' union and remains the largest national-level union organization in Poland, with roughly 620,000 members as of 2012. Compared with the other two major trade unions, Solidarność's constituency is predominantly blue-collar, with higher-grade employees being less present. Solidarność maintains a parallel organizational structure: sectoral and territorial. The company and inter-company unions are organized into basic branch structures, which are further grouped in units called secretariats. The territorial structure comprises 38 regions. The largest branch secretariats are (data for 2006): mining and energy (87,000 members), science and education (79,000), and transport (52,000) (Gardawski *et al.* 2012).

The All-Poland Alliance of Trade Unions (OPZZ) was founded in 1984, replacing the former official trade unions dissolved in 1980. OPZZ is a confederation of 89 national unions and federations. It ranks as the second largest national-level union organization, with an estimated 500,000 members. Traditionally, OPZZ has attracted specialists and white-collar workers, which differentiates it from Solidarność. It has a parallel organizational structure: sectoral and territorial. In the sectoral dimension, 89 national-level federations and general unions belong to the confederation.

In the territorial dimension, organizational units exist at two levels of administrative division, an upper unit at the regional level and a lower unit at the district level. The largest member organizations of OPZZ are: the Polish Teachers' Union (*Związek Nauczycielstwa Polskiego*, ZNP) with 255,000 members (2008), the Trade Union of Miners in Poland (*Związek Zawodowy Górników w Polsce*, ZZG) with 33,000 members, and the Federation of Healthcare and Social Care Employee Unions (*Federacja Związków Zawodowych Pracowników Ochrony Zdrowia i Pomocy Społecznej*, FZZPOZiPS) with 21,000 members (Gardawski *et al.* 2012).

The Trade Unions Forum (*Forum Związków Zawodowych*) was established in 2002. It is a confederation of independent unions and federations. In 2012 Forum claimed to have over 400,000 members including many specialists and white-collar workers. The confederation comprises mostly unions from the public sector. Forum emerged as an alternative to the two older national unions, building its identity as a confederation without direct political links. In a manner similar to OPZZ, Forum also has a parallel organizational structure: sectoral and territorial. In the sectoral dimension, 89 national-level federations and general unions belong to the confederation. In territorial terms, organizational units exist at two levels of administrative division, an upper unit at the regional level and as lower unit at the district level. The branches with the largest number of unions affiliated to Forum are: manufacturing, health-care, transport and public services (Gardawski *et al.* 2012). All three major nationwide union organizations belong to the European Trade Union Confederation (ETUC): Solidarność joined first (in 1991), followed by OPZZ (2006) and Forum (2011).

The evolution of CSR

The term CSR first appeared in the public discourse in Poland in the early 1990s, following the launch of the socio-economic transformation. According to Gasparski (2005), the term had been introduced into academic debate in 1994. However, issues of business ethics had been nurtured by the world of academia in Poland even prior to the Second World War, as the moral aspects of economic activity had been increasingly discussed by philosophers. Growing interest in CSR among academics was paralleled as the business community in Poland also became familiar with the concept. Yet, in the early phase of transformation, CSR did not make a breakthrough into the mainstream of public discourse. Only when the early stage of transformation, marked by primitive capital accumulation, came to an end, did companies show concern for doing business in a socially responsible way. Before 2000 there was 'silence and complete lack of interest' in CSR (UNDP 2007: 22).

In the early 2000s, the original ambivalence was replaced with a definitive, albeit largely negative, stance towards CSR, seen as a kind of blasphemy against the overwhelming faith in the 'free market'. In the final years of EU accession, attitudes began to change, and CSR became quite a fashionable concept, although this fashion rarely translated into action. The initial phase of EU membership brought numerous CSR-related projects, implemented by companies in a rather uncoordinated manner. In the latter part of the decade, a trend towards integrating CSR into corporate strategies became visible (UNDP 2007). Unfortunately, the arrival of the global economic crisis called the further progress of this process into question. Although Poland has not slipped into recession, companies remain under pressure from the unfavourable economic climate.

A more detailed account of the obstacles to CSR implementation in Poland is provided by Filek (2008), who divides the barriers into four categories: methodological, theoretical, practical and country-specific. The methodological barriers are said to stem from the ambiguity of the CSR discourse and from a wide range of self-constructed definitions of the concept circulating within the business community, which seriously hinders the prospects for a consensus over the meaning of CSR. The theoretical barriers are allegedly a result not only of the cultural legacy of authoritarian state socialism and a state-controlled economy but also a neophyte faith in the 'invisible hand of the market', instilled in entrepreneurs and managers by the education system and labour market of the 1990s. The practical obstacles supposedly stem from the supremacy of the success-at-any-cost orientation of business, a reluctance to implement ethical principles in daily business activities, and the wide social and economic disparities in Polish society. Finally, country-specific impediments are said to result from mistrust of institutions (to which companies are considered to belong), poor drafting of legislation, failures of the educational system (where CRS is neglected), and ignorance of the economic conditions of companies (whose management tend to believe they cannot afford such a luxury as CSR) (Filek 2008). This view is reinforced by an empirical analysis according to which there is a wide prevalence of an 'amoral organizational culture' among Polish enterprises (Szczupaczyński 2011).

Public opinion on CSR has changed over time. The popularity of the concept was subject to survey research during the 2000s, which consistently confirmed CSR to be a rather mysterious term within society. In 2007 a large nationwide survey ($n = 1{,}021$) revealed only 30 per cent of workers replying positively to the question of whether or not CSR standards were followed in their workplace. The rate of positive answers was considerably higher among respondents employed in enterprises with foreign capital. However, when asked about phenomena which could be considered functional equivalents of CSR, such as codes of ethics in their workplace, and whether there was a protective approach towards the natural environment at the workplace, the majority replied in a positive way (62 per cent and 72 per cent, respectively) (Gardawski 2009). It is noteworthy that the concept is barely known among young people, a 2009 survey revealing that 63 per cent of respondents aged 18–25 had never encountered the term CSR (FOB 2009).

Public authorities became interested in CSR following EU accession. In 2009 the special Committee for Corporate Social Responsibility (*Zespół do spraw Społecznej Odpowiedzialności Przedsiębiorstw*) at the Ministry of Economy was established by a decree from the prime minister, although it was resolved in 2013. It issued a special policy document 'Recommendations for the Implementation of Corporate Social Responsibility Principles in Poland' in 2011. Trade unions are addressed only in one of the recommendations, in terms of 'engaging trade unions in creating occupational pension schemes offered by companies' (Committee for Corporate Social Responsibility 2011: 20). It is hard to resist the impression that the role for unions envisaged by the official document is quite narrow.

The link between CSR and industrial relations has mostly been neglected in the mainstream CSR debate. Correspondingly, CSR has rarely featured in union discourse. Finally, the relationship between organized labour and CSR has seldom become a subject of academic investigation and reflection (Czarzasty and Warchał 2010; Męcina 2011). In the mainstream debate, industrial relations issues were first embraced in the 2010 edition of an annual report by the Responsible Business Forum (*Forum Odpowiedzialnego Biznesu*, FOB), to which trade union representatives made their contributions (the report has been published annually since 2002) (FOB 2010). In the previous edition of the report, a survey is cited, according to which socially responsible businesses should first and foremost 'treat their employees well', as nearly 80 per cent of the sample declared (FOB 2009).

Methods: unions interviewed

Due to organizational constraints and the scarcity of data on trade union involvement with CSR, the research took primarily an exploratory form. The trade unions covered were selected on two criteria: first, association to one of the three main representative national-level organizations (Solidarność, OPZZ and Forum); second, involvement in CSR-related initiatives and projects, identified using secondary data analysis and through personal inquiries among union personnel, with the aim not only to set up interviews directly but also to reach out to other unions by creating a snowball effect.[1] Altogether six organizations responded to the inquiries. The following unions were interviewed:

- 'Solidarność': the largest national-level union covering mainly blue-collar workers with roughly 620,000 members as of 2012. Interview with a policy officer at the National Committee;
- FZZ, Trade Unions Forum: a confederation of independent unions and federations organizing white-collar workers, in particular in the public sector. In 2012, it claimed to have over 400,000 members. Interview with a Vice Chairman;

- KP, Confederation of Labour – an affiliate of nationwide trade union confederation OPZZ. KP is an all-grade, cross-occupational trade union with 15,000 members. Interview with a National Board member, Treasurer General;
- 'Budowlani' trade union – also an OPZZ affiliate. It is a leading union in the construction industry, with nearly 14,000 members. Interview with a Secretary General;
- ZZMK, Trade Union of Locomotive Drivers in Poland – an OPZZ affiliate. ZZMK is one of the major trade unions in the railway sector with approximately 10,000 members. Interview with a policy officer at the National Committee;
- OPZZ Silesia, the regional council of OPZZ in Silesia, interview with a Chairman.

An explanation is needed as to why OPZZ itself, being one of the three central-level social partners discussed in the chapter, is absent from the sample, while only its affiliates are covered. This is because no organizational unit or executive post within the confederation's headquarters is responsible for CSR matters, although one of the deputy chairpersons has CSR issues assigned to their domain. Furthermore, no CSR related initiatives in which OPZZ has been directly involved can be named, even though the headquarters was approached to provide details of such initiatives.

Although a low responsiveness itself does not allow us to determine the level of CSR awareness among trade unions, not to mention their active involvement in CSR-related initiatives, it may still serve as a signal of the current state of affairs in this field of analysis. The additional material collected in the course of the field research included official publications prepared as part of European Social Fund (ESF)-funded projects carried out by the unions in co-operation with other partners in order to advertise those projects and disseminate the results of the research (where applicable), as well as learning materials prepared for participants in training conducted under the projects.

Union understanding of CSR

The research revealed that the involvement of trade unions in CSR in Poland is very moderate. Such a claim is justified not only by the low responsiveness to the research, but also by the content of the answers. On the one hand, the concept still appears to be a relative novelty to the unions interviewed; yet on the other hand, there is a great deal of angst and suspicion about CSR. According to the unions, the CSR concept is not well known or correctly understood by employees, union members or employers. First of all, the unions confirm they are familiar with the notion of CSR but remain sceptical about the level of knowledge of CSR (and more importantly, its content) within the public, who are 'largely oblivious to the phenomenon' (OPZZ Silesia). Second, there is a tendency to maintain that the terminology (and, subsequently, rhetoric) dominating the domestic debate on the subject stem from EU discourse (they are not homegrown and, as a consequence, remain hard to communicate to an ordinary union member, not to mention a common employee). All the interviewees agreed that there is a lack of consensus regarding the meaning of CSR. A typical comment was:

> While the academic community is able to define it properly, to many employers CSR is just about charity actions, and some identify environmental actions and initiatives as a feature of CSR, but employees to a large extent are either ignorant about CSR or, if they know about it, are usually hesitant in their approach.
>
> (Budowlani)

The trade unionists interviewed share a belief that in the eyes of employers CSR is equivalent to 'charity' or 'philanthropy'. From the unions' perspective, the approach of companies to CSR is mainly instrumental, because, as they see it, business is interested in and willing to engage in CSR only as long as it proves to be a viable public relations vehicle. In other words, CSR is a venture worth putting money into when it allows the company to maintain an image of being 'socially responsible'. This view is reinforced by empirical research, revealing that at company level CSR initiatives are predominantly fostered by managers and departments dealing with PR issues (Forum Odpowiedzialnego Biznesu and Polskie Stowarzyszenie Public Relations 2006). The majority of unions studied tended to identify the dominant approach of companies as 'selective', which one respondent described as 'actions aiming at some stakeholders, with a view of maximizing good publicity, and employees are usually not the target' (KP).

From the unions' perspective, the origin of a company's capital is an important factor in differentiating its approach towards CSR. Companies with foreign capital, especially multinationals, tend to display a higher level of CSR awareness than those owned exclusively by domestic shareholders. The size of a company and its volume of employment is also a significant indicator of company involvement in CSR: 'Differences between companies are observed not only in terms of size but also country of origin of the capital, and sector' (Solidarność). Or: 'It usually works better with the foreign-owned companies' (FZZ). However, 'better' does not necessarily mean 'more satisfactorily', as the approach of the multinationals is also subject to criticism, the unions noting a reluctance on the part of businesses to include employment and labour-related issues in their reporting activities: 'Both in theory and practice, it is easier to address environmental issues than the social ones' (Solidarność). This observation is reinforced by the fact that labour relations issues are neglected by the companies that are certified as being socially responsible in their reporting activities.

Union engagement with CSR

Although modest in number, there are CSR-related initiatives involving the social partners at sectoral level. Both Solidarność and Budowlani mentioned the example of the 'Joint Declaration on the Agreement for Workplace Safety in the Construction Sector' ('*Deklaracja w sprawie porozumienia dla bezpieczeństwa pracy w budownictwie*') of 26 August 2010, signed by seven major companies in the sector, without trade unions or other stakeholders but generally supported by the unions, as Budowlani claim. The respondents from OPZZ affiliates claim that there is little interest in CSR at sectoral level, and that internal debate is generally instigated at national level:

> There has not been much interest in CSR in recent years in our union, and what was happening took place in the headquarters, while sectoral structures seem rather indifferent. No resolutions related to the subject were passed.
>
> (OPZZ Silesia)

On the other hand, collaboration between trade unions and employers (or their organizations) takes place within the framework of the European Social Fund (ESF), in particular under the Operational Programme Human Capital. This is confirmed by the timeline of union involvement with CSR, as reported in the interviews. Except for Solidarność, which first encountered CSR in an institutional way through the ETUC, when the topic had become a subject of interest at the European social dialogue level, and ZZMK, which, by contrast, firmly states it is not interested in CSR and does not expect to change its orientation in the foreseeable future, the other organizations declared their involvement with CSR to have begun either in 2008 or 2009.

Notable examples of joint ESF-financed projects[2] carried out by the unions and employers include 'Promoting Corporate Responsibility Standards at the Company Level' ('*Promocja standardów społecznej odpowiedzialności w przedsiębiorstwie*') carried out by NSZZ, Solidarność and the central-level employers' organization, the Polish Confederation of Private Employers Lewiatan (*Polska Konfederacja Pracodawców Prywatnych 'Lewiatan'*)[3] in 2009–2010, and 'Ethics and Business' ('Etyka i biznes') completed by Solidarność and the Polish Crafts Union (*Związek Rzemiosła Polskiego*, ZRP) in 2009–2010. The former project's objectives included the development of an analytical framework suitable for assessment of good practices, which was tested on a sample of companies from the small and medium sized enterprise (SME) sector. Solidarność was consulted on the employment relations dimension of the framework, and their contribution materialized in a process called 'Obligations to Employees'. The latter project was training-oriented, and aimed at disseminating knowledge on CSR, in connection with the rights guaranteed to employees by law. It targeted both employees and employers, in order to raise CSR awareness within the two categories of recipients.

Besides employers, trade unions also co-operate with non-governmental organizations (NGOs). Examples of ESF-funded projects implemented jointly by unions and NGOs include 'Generations in the Workplace: Good Practices in the Field of Capacity Building of Young and Mature Employees' (*'Pokolenia w miejscu pracy. Dobre praktyki w obszarze rozwoju potencjału młodych i dojrzałych pracowników'*) by Solidarność and CSRinfo; and 'Corporate Social Responsibility and the Work Environment in the Mazovia Region' (*'Społeczna odpowiedzialność biznesu (CSR) w środowisku pracy w woj. Mazowieckim'*) by the Confederation of Labour and Centrum CSR foundation. The former project focused on enhancing the adaptability of people within those age brackets (that is, the youngest and those nearing the retirement age), who are considered particularly prone to unemployment and non-favourable employment conditions, by carrying out an on-line survey to examine empirically the state of employment conditions offered to young people, as well as to investigate good practices of employers in that field. In the latter project, a research component was also included, unlike other projects which mainly focused on training. The influx of EU funds which became accessible after EU enlargement (especially with the launching of the 2007–2013 EU budget) is a factor which boosted the interest of the social partners, including trade unions, in CSR-related initiatives: 'When the European money that could be channelled into projects on CSR appeared, it was an impulse [for the unions] to get involved' (OPZZ Silesia).

Based on the results of this research, the trade unions' approach to CSR may be described as ambiguous, if not a little schizophrenic. On the one hand, the unions remain attracted to various initiatives aimed at promoting CSR, in particular if there are financial incentives involved. In such cases, they do not express any reservations about entering into partnerships with employers. On the other hand, they look at CSR with anxiety, perceiving it as a sort of 'Trojan horse' that allows employers to bypass the traditional institutions of collective bargaining and social dialogue:

> CSR is not seen as a particularly important field of activity. There is some concern, though, that CSR may become a substitute for social dialogue, and some employers may even use it to justify and legitimize the absence of such dialogue. [. . .] The unions in general are not interested in taking an active part in developing CSR policies within companies, because from their point of view it is a threat to their position and to social dialogue.
>
> (Budowlani)

> In the long run, [CSR] is going to weaken the position of trade unions (like, what do we need unions for, when everything is fine?) but for today, unions may benefit from CSR initiatives.
>
> (OPZZ Silesia)

Likewise, unions are supportive of certain aspects of CSR, while being critical of many others. Not surprisingly, unions favour those features impacting internal stakeholders (especially employees), while being critical of those which, in their opinion, do not require strong commitment on the part of management, and can be implemented unilaterally, without securing the co-operation of many stakeholders, and merely produce PR effects: '[Supportive:] freedom of association, human rights in the workplace. Critical: voluntary nature of CSR initiatives' (Solidarność).

Union policies on CSR

None of the unions approached treat CSR as a strategic priority, as manifested by the lack of relevant CSR policies or documents. All the unions admit to being familiar with ISO 26000, yet that knowledge is restricted to a narrow circle of leaders and experts only, while to rank-and-file members the guidance document remains a mystery. FZZ states that ISO 26000 is 'currently being analysed'. Moreover, no further details were revealed as to whether, and to what extent, the guidance helps the unions develop collaboration with employers.

Union engagement with CSR has thus far hardly been reflected in their organizational structures. Only Solidarność claims to have one member of staff in the National Committee whose duties include 'CSR in a broad sense', but no separate organizational unit exists, so the post is a part of the International Relations Department. Aside from Solidarność, no functional posts whose scope of responsibilities would embrace CSR-related matters in the headquarters of the unions studied exist. In the political dimension, OPZZ has assigned CSR to the domain of one of their deputy chairpersons. The other unions do not have any member of staff with formally allocated responsibility for CSR matters. This is considered a problem, judging by the comment that 'no such post exists, there is no expert on board, thus what we do in this regard is quite unprofessional' (OPZZ Silesia). Involvement in the ESF-funded projects has, however, produced some learning effect, because 'there are union activists who know more about those issues, thanks to their participation in the projects' (Budowlani).

The results of the projects also tell us more about unions' attitudes towards CSR, and their views on how to promote and implement socially responsible business practices involving organized employee representation. For example, in the publication prepared for the abovementioned project 'Promoting Corporate Responsibility Standards at the Company

Level' (also intended to serve as a guidebook for enterprises), one can find the following passage (Szymonek 2010: 74):

> In the CSR debate, there are several areas at which unions look with special attention. In the unions' opinion, CSR should rely on high-quality employment, labour relations, skills development and continuing improvement of employee qualifications through vocational training, which altogether should be treated as an investment in human capital of a company. [...] Respecting [the rights of] trade unions, works councils or European works councils, non-discrimination of union activists, engagement in collective bargaining, and concluding collective agreements are all merits of a socially responsible company. A company that does not comply with the ILO conventions cannot be considered socially responsible.

Since 2007, an 'Employee-friendly Employer' certificate is granted under the auspices of NSZZ Solidarność, to companies respecting and promoting social dialogue, in particular those which show preference for steady employment, comply with the law and labour standards, and observe the employees' right to union association. The certification procedure is launched either on the recommendation of an enterprise-level trade union or by employers themselves, as long as they have official support from the unions. By 2013, nearly 80 employers had received the certificate.

A new direction in the unions' activities within CSR seems to have emerged recently, with the UEFA Football Championship (Euro 2012) being a pivotal moment. Prior to the tournament, the chairman of Solidarność, Piotr Duda, met the UEFA head, Michel Platini, to discuss issues of labour relations and working conditions in the companies sponsoring Euro 2012. The event's importance was particularly high due to the fact that among the sponsors were companies like Biedronka, a leading discount chain in Poland. Chairman Duda sent an official letter to UEFA addressing the issue of alleged anti-union practices of the company, which eventually led to the meeting on 9 March 2011. While the meeting received substantial media coverage, the interest of the public seems to have faded once the tournament ended.

Discussion

A picture of a trade union approach towards CSR has been sketched on the basis of original findings from the field research and secondary data analysis. This has revealed that, in general, CSR still remains *terra incognita* to a large part of the Polish trade union movement, and those few unions which are familiar with the concept (and claim to have gathered relevant experience) approach the very idea of CSR with caution. Trade unions' attitudes towards CSR are clearly ambivalent. On the one hand,

CSR is suspected of being a tool deliberately used by employers to undermine the position of the trade unions. On the other hand, trade unions cannot resist the temptation to take part in various CSR-related endeavours, often in co-operation with NGOs but also with employers and their associations.

Issues of work and employment relations are virtually absent in the social reporting of companies in Poland. Furthermore, despite the fact that instruments – such as the UN Global Compact, the Global Reporting Initiative (GRI), codes of conduct or certification (e.g. ISO 26000 or SA8000) – are known to union leaders (but not to the wider circle of union members, and still less to non-unionized employees), their knowledge is quite superficial and the detailed content of such documents (such as Principle 3 on freedom of association of the Global Compact or G3 Guidelines of the GRI) remain largely unheard of. The low level of CSR awareness and possession of detailed knowledge on the subject among union leaders may be explained by an inadequate proficiency in foreign languages, especially English, which, combined with the fact that the CSR discourse is dominated by the managerial literature (where labour and employment related topics are neglected), poses a serious barrier for union activists in terms of expanding their horizons. As a consequence, rank-and-file union members cannot rely on the knowledge disseminated through institutional channels.

When discussing trade unionism in the context of CSR, one needs to remember the employment structure of Polish enterprises: approximately 96 per cent employ less than 10 staff, and roughly 40 per cent of the national workforce work for micro-firms. Due to the legal constraints on union establishment (at least 10 workers are required to found a new union at company level) and participation (ineligibility of certain categories of people in employment, such as the self-employed or individuals working on the basis of civil law contracts, for union membership), substantial numbers of employees hardly have any access to union representation. Micro-firms are also not commonly engaged in CSR activities, although there is some ready-made expertise available to such entrepreneurs (Gasiński and Piskalski 2009).

In the course of devising their CSR policies, trade unions should also be aware of the divergent preferences of public opinion with regard to various CSR practices. As survey research carried out as part of an ESF-funded project by the KP in late 2010 reveals, people in employment exhibit different attitudes towards CSR practices which can be implemented by companies in a top-down manner, without the active involvement of employees, from those which can be developed only with employees engaged. Whereas the former (such as work-life balance, health and safety education and training, transparent information about the economic condition of the company and restructuring plans, and helping local communities) draw support from an overwhelming majority of the employees, the latter (such as increasing employee participation, empowerment of employees, and, in particular, employee volunteering) are approached with less enthusiasm. Although participation and empowerment gather more positive support than volunteering (which is rarely a feature of workplace conditions and is very unwelcome in the eyes of the respondents), this still contrasts with the nearly unanimous acceptance expressed towards the practices from the first category. In the same survey respondents revealed a strong preference for a non-adversarial type of trade union.

Conclusions

Trade unions in Poland have to cope with an array of challenges. CSR is an issue of relatively minor importance for organized labour, which is hardly surprising when considering that unions face dramatically low (and still falling) density, 'ageing' of the union movement, marginalization of collective bargaining in general and – at the sectoral level in particular – the recent deterioration of tripartite social dialogue, together with polyvalent attitudes on the part of the main, national trade unions' leadership towards politics. To some trade unionists, CSR is still an essentially 'foreign' concept, which they tend to perceive more as a non-affordable luxury or even as mere capitalist propaganda, and hence as a threat to, rather than an opportunity for, trade unions.

Nevertheless, there are two aspects of CSR which are apparently seen in a quite a favourable way by the union movement. First, CSR is seen as providing a chance to catch self-proclaimed 'socially responsible' companies (whose legitimacy as such is often reinforced by some external stakeholders like NGOs and other non-public institutions whose main domain is CSR) red-handed when they either fail to live up to the standards they declare or simply forget about them, and thus need to be publicly reprimanded (such as the campaign preceding EURO 2012). Second, in recent years CSR has proved a viable vehicle for accessing additional financial resources from the ESF and, as the evidence shows, unions are not reluctant to engage in co-operation and partnerships with employers and NGOs in ESF-funded projects.

Notes

1 Such attempts involved the distribution of questionnaires among the leaders of member organizations of OPZZ during union conferences and summits in 2012. Two of the interviews eventually completed (number 5 and 6 on the list) are the result.

2 At the end of March 2013, in the official register of projects implemented under the ESF financing scheme within the 2007–2013 EU budget, there were a total of 16 projects approved and subsequently carried out by trade unions as project leaders (author's own calculation), not to mention an unspecified number of projects in which trade unions were involved as partners.

3 On 1 January 2013 the organization changed its name to *Konfederacja Lewiatan* (Confederation Lewiatan).

References

Bohle, D. and Greskovits, B. (2012) *Capitalist Diversity on Europe's Periphery*, Ithaca, NY and London: Cornell University Press.

Committee for Corporate Social Responsibility (2011) *Recommendations for the Implementation of Corporate Social Responsibility Principles in Poland*, Warsaw: Committee for Corporate Social Responsibility, Ministry of Economy.

Crowley, S. and Ost, D. (eds) (2001) *Workers after Workers' States: Labor and Politics in Postcommunist Eastern Europe*, Lanham: Rowman & Littlefield.

Czarzasty, J. and Warchał, M. (eds) (2010) *Etyka a biznes: Społeczne aspekty podnoszenia potencjału adaptacyjnego przedsiębiorstw oraz pracowników*, Katowice: Śląsk.

European Commission (2010) *Industrial Relations in Europe in 2010*, Brussels: European Commission.

Forum Odpowiedzialnego Biznesu and Polskie Stowarzyszenie Public Relations (2006) *Co PR-owcy myślą o CSR?* Online. Available: http://odpowiedzialnybiznes.pl/public/files/csr_pr_raport_2006.pdf (accessed 7 June 2013).

Filek, J. (2008) 'Przyczyny małego zainteresowania ideą CSR w Polsce', in M. Bąk and P. Kulawczyk (eds), *Społeczna odpowiedzialność biznesu w małych i średnich przedsiębiorstwach*, Warsaw: IBnDiPP, EQUAL.

FOB (2009) *Odpowiedzialny biznes w Polsce. Dobre praktyki*, annual report, Warsaw: Forum Odpowiedzialnego Biznesu.

FOB (2010) *Odpowiedzialny biznes w Polsce. Dobre praktyki*, annual report, Warszawa: Forum Odpowiedzialnego Biznesu.

Gardawski, J. (2003) *Konfliktowy pluralizm polskich związków zawodowych*, Warsaw: Friedrich Ebert Foundation.

Gardawski, J. (2009) *Polacy Pracujący*, unpublished research report.

Gardawski, J., Mrozowicki, A. and Czarzasty, J. (2012) 'History and current developments of trade unionism in Poland', *Warsaw Forum of Economic Sociology*, 3:1(5): 7–50.

Gasiński T. and Piskalski, G. (2009) *Zrównoważony biznes. Podręcznik dla małych i średnich przedsiębiorstw*, Warszawa: Ministry of Economy of the Republic of Poland.

Gasparski, W. (2005) 'Business expectations beyond profit', in A. Habisch, J. Jonker, M. Wegner and R. Schmidpeter (eds) *Corporate Social Responsibility across Europe*, Berlin: Springer.

King, L.P. (2007) 'Central European capitalism in comparative perspective', in B. Hanké, M. Rhodes and M. Thatcher (eds) *Beyond Varieties of Capitalism: Conflict, Contradictions and Complementarities in the European Economy*, Oxford: Oxford University Press, 307–327.

Meardi, G. (2002) 'The Trojan horse for the Americanization of Europe: Polish industrial relations towards the EU', *European Journal of Industrial Relations*, 8(1): 77–99.

Męcina, J. (2011) 'Standardy w stosunkach pracy i dialog społeczny a społeczna odpowiedzialność biznesu', in M. Bernatt, J. Bogdanienko and T. Skoczny (eds) *Społeczna odpowiedzialność biznesu. Analiza krytyczna*, Warsaw: Wydawnictwo Naukowe Wydziału Zarządzania Uniwersytetu Warszawskiego.

Morawski, W. (1995) 'Korporatyzm: wyłanianie się nowych stosunków pracy w Polsce', in T. Kowalik (ed.) *Negocjacje. Droga do paktu społecznego*, Warsaw: IPiSS.

Mykhnenko, V. (2007) 'Poland and Ukraine: institutional structures and economic performance', in D. Lane and M. Myant (eds) *Varieties of Capitalism in Post-Communist Countries*, Basingstoke: Palgrave Macmillan, 124–145.

Noelke, A. and Vliegenthart, A. (2009) 'Enlarging the varieties of capitalism: the emergence of dependent market economies in East Central Europe', *World Politics*, 61: 670–702.

Ost, D. (2000) 'Illusory corporatism in Eastern Europe: neoliberal tripartism and post-communist class identities', *Politics and Society*, 28(4): 503–530.

Sroka, J. (2000) *Europejskie stosunki przemysłowe w perspektywie porównawczej*, Wrocław: Wydawnictwo Uniwersytetu Wrocławskiego.

Szczupaczyński, J. (2011) 'Bariery etycznego zarządzania w opinii polskich menedż erów i przedsiębiorców', *Przegląd Organizacji*, 1(852): 12–16.

Szymonek, J. (2010), 'KK NSZZ "Solidarność" wobec zagadnień CSR', in *Model rozwoju społecznej odpowiedzialności przedsiębiorstwa. Poradnik metodyczny*, Warsaw: PKPP Lewiatan.

Towalski, R. (2011) *Dialog społeczny w Europie Środkowej i Wschodniej w procesie integracji europejskiej (na przykładzie krajów Grupy Wyszehradzkiej)*, Warsaw: SGH.

UNDP (2007) *Corporate Social Responsibility in Poland. Baseline Study*, Warsaw: United Nations Development Programme.

9 Slovenia

CSR as a luxury in tough economic times

Urša Golob, Klement Podnar and Miroslav Stanojević

> CSR should be seen not only as something imposed by law and exercised through union pressure on companies to abide by the law … it should also be seen as a willingness expressed on the corporate side to do something more.
>
> (SDGD, Trade Union of Construction Industry Workers of Slovenia)

Introduction

Slovenia is one of the relatively successful new European Union member states and one of the few transition countries to join both the EU and the Eurozone with a fairly robust economy (Crowley and Stanojević 2011). It also has a strong trade union movement that dates back to the previous socialist regime and a high trade union density compared with the other transition countries. It is therefore positioned alongside countries with longer traditions of strong unionization, such as neighbouring Austria and Italy (Fulton 2011). Although this should indicate a predisposition to develop corporate social responsibility (CSR) practices at a national level, a brief look at Slovenia shows a different picture. Despite the emphasis placed on CSR by the EU institutions, it seems that this debate remains a challenge for Slovenia. It also means that beside the uneven practice of CSR at corporate level, there is still room to develop the debate further and include relevant actors in multi-stakeholder dialogue. In particular, trade unions should be involved in shaping the meanings and representations of CSR (Justice 2002).

However, it seems that trade unions in Slovenia are not a visible stakeholder when it comes to CSR. Although one could argue that employee-related issues, which are at the centre of union activities, are strongly embedded in the internal dimension of CSR (Golob 2011b), they have never been explicitly linked to CSR in trade union discourse. Similar union attitudes towards CSR have been observed in other countries analysed in this volume. However, the reasons for this trend in Slovenia may be very different from those in other countries and reflect the country's particular institutional context.

National business system

Under Hall and Soskice's 'varieties of capitalism' framework (2001), Slovenia is characterized as a 'co-ordinated market economy' (CME). This is rare among the post-communist transition countries (Feldmann 2006). Slovenia's system of institutional co-ordination seeks to achieve a balance between marketization and social protection, with all the main actors – business, labour and other social groups – accepted as partners. This has ensured relative political and economic success through membership of the European Union (EU) and European Monetary Union (EMU) in 2004 and 2007 respectively (Bohle and Greskovits 2007). Among other things, as a fairly typical CME country, Slovenia maintains relatively high employment protection, social dialogue with centralized wage bargaining, and long-term capital and bank-based finance for companies (Feldmann 2006). The character of Slovenia's CME has its roots in the inherited structure of the Slovenian economy and a legacy of self-management within companies, which has further resulted in strong workplace participation, in particular through work councils that mirror the German model (Crowley and Stanojević 2011).

However, while workers' participation has been formalized and practised to some extent, the current economic situation in Slovenia reveals certain problems over how the provisions are implemented and how owners and management treat the workforce (Gostiša 2012). This is related to often non-transparent corporate governance practices in Slovenian companies (Djokic 2013). As Djokic (2013) observes, a high increase in debt in Slovenian companies (as a percentage of GDP), negative profits, very low short-term investments and poor financing of current operations are strong indicators that, over the last 10 years or so, corporate assets and funds have been spent not on developing companies but rather on management buyouts or on generating premiums on share sales to outside investors.

These circumstances did not help protect Slovenian companies when the global economic crisis hit in 2008. A decline in profits and lower property values have been hindering company competitiveness for several years and, consequently, are starting to have a negative impact on industrial relations both within companies and at sectoral level. Hence, the challenge Slovenia is now facing is how to prevent a further erosion of its institutions of co-ordination and how to change its development paradigm to secure a generous welfare regime (Stanojević 2011a, 2011b).

Industrial relations system

One of the key reasons for the present state of industrial relations in Slovenia is its institutional legacy. In the 1990s, there was no deep transitional recession and no disruption of existing networks; the transition process was relatively smooth and not as radical as in some other post-communist countries. The institutional, co-ordinative practices that emerged were based mainly on the key organized economic interests, such as robust unions and employers' associations, being involved in the design and implementation of national economic and social policies. These policies were primarily focused on job protection, that is, on ensuring low unemployment rates and gradually reducing relatively high inflation, based on systematic co-operation between the social partners. The social partnership infrastructure was strong on both sides (Feldmann 2006): while unions were already regarded as important actors in Slovenian macroeconomic policy, the compulsory membership of companies in the Slovenian Chamber of Commerce had created a well-organized business structure and a strong employers' organization responsible for wage bargaining. All this led to economic policies and reforms founded on gradualism, where the state played an important role in cushioning shocks and co-ordinating adjustment. Privatization involved workers, who contributed to the emergence of the corporatist model of industrial relations that included comprehensive collective bargaining and legally binding tripartite agreements between unions, employers' organizations and government (Crowley and Stanojević 2011; Feldmann 2006).

Hence Slovenia started its EU membership as a country with three distinctive industrial relations features that made its economy closely resemble a CME: first, collective bargaining and tripartite agreements; second, the requirement for larger firms to have works councils; and third, the highest trade union density among the transition countries joining the EU. Although Crowley and Stanojević (2011) argue that unions in Slovenia remained strong actors over the years, acting rather successfully to preserve elements of the welfare state, after 2007 the context of neo-corporatist regulation changed radically and was eroded in the face of widening social differences, cleavages and conflicts. This was in part the result of the right-of-centre government policies in force until 2008, the global economic crisis, the pressures of Eurozone membership, the recent decline in union density, and corporate governance issues within Slovenian companies. Despite all these threats, the main force behind the co-ordination principles remains the ability of labour to mobilize (Crowley and Stanojević 2011).

Even in the former Yugoslavia, trade unions were part of the movement that first articulated workers' discontent, and this created a well-established trade union movement in Slovenia (Stanojević 2011b). After independence in the 1990s, trade unions were under pressure from political dissidence and personal interests, which caused them to fragment. Hence Slovenia's trade union movement is now rather like other EU countries. The main structures at national level include seven union confederations, with some political and industrial rivalry between them (Fulton 2011). There are also several autonomous unions. The seven trade union confederations in Slovenia are: ZSSS, the Association of Free Trade Unions of Slovenia;

KNSS, the Confederation of New Trade Unions; PERGAM, the Confederation of Trade Unions of Slovenia; KS-90, Trade Union Confederation 90 of Slovenia; Alternativa, the Slovene Union of Trade Unions; Solidarnost, the Union of Workers' Solidarity; and KSJS, the Confederation of Public Sector Trade Unions. ZSSS, KNSS, PERGAM and KS-90 were formed at the beginning of the transition, while Alternativa, Solidarnost and KSJS came into being later in the new millennium.

The distribution of union members among the main confederations is hard to assess because of a lack of official membership statistics. The largest confederation is ZSSS, which officially states that it has around 300,000 members. However, this is contested, and a more realistic estimate is about half the stated figure – between 150,000 and 160,000 members (Stanojević 2011b). This represents around 50 per cent of all union members in Slovenia. ZSSS is organized into 22 affiliates: eight in manufacturing, six in private sector services, six in the public sector, and two covering other groups, such as pensioners. The second largest confederation, KSJS, which is a public-sector workforce organization, accounts for around 25 per cent of total Slovenian union membership, while each of the other five remaining confederations represents up to 5 per cent of the national figure (Fulton 2011). Thus, the two major confederations (ZSSS and KSJS), together with the other two smaller confederations (KNSS and PERGAM), cover almost 90 per cent of the total unionized population in Slovenia. The remaining employees not covered by these four confederations belong to autonomous company unions, the smaller autonomous white-collar sector and/or occupational unions, and the remaining small confederations (Stanojević 2011b).

The minimum condition for union confederation representation at national level (in collective bargaining and within the tripartite concertation process) is to have at least two branch affiliates that cover at least 10 per cent of employees from their sector. An autonomous branch of a national union organization (not included in a confederation) can acquire official recognition if it covers at least 15 per cent of the workforce within a sector. Once confirmed as representative organizations, these unions keep their status irrespective of subsequent changes in their membership (Stanojević 2011b). The seven confederations that are representative at national level sit on the tripartite Economic and Social Council (*Ekonomsko-socialni svet*, ESS), made up of representatives of the unions, employers and the government. ZSSS has two seats and all other confederations have one seat each. The extent to which the confederations are representative across the economy varies markedly. For example, while 19 out of 22 unions affiliated to ZSSS are listed as representative, some of the smaller confederations are representative of only one or two industries each.

Although some union membership figures have been mentioned, strong competition between trade unions makes it difficult to provide precise numbers. No official figures on trade union density exist. The latest estimate from ICTWSS, the Institutional Characteristics of Trade Unions, Wage Setting, State Intervention and Social Pacts database, puts general union density in Slovenia in 2008 at 29.7 per cent of the total working population (Fulton 2011). Data obtained from Slovenian public opinion surveys, however, show that the density in Slovenia was 26.6 per cent in 2008 (Stanojević 2011b) and 25.6 per cent in 2011 (Public Opinion Research Centre 2011).

As noted by Stanojević (2011b), the decline in general trade union density was substantial from the 1990s onwards, falling from around 66.5 per cent of employees in 1991 to 25.6 per cent in 2011. The main reason was the strong decrease in unionization in manufacturing industry, while public sector unions maintained their membership levels. Interestingly, another substantial decline followed the country's full integration into the EU and the Eurozone. From 2003 to 2008, during the years of economic prosperity, Slovenian unions lost around one-third of their membership. Nevertheless, it should be noted that the union membership rate among the working population is still one of the highest amongst new EU member states.

The evolution of CSR

The issue of CSR entered into debate only recently, and some initiatives to put it on the agenda have been emerging. One such initiative, led by non-governmental actors, has been to develop a national strategy for CSR to be co-ordinated by the Network for Corporate Social Responsibility Slovenia (MDOS). This initiative was inspired by the European Commission's new CSR strategy (European Commission 2011), part of which emphasizes the importance of national and subnational CSR policies and strategies. Until recently, Slovenia had not considered such measures at any level. Political awareness of CSR at the state, as well as at the local, level was quite low.

The recent push towards CSR is now obvious from the activities of several Slovenian companies and other drivers, such as NGOs, academic institutions and the media. Two conferences are organized every year by separate non-profit organizations involved in promoting CSR; one was first organized in 2006 and the other in 2008. The business daily *Finance* introduced its annual ranking of the most socially responsible companies in Slovenia in 2005. The ranking is based on a questionnaire sent to a range of companies. Those who respond are publicly listed as socially responsible. Furthermore, the Institute for the Development of Social Responsibility (IRDO) organizes the national CSR award, HORUS, and MDOS is also promoting the European CSR Award Scheme, introduced in 2012.

Despite these recent initiatives, CSR debate at a national level is still fairly insignificant compared with that in other EU countries. Hrast (2012) argues that it could take up to 10 years for it to become an established and widely recognized concept in Slovenian society, as in the case of other countries where CSR is more developed. The reasons for this are mainly institutional and have their roots in the socialist regime and in the transition period (Golob and Bartlett 2007). The Slovenian socialist regime was much more liberal than that of other former communist countries and was characterized by strong concern for workers and for the community in general. At that time, some issues that would today be labelled as CSR were high on the agenda. However, after the transition to a market economy, many of the new privately owned companies did not actively express a willingness to participate in socially responsible practices, as they were more concerned with making profits. At the same time, public expectations of businesses were usually limited to their role in creating jobs (Golob and Bartlett 2007). Some of the reasons for the reluctance to discuss CSR issues may also be related to the low level of political responsibility and the absence of ethical values among the political elite (Jaklič 2003). Public interest in CSR has also been rather limited.

Existing research on CSR has focused mainly on consumers (Podnar and Golob 2007; Golob 2011a), employees (Golob 2011b), companies (Golob and Valentinčič 2008) and the media (Becela *et al.* 2012). Studies involving consumers show that they are most concerned with the legal, ethical and philanthropic aspects of CSR. The results of a study into consumers' CSR associations during the economic crisis confirmed that CSR-related issues tend to be context- and country-specific. Consumers cited issues related to basic business operations that seem to be more important in the context of the economic crisis: company efficiency and integrity, honesty and transparency, and fair treatment of employees and customers (Golob 2011a).

Another study conducted among employees in Slovenian companies revealed the relative importance of the internal dimension of CSR for job satisfaction (Golob 2011b). The internal dimension of CSR, as proposed by the European Commission in the *Green Paper* (2001), emphasizes that CSR practices primarily involve employees and relate to issues such as investing in human capital, health and safety, and managing change, while environmentally responsible practices relate mainly to the management of natural resources used in production. The external dimension of CSR, however, involves a wide range of stakeholders in addition to employees and shareholders: business partners and suppliers, customers, public authorities and NGOs representing local communities, as well as the environment.

The same study also pointed out that some institutional and organizational factors, such as a strong union presence, as well as how successfully the company manages its operations, are fairly strongly correlated with both the internal and the external dimension of CSR. Unsurprisingly, however, the correlations between union activities and the internal dimension of CSR were significantly higher (Golob 2011b). Furthermore, a study on CSR reporting practices in some Slovenian companies indicates that they are mainly concerned with practices related to employees, the natural environment, sponsorships and donations and, to some extent, care for the local community (Golob and Valentinčič 2008).

CSR was introduced in Slovenia in the beginning of the new millennium by some of the largest companies and subsidiaries of multinationals as a management tool. The implementation of specific CSR-related practices in these companies can be seen as a form of institutional isomorphism (DiMaggio and Powell 1983). For instance, companies were copying practices from other 'model' companies that they thought of as successful or more legitimate. The business media and different types of CSR awards supplement this type of institutional isomorphism. Although the EU's CSR strategy places companies at the centre of such activities and sees it as a strategic approach, which is increasingly important to competitiveness (European Commission 2011), it cannot be said that the EU perspective is entirely corporate-centred (De Geer *et al.* 2009). To prevent businesses from filling CSR with arbitrary content, the EU strategy also recognizes the importance of strong engagement with relevant stakeholders, such as NGOs and trade unions, the role of public authorities, and the importance of national CSR policies developed by way of multi-stakeholder dialogue (European Commission 2011).

Given the fact that the CSR debate within Slovenian trade unions seems to be rather limited, research on CSR and trade unions is almost non-existent. The first trade unions to use the CSR concept in Slovenia were SKEI and KNG (see below). The introduction of the concept was made via their international partner institutions and presented at the SKEI trade union national conference in 2002.

Methods: unions interviewed

The sampling frame for face-to-face interviews conducted between October and December 2011 comprised national union confederations and selected sector-level unions. We interviewed representatives of two confederations – ZSSS, the principal union confederation, and KNSS, the third largest confederation for the private sector.

With regard to the sector-level unions, four affiliates of ZSSS were selected to provide examples of unions engaged in both domestic and global markets. The study also took into account the specific circumstances and structure of the Slovenian economy, in which large companies from the metalworking, mechanical engineering and chemical/pharmaceutical industries are heavily export oriented (Stanojević 2011a), while other industries have a traditionally domestic orientation and are especially vulnerable to the economic crisis. The full list of unions and confederations interviewed is as follows:

- ZSSS, Association of Free Trade Unions of Slovenia – the principal union confederation in Slovenia, representing 22 unions with approximately

150,000 members. Interview with the executive secretary for international relations, strategic development and membership, who is also in charge of CSR in the union;

- KNSS, Confederation of New Trade Unions of Slovenia – the third largest confederation for the private sector, consisting of eight regional unions and representing around 14,000 workers. Interview with the union's president;
- SKEI, Trade Union of the Metal and Electrical Industry of Slovenia – the biggest Slovenian sector-level union and represents around 35,000 workers. Interview with the union's president;
- KNG, Chemical, Non-metal and Rubber Industries Trade Union of Slovenia – has around 11,000 members. Interview with the union's president;
- SDGD, Trade Union of Construction Industry Workers of Slovenia – represents a very 'vulnerable' industry with many scandals and corporate breakdowns and has, as an estimate, fewer than 5,000 members. Interview with the union secretary;
- SDPZ, Union of Transportation and Telecommunication Workers of Slovenia – estimated to represent around 5,000 to 6,000 workers. Interview with the general secretary.

Union understanding of CSR

Interviewees' responses suggest that CSR is still a fairly recent phenomenon in Slovenia. The conversations revealed a familiarity with the basic idea of CSR, although respondents usually did not refer to it by this name but spoke instead about specific areas that come under the CSR umbrella. According to the executive secretary of ZSSS: 'some traces of CSR were always present in collective bargaining from 2000 on, but not necessarily under this term'.

According to the interviewees, CSR in Slovenia is understood mainly as community involvement, sponsorships and donations. All respondents agreed that there seems to be no common definition of the term, no consensus surrounding it and, consequently, no special affinity towards CSR. Moreover, some respondents believed that various actors have not contested it because of ignorance, while others mention that employers are contesting it by strictly emphasizing its voluntary nature:

> This is all what they opt for, competition, this liberal mantra, competition, competitiveness. When I explained our understanding of CSR, he [the employers' representative] said, 'no way can we include all this' he said, 'this will hinder our competitiveness'.
>
> (ZSSS)

Some of the interviewees had a similar attitude, which implies they have passively accepted the voluntary nature of CSR by emphasizing that it is not on the agenda in times of crisis. Others, however, commented that the unions understand CSR mainly in terms of care for employees. As the president of SKEI pointed out: 'I think this comes about naturally this way'. They did note that larger, successful firms tend to implement CSR by means of taking care of employees and even cited a few examples of good practice. However, the general secretary of SDPZ added that this had been happening before the financial crisis hit. Overall, CSR as a concept was not seen as particularly effective or, as one interviewee said, as no more than 'words on paper'. Nevertheless, in the view of the interviewees, CSR should not be something only imposed by laws, regulations, and by trade union pressure on companies to conform to the laws. Rather there should be willingness on the side of the companies to go beyond the laws and do something more. However, this is not often the case. A representative of one of the sectoral unions felt that the legal framework very much dictates the terms of CSR. The legal argument of CSR was also discussed from a different angle: the laws provide grounds for the unions to be active and to legitimize their role as a source of CSR-related pressure.

The view of interviewees was that CSR differences exist mainly at company rather than at sector level. However, according to the confederation interviewee, some sectors clearly lag behind (especially the construction industry) while others are more advanced (such as the metalworking and chemical industries). Furthermore, companies that have developed a trusted brand or are part of the supply chains of big multinationals appear to be more responsible. In terms of attitudes towards CSR, the president of SKEI emphasized the interesting point that, implicitly, CSR was considered part of the employers' agenda. This also indicates that some unions might not necessarily think of their activities as being part of the CSR concept. She said:

> It seems to me that from the perspective of our members, CSR is something done by someone else. Someone else must be doing it. Someone else should try so that I will be better off and I don't have to do much for it.

Union policies on CSR

Unions have no official documents or policies on CSR-related issues, apart from some basic materials prepared for member education purposes at seminars and conferences. Their CSR actions are thus based on more or less unwritten rules and are not very systematic. The exception, however, are policies that relate to their own mission, but these are not explicitly linked to CSR. The policies listed in their documents address mainly social dialogue, forms of social policy (such as social security, equal opportunities, and health and safety at work), wages and employment legislation. However, the confederation ZSSS did try to discuss CSR more explicitly and systematically in 2007, when the topic was included in the programme for the national congress. The initiative was taken by the executive secretary, who took a personal interest in the matter:

> I started with this, I read the *Green Paper* and so on, saw the examples of good practice, it was all a little less than a hobby.... And then, when I explained the concept to others, it slowly gained attention.

One of the major confederation attempts to address CSR systematically was made on this basis. ZSSS outlined some CSR guidelines and took the initiative to include them in the draft social agreement in 2007. However, the employer representatives on the Economic and Social Council objected and insisted that this part should be excluded from the agreement.

All interviewees agreed that unions could be only a limited source of pressure in favour of CSR. As the interviewee from KNG said:

> We try to understand or hear [about CSR], but maybe do not know how to deal with it or have no vision of it. There are always some other interests that come before this.

Most interviewees agreed that when trade unions do address CSR-related topics they cover mainly aspects related to employee issues. Hence, their actions seem to be particularly supportive of the internal dimension of CSR, as the general secretary of the union in the construction industry observed:

> We would like this to be a relationship with employees, especially in terms of treating employees better than is currently done, that it wouldn't be always necessary to negotiate or force them by law, that is, forcing employers with a stick to improve working conditions.
>
> [and]
>
> Our policies are directed towards employees in particular. Here we can have some influence while for everything else our impact is fairly limited. This is sort of our domain, competence and scope, and other things are mainly out of our reach.

Related to this point, the president of SKEI questioned union-specific social responsibility and admitted that this might be an indicator that unions' interests are too narrow for them to be perceived as socially responsible. The president of KNG added that CSR policies are more wishful thinking than substance:

> These are the topics that are not on the table. And not only that, the main level of activity is now seen as negotiations for collective

> agreements on basic things. When we try to bring this to a higher level, there is no real understanding. We do try. But I do not have anything to say here, really. Except that this must be a challenge for the future. Unfortunately.

Hence, 'existential' issues (that is, survival of workers and their families, redundancies, wages and so on) are highest on the trade union agenda, which prevents unions from taking a more proactive stance towards broader CSR issues. While unions are particularly supportive of the internal CSR dimension, they also cited local community interests and the natural environment, though to a lesser extent. Interviewees did not see CSR as something that would undermine their policies; quite the opposite. They believed that it is a very important issue for trade unions and that it should be more broadly accepted by their members. Interviewees commented that seeing the 'business case' for CSR makes a lot of sense and pointed out that it is about long-term success, which is beneficial for all parties involved – employees, owners and management. Two interviewees mentioned positive outcomes in terms of more committed employees who are willing to stick with the company in hard times and cited examples of such companies.

Though some of the interviewees asserted that CSR is implemented mainly as corporate strategy and is not based on a dialogue with trade unions, others believed that dialogue is the only way for CSR policies to be accepted and that this is the policy of several trade unions organized at the level of a company. The president of KNG mentioned a few examples, such as the 'family-friendly employer' certification, which promote CSR and have been implemented with the collaboration of union representatives in the company. However, these are not explicitly perceived as CSR policies. In terms of CSR training, the executive secretary of ZSSS asserted that the confederation is trying to integrate CSR topics into seminars and educate members. However, the response is rather weak; self-interest and narrow employee interests normally prevail. The SDGD secretary illustrated employee reasoning, acknowledging that there is a strong need to educate members and others involved: 'If our company starts to take care of the environment, what will happen to our salaries?'

Overall, representatives of unions in more export-oriented industries were slightly more involved in CSR and show that the concept has been promoted to union members to at least some extent. The construction industry, by contrast, tends to be the least CSR-driven, facing severely irresponsible practices by companies. According to interviewees, the widest differences in implementing CSR and the influence of unions are related to company size and overall business success, with larger and more successful companies being more likely to take CSR-related issues seriously.

Union engagement with CSR

Trade unions in Slovenia have no strategies to engage actively and purposefully in CSR, although some ad hoc projects do exist, and there is only minimal collaboration with other stakeholders in this regard. As one of the interviewees observed:

> I cannot say that there is no engagement; it is just not a strategic focus for this union. Too much depends on the individuals, nothing is really planned and there is no direction. All you do is catch some ideas somewhere and then you try to bring them to life in your company and in your union. Now that's what I do, basically.
>
> (KNG)

There are notable sectoral differences in how unions engage with CSR-related practices. Some examples were cited by the union representatives in the chemical and metalworking industries, as well as in transport and telecommunication services. For example, the representative of the union in transport and telecommunication services argued that, because the union covers such different industries, some variation exists even within the union when issues are brought to the company-level representatives. The same interviewee also mentioned two factors that often determine the scope of representatives' engagement: one related to the size and public visibility of the company and the other to the money available for CSR-related practices. These are often considered a luxury and not something that should be a necessity, even when it comes to the question of employees' wellbeing. The interviewee from SDGD commented on another case of union engagement related to the working and living conditions of migrant workers, where construction sector unions joined forces to help raise awareness of the issue in the media and in society. This particular action was also supported by the ZSSS confederation.

Interviewees were thus in agreement that it is easier to implement projects in larger companies that are more concerned with their reputation and more aware of their role in society. An interesting CSR-related practice was implemented by SKEI and was considered to be quite effective. As the SKEI leader explained: 'I suppose one of those things we implemented worth mentioning affects the social responsibility of the company: our company blacklist'. Companies are blacklisted when they do not respond to the union's notifications about their actions being unlawful or harmful to their employees. As a counterweight, SKEI also publishes on its website a 'whitelist', with the examples of good practices.

There are also some other projects, such as environmental projects in the chemical and transportation industries, where trade unions are involved as one of the project partners. Otherwise, collaboration with other NGOs is far from extensive. The leader of KNG even cited an example of a potential conflict between that union and a local environmental organization that arose from unsupported claims and demands made by local environmentalists and a campaign initiative:

> We knew what was going on and we discussed it and decided to go against the campaign initiative ... their attacks were unjustified. We called in the official institutions and media and urged them to examine the matter, and then their evaluations should be respected ... when a thousand jobs are potentially at stake ... I mean, let's put things on the table once and for all; it is just so that, too often, anything goes.

Although all interviewees expressed a wish for more CSR debate and greater union engagement in CSR-related issues, they were also very sceptical about it in the current economic conditions. They mentioned a number of other obstacles that might hinder CSR debate and engagement: these included the crisis of moral values, inadequate social dialogue and a shrinking welfare state. In addition, interviewees felt that other social actors, such as state officials, employers and political parties, were not really interested in CSR topics and, consequently, there was no systemic support for the issue.

Discussion

The comments gathered in the interviews show that CSR is seen by Slovenian trade unions as an important, albeit rather abstract, concept. Nevertheless, the interviewees' comments suggest that CSR is seen as something that complements trade union objectives (Justice 2002). In addition, this study supports the claim that internal company aspects prevail in how trade unions relate to the CSR concept (Preuss *et al.* 2006). Interviewees commented that it is quite natural for their main focus to be on the internal dimension of CSR, as this reflects their mission; however, their efforts are not explicitly categorized as CSR. They also stressed how important it is for unions to engage in issues beyond their traditional agenda, such as environmental concerns that are, ultimately, also important for the workers themselves.

At the same time, the unions are rather sceptical about the impact of CSR. The main reason, explicitly stated by union representatives, was the financial and economic crisis; in such circumstances, other existential issues seem to be higher on the agenda. However, it can be noted from their answers that even before the crisis, unions focused primarily on preserving their existing rights and political power. Thus, as is evident from interviewees' answers, they are unable to go beyond defending basic labour standards apart from sporadic attempts to implement some aspects of CSR. This does not, however, necessarily mean that trade unions are agenda setters; it shows, rather, that they are forced to accept the agenda set by other players, such as employer organizations and the state, and can thus be seen more as a victim of the prevailing circumstances. One indicator of this is also the failure of ZSSS to embed CSR elements in the tripartite social agreement, as noted by the ZSSS executive secretary.

This also points to the rather ambivalent role of trade unions with respect to CSR and leads to a paradoxical situation: while they may see themselves as important drivers of CSR – and, under the institutionalist explanatory model of CSR (Gjølberg 2009), they should be seen as such – they tend in reality to lack the power to shape its agenda. This is a situation similar to that in the eastern European countries (Preuss *et al.* 2006). While it contradicts the assumption that a strong CSR presence may exist in the CME countries due to the comparative institutional advantages of the political and economic systems, it also supports Gjølberg's (2009) empirical findings that strong unions in CME countries do not guarantee a better CSR performance by companies. As further argued by the same author, the main driver behind the successful implementation of CSR in a country may be the country's cultural characteristics, such as its values and norms. Values such as environmentalism, tolerance, trust, and social activism and participation have proved to be the most important correlates of well-developed CSR practices (Gjølberg 2009).

The relative lack of such values in a country like Slovenia (Hlebec and Mandič 2005), which only recently emerged from its transition period and was, after a short economic boom, pushed into economic crisis, can therefore help explain both the enforced context in which trade unions are supposed to act and the absence of any strong CSR initiatives that would go beyond the 'cosmetic' and strictly voluntary nature of CSR.

Conclusions

This chapter has provided a short overview of CSR perceptions and activities among Slovenian trade unions. Given the volume of debate about CSR within the EU and a recent push towards CSR in Slovenia, as well as the emerging debate about the direction of the labour movement, unions should maintain (or acquire) an important role in CSR debates. This relates to the argument advanced by Burchell and Cook (2006) that trade unions have been important actors in the multi-stakeholder dialogue when the meaning of CSR in the EU *Green Paper* was negotiated. A broader interpretation of the concept has been accepted to encompass dimensions that are far beyond the meanings championed by the business community and includes considering the workforce and the input of other stakeholders into business practices (Burchell and Cook 2006).

One way for unions to use CSR is to promote 'a culture of legal compliance and respect for standards, as well as to promote good industrial relations' (Justice 2002: 5). In order for CSR to contribute to union viability (Dawkins 2010), Slovenian unions should strive to implement an 'institutional response face' (Freeman and Medoff 1984) and implement, organize or even document an operational strategy that goes beyond the service approach, which is concerned solely with basic issues of employees and ignores the interests of outside stakeholders (Dawkins 2010). Such an approach would allow them not only to be reactive to social issues but also to be initiators of developing solutions. This might, however, be hard to achieve, because they would have to change the context in which they try to operate and the constraints they face in relation to other partners. Hence, based on the development of CSR in Slovenia and the arguments put forward by the interviewees in our study, we could argue that the future engagement of trade unions in CSR is uncertain at best. The question is also how CSR as a concept and practice will succeed in becoming an important part of the public agenda given the lack of understanding and the interdependence among stakeholders – a prerequisite for finding ways to build relations beyond those based on power or narrow interests.

References

Becela, M., Gajić, J. and Golob, U. (2012) 'Pomen družbene odgovornosti na področju medijske industrije', in A. Hrast, M. Mulej and S. Kojc (eds) *Innovation of Culture toward More Social Responsibility: The Way out of Socio-Cultural Crisis*, Maribor: IRDO.

Bohle, D. and Greskovits, B. (2007) 'Neoliberalism, embedded neoliberalism and neocorporatism: Towards transnational capitalism in Central-Eastern Europe', *West European Politics*, 30(3): 443–466.

Burchell, J. and Cook, J. (2006) 'Confronting the "corporate citizen": shaping the discourse of corporate social responsibility', *International Journal of Sociology and Social Policy*, 26(3/4): 121–137.

Crowley, S. and Stanojević, M. (2011) 'Varieties of capitalism, power resources, and historical legacies: explaining the Slovenian exception', *Politics and Society*, 39(2): 268–295.

Dawkins, C.E. (2010) 'Beyond wages and working conditions: a conceptualization of labor union social responsibility', *Journal of Business Ethics*, 95(1): 129–143.

De Geer, H., Borglund, T. and Frostenson, M. (2009) 'Reconciling CSR with the role of the corporation in welfare states: the problematic Swedish example', *Journal of Business Ethics*, 89(3): 269–283.

DiMaggio, P.J. and Powell, W.W. (1983) 'The iron cage revisited: institutional isomorphism and collective rationality in organizational fields', *American Sociological Review*, 48(2): 147–160.

Djokic, D. (2013) 'Corporate governance after 20 years in Slovenia', *Montenegrin Journal of Economics*, 9(2): 121–126.

European Commission (2001) *Green Paper Promoting a European Framework for Corporate Social Responsibility*, Luxemburg: Office for Official Publications of the European Communities.

European Commission (2011) *A Renewed EU Strategy 2011–14 for Corporate Social Responsibility*, Brussels: COM 681.

Feldmann, M. (2006) 'Emerging varieties of capitalism in transition countries: industrial relations and wage bargaining in Estonia and Slovenia', *Comparative Political Studies*, 39(7): 829–854.

Freeman, R.B. and Medoff, J.L. (1984) *What Do Unions Do?* New York: Basic Books.

Fulton, L. (2011) *Worker Representation in Europe*, Labour Research Department and ETUI online publication. Online. Available: www.worker-participation.eu/National-Industrial-Relations/Across-Europe/Trade-Unions2 (accessed 4 September 2012).

Gjølberg, M. (2009) 'The origin of corporate social responsibility: global forces or national legacies?', *Socio-Economic Review*, 7(4): 605–637.

Golob, U. (2011a) 'Towards an institutional view of mapping corporate social responsibility meanings', *Teorija in Praksa*, 48(6): 1573–1583.

Golob, U. (2011b) 'Institucionalno uokvirjanje družbene odgovornosti v slovenskih podjetjih: vidik zaposlenih', Working Paper, University of Ljubljana, Faculty of Social Sciences.

Golob, U. and Bartlett, J.L. (2007) 'Communicating about corporate social responsibility: a comparative study of CSR reporting in Australia and Slovenia', *Public Relations Review*, 33(1): 1–9.

Golob, U. and Valentinčič, N. (2008) 'Longitudinalna analiza poročanja o družbeni odgovornosti: Primer izbranih slovenskih družb', in A. Hrast and M. Mulej (eds) *Prispevki družbene odgovornosti k dolgoročni uspešnosti vseh udeležencev na trgu*, Maribor: IRDO.

Gostiša, M. (2012) 'Slovenski menedžment in "stroški na dveh nogah"', *Ekonomska demokracija*, 17(4): 2–3.

Hall, P.A. and Soskice, D. (2001) *Varieties of Capitalism: The Institutional Foundations of Comparative Advantage*, Oxford: Oxford University Press.

Hlebec, V. and Mandič, S. (2005) 'Socialno omrežje kot okvir upravljanja s kakovostjo življenja in spremembe v Sloveniji med letoma 1987 in 2002', *Družboslovne razprave*, 49/50: 263–285.

Hrast, A. (2012) 'Poslanstvo inštituta IRDO in Slovenske nagrade za družbeno odgovornost HORUS', paper presented at 24th Forum of Excellence, Otočec, May 2012.

Jaklič, M. (2003) 'Prevzeti (etično) odgovornost', *Delo: Sobotna priloga* (28 June).

Justice, D.W. (2002) 'Corporate social responsibility: challenges and opportunities for trade unionists', *Corporate Codes of Conduct*, Paper 9. Online. Available: http://digitalcommons.ilr.cornell.edu/codes/9 (accessed 4 September 2012).

Podnar, K. and Golob, U. (2007) 'CSR expectations: the focus of corporate marketing', *Corporate Communications: An International Journal*, 12(4): 326–340.

Preuss, L., Haunschild, A. and Matten, D. (2006) 'Trade unions and CSR: A European research agenda', *Journal of Public Affairs*, 6(3/4): 256–268.

Public Opinion Research Centre (2011) *Slovenian Public Opinion Survey 2011/1*, unpublished summary report, University of Ljubljana, Faculty of Social Sciences.

Stanojević, M. (2011a) 'Evropeizacija slovenskega (neo)korporativizma', Working Paper, University of Ljubljana, Faculty of Social Sciences.

Stanojević, M. (2011b) 'Historical development of trade unions in Slovenia', Working Paper, University of Ljubljana, Faculty of Social Sciences.

10 Spain

An opportunity to improve working conditions through CSR

Xavier Coller, Jesús Cambra-Fierro, Thomas Gualtieri and Iguácel Melero-Polo

Only a minority of companies introduces CSR into their global corporate strategy.

(UGT, General Union of Workers)

Introduction

The driving forces behind the implementation of CSR practices in Spain are political institutions (national and regional parliaments and governments) and the policies advanced by economic actors like large (and to a much lesser extent medium-sized) companies and, especially, the two largest trade union federations — Unión General de Trabajadores (UGT, General Union of Workers) and Comisiones Obreras (CCOO, Workers' Commissions). Agreements between governments, employers' associations and unions are central to the Latin or mixed capitalist model that characterizes Spain, and they are also the umbrella under which certain CSR initiatives are taken. However, the voluntary nature of these initiatives, the relatively small size of firms and the economic crisis are perceived as a brake on the extension of CSR practices. Furthermore, the central role of unions in the Latin capitalist model is changing, partly as a result of the crisis and the reform policies implemented by the conservative government since its election in 2011.

Spanish trade unions perceive CSR as an opportunity to improve working conditions and render companies more accountable. They participate or have set up research centres (*observatorios*) to help disseminate information on CSR and monitor appropriate corporate policies. CSR is perceived as a key factor in the survival of companies and in the expansion of unions' relevance. However, unions also acknowledge that CSR provides an opportunity for companies to improve their public image, and to promote a set of principles that may not necessarily lead to genuine improvements in their business practices.

National business system

Since the restoration of democracy (1977–1979), a sort of 'consensus capitalism' (Renshaw 1991) has fostered the development of a weak welfare state, originally modelled in the early 1980s on the north and central European social democratic traditions. Accordingly, various authors have seen Spain as either approaching the co-ordinated market economy (CME) model without some of its formal elements (Royo 2007, 2008), or as part of an intermediate category dubbed 'Latin capitalism', 'mixed market economy' or 'state-influenced market economy' (Rhodes and Apeldoorn 1998; Molina and Rhodes 2006; Schmidt 2009), in which the state is seen as a leading or highly influential actor, as in France or Italy. Despite the deregulation years of conservative governments (1996–2004), Spain can be placed closer to the CME model than the liberal market economy (LME) model (Hall and Gingerich 2009) owing to the role of the state in the economy, its system of industrial relations and the development of its social protection schemes. Collective agreements between unions and employers' associations (with the possible involvement of national and regional governments) have been central to the evolution of this variety of capitalism. These developments have been politically driven, given the internal structure of the business system, which is tilted toward small, highly local companies.

According to the Spanish National Institute of Statistics (INE), 99.9 per cent of Spanish companies employ fewer than 250 workers and 95.5 per cent are micro-companies employing fewer than 10 workers (the average for the European Union is 92 per cent). Around 80 per cent belong to the services sector. Family businesses are the rule rather than the exception, and corporate governance is based largely on personal or family ownership. Contrary to what might be expected, the small size of companies has facilitated a pragmatic modernizing model of capitalism based on the creation of key alliances with multinational companies (MNCs) and the development of business groups (Guillén 2001). To a large extent, these alliances have fostered the incorporation of industrial relations practices alien to local traditions (Ortiz and Coller 2010), but have also provoked a high level of dependence of small and medium-sized enterprises (SMEs) on large corporations in their supply chains.

Spain's economy has been moving towards the (weak) LME pole as a result of a number of de-regulatory reforms that the government has implemented since the Popular Party (*Partido Popular*) took power in 2011. This transformation has affected the dynamics and the role of unions and employers' associations in the national business system, perhaps leading towards what has been called 'disorganized decentralization' (Traxler 1995). Centralized bargaining between unions and employers is still the main form of regulating industrial relations, but the labour reform of 10 February 2012 has weakened these agreements. For instance, it is now easier for a company to opt out of collective agreements at the national and industry level. Once a particular collective agreement has expired, it no longer remains in force until a new one has been negotiated, and a company may instead choose another one (for instance, at the industry level) that is closer to its interests. The consequences of this labour reform overlap with other side effects undermining the role of unions in the industrial relations system. For instance, since redundancies are cheaper for the company, and short-term temporary hiring has become easier, the potential membership for unions diminishes, as accordingly do their finances.

Industrial relations system

In contrast to other countries characterized as LMEs, the industrial relations system in Spain is based on the predominance of centralized bargaining of collective agreements between unions (the two largest, UGT and CCOO) and the main employers' associations (Spanish Confederation of Employers' Organizations (CEOE) and Spanish Confederation of Small and Medium-Sized Companies (CEPYME)) at national, regional and industry levels. Unionized companies (usually the largest) tend to negotiate their own collective agreements. It is not mandatory to have a workers' representative in companies employing five or fewer workers. Various laws protect the presence of unions in companies through elections, though there are ways to evade the presence of unions in smaller firms while meeting the relevant legislative requirements, such as the creation of unions organized by managers (Miguélez and Prieto 1999). In this context, the industrial relations system is characterized both by the strength of the unions in the public realm and by their weakness at plant level. The lack of a general trade union culture (free unions were not recognized as social actors until democracy was restored in the late 1970s) and the reluctance of SMEs to become unionized may explain this paradox. However, over the last few decades, organizational learning processes have led unions to renew leaders and strategies, helping them to converge with some of the main European trade unions in terms of membership, influence, representativeness and workers' coverage (Beneyto 2010).

Union membership has grown over the years but in a different way from other countries (Blanchflower 2007). Thanks to a period of economic growth from 1990 to 2008 and the consolidation of permanent jobs, union membership rose from 1.5 million to the current three million workers (Beneyto 2010). This growth has allowed unions to gain a presence in companies (especially the large ones) and improve their finances, although a good proportion of union revenues come from national and regional governments. However, union density is quite low when compared with European standards: only a fifth of the employed workforce (19 per cent) is a union member while the European average is 25 per cent (EFILWC 2010).

Table 10.1 The main trade unions in Spain

Union	*Members*	*Representativeness (%)*
CC.OO	1,139,591	37.8
UGT	1,242,200	35.8
ELA-STV (Basque nationalist)	105,312	3 (national level)/ (36 Basque Country level)
USO (Christian oriented)	120,000	2.9
CSI-CSIF (public sector)	n.a.	1.8
CIG (Galician nationalist)	n.a.	1.6
LAB (radical Basque nationalist)	n.a.	1.3
CGT (anarchist)	60,000	1.3
FETICO (Commercial workers)	n.a	1.3
Others		13.1

Source: Authors' calculations based on data provided by the Ministry of Labour and the trade unions.

Note
Representativeness is calculated as the proportion of delegates/representatives at national level.

More than 3,500 unions exist in Spain, which are organized along ideological, national, professional and corporate divisions. However, two stand out from the rest in terms of membership, role and social impact: the General Workers' Union (UGT), founded in 1888, and the Workers' Commissions (CCOO), founded in the mid-1950s as a clandestine organization dependent on the Communist Party (PCE). Both these unions have over 230,000 worker representatives, around 75 per cent of the 286,000 total across the country. CCOO has a slightly larger share of representatives than UGT, as can be seen in Table 10.1. Both unions have a similar internal structure. They are organized by industry and territory (following the territorial division of Spain into 17 autonomous communities). The bulk of their membership is found in large companies, among permanent workers, in the public sector rather than the private one, and in industry more than in the service sector (García-Olaverri and Huerta 2011:13). In small private companies, union membership is so low that it could be considered symbolic (Observatorio RSC-UGT 2012a).

The weakness of unions in terms of membership and coverage of workers at the company level is counterbalanced by two factors that enhance their strength. First, they are formally recognized as bargaining partners by the government and employers' associations for the purposes of negotiating far-reaching collective agreements that help regulate the economy and the labour market. Second, in the absence of strong political parties capable of mobilizing citizens, trade unions have become a counterbalancing power to successive governments. They have become leaders in mobilizing citizens against the effects of the recent economic crisis and some of the policies that the government has implemented. Just one month after the government passed the labour reform of 10 February 2012, the main unions organized a general strike in protest, with another a few months later.

The evolution of CSR

The debate about CSR in Spain took an institutional turn when two socialist members of parliament proposed a bill on CSR in 2002. The bill became the basis of a parliamentary committee (2005), on which experts from unions, companies and universities analysed the opportunities for CSR. The result of this joint effort was the White Paper on Corporate Social Responsibility (*Libro Blanco sobre Responsabilidad Social Empresarial*), the first set of analyses and recommendations approved by a parliament in Europe (2006). The White Paper suggests that public policies on CSR should be based on norms fostering initiatives that companies could adhere to voluntarily. However, these recommendations have had a limited impact, since only a short article contained in, first, the Law for a Sustainable Economy (LSE) and, second, the Law for Corporate Social Responsibility passed by the Parliament of Extremadura have translated the initial political concern for CSR into legislation.

The LSE sets out the role for national government in promoting CSR in two principal ways: the requirement to disseminate information about CSR and best practices associated with it, and promoting the analysis of its effects on the overall competitiveness of companies. For that purpose, Article 39 of the LSE indicates the areas on which CSR should focus:

> transparency in the management of firms, good governance, commitment to the environment and local issues, respect for human rights, improvement of labour relations, promotion of the integration of women, real equality between men and women, equal opportunities, universal accessibility for the handicapped, and sustainable consumption.

However, actual regulation of CSR has taken place only at one regional level, when the regional parliament of Extremadura passed the first Law regulating CSR issues (Law for Corporate Social Responsibility) in 2010. The law encourages the voluntary implementation of CSR policies through the creation of two incentives: the acknowledgement in an official record that the firm complies with CSR (a 'label' that grants certain tax benefits, publicity and priority in accessing public subsidies) and the award of an official prize for CSR-compliant firms. Additionally, the law facilitates the creation of a research centre for the implementation and monitoring of CSR policies in Extremadura. This law is perhaps the clearest document in Spain indicating how CSR is perceived, namely as covering ethics and values, industrial relations and human resource management (including issues like diversity management and equality, affirmative action, job stability and security, and work-life balance), the incorporation of the organizational environment into the management of the firm, stakeholder relations (including local contracting) and CSR reporting.

Overall, the law outlines a set of principles for companies to voluntarily operate CSR-oriented policies, though by the time of writing this was still an isolated example. However, the conservative government has plans to promote two initiatives whose implementation is still uncertain (Santiago 2013). First, the National CSR Strategy (*Estrategia Nacional de Responsabilidad Social de las Empresas*) establishes a link between CSR, sustainability and competitiveness, and is addressed to SMEs in an attempt to generate jobs. The second initiative, the Plan for Companies and Human Rights (*Plan de Empresas y Derechos Humanos*) focuses on the protection of human rights in Spanish companies, whether operating solely in Spain or abroad.

Institutionally, the most significant CSR initiative is the National Council for Corporate Social Responsibility (CERSE, *Consejo Estatal para la Responsabilidad Social Empresarial*), which was created in 2008 within the Ministry of Labour, although it has been virtually inactive since April 2013. This Council advises the minister, but has no executive function, and became a forum for exchanging ideas rather than a proactive actor promoting CSR and identifying best practices. It comprises 56 members from different arenas, such as government, trade unions, employers' associations and other organizations related to CSR. The precursors of the Council are the Social Dialogue Round Table (SDT, *Mesa para el Diálogo Social*) and the Experts' Forum (EF, *Foro de Expertos sobre la Responsabilidad Social Empresarial*). The SDT was created in 2008 by the socialist government after the unions (UGT and CCOO), employers' associations (CEOE and CEPYME) and government decided to incorporate CSR into the issues dealt with by the Committee for Monitoring and Evaluating the Social Dialogue (*Comité de Seguimiento y Evaluación del Diálogo Social*). The EF is a less formal entity created by the Minister of Labour in 2005. Members include representatives from several regional administrations, university professors, members of NGOs and companies. The main output of the EF is the Report of Experts on CSR (*Informe del Foro de Expertos en Responsabilidad Social de las Empresas*), which sets out an operational definition and landscape for CSR, and gathers recommendations to promote it in companies and the public sector.

Independently from government, there are certain other initiatives in which trade unions play an important role. Perhaps the most relevant is the CSR Research Centre, in which NGOs (such as Greenpeace, Oxfam and the Red Cross), universities, experts and CCOO collaborate to produce and exchange ideas to promote CSR initiatives (Observatorio RSC 2013). CCOO monitors CSR policies in different organizations and produces a ranking, paying attention to issues like presence of women on boards of directors, transparency of information concerning board decisions, size and type of vote in shareholders' meetings, independence of the chair of the board of directors, and so on. UGT created its own research centre in 2006 to promote and monitor CSR practices (Observatorio RSE-UGT 2013). Rather than participating in an independent centre, UGT has developed an internal section in charge of CSR issues, which monitors CSR and trains worker representatives to introduce CSR issues into collective bargaining agendas. In both centres, the aim is to generate ideas, promote initiatives, monitor practices and become advocates of CSR policies so that they are reflected in company conduct. Training and dissemination of best practices is a key task for both centres, although the economic crisis has deferred these intentions.

Apart from these union activities there are further initiatives designed to promote CSR-related issues and generate some level of concern in society. Certain universities have adopted relevant initiatives – for example, the universities of Murcia and La Coruña both created chairs related to CSR issues – while others (such as Extremadura, Málaga and Castilla-La Mancha) created offices responsible for developing CSR. In 2013, the Spanish Association for Managers of Social Responsibility (DIRSE, *Asociación Española de Directivos de Responsabilidad Social*) was founded to spread and exchange ideas and experiences around CSR policies and practices. Finally, some regional administrations have also created either specific centres (as in Galicia or Extremadura) or particular departments (like the Catalan government) in charge of these issues.

CSR policies are still at their early stage of development and are usually related to the internationalization of large companies in banking (BBVA, Santander), communications (Telefónica) and energy (Repsol, Endesa). Some studies have shown that the number of companies implementing some sort of CSR policy at least nominally has grown in different ways according to size and industry (Fraj-Andrés *et al.* 2012). Large companies consolidate their presence in the main international sustainability rankings. For instance, Telefónica was sector leader in the *Dow Jones Sustainability Index* in 2010, while Repsol YPF achieved this position in both 2011 and 2012. In *Tomorrow's Value Rating*, Santander and Telefónica appear in the third group of the rankings and Rio Tinto in the fourth. All companies grouped in the IBEX-35 (the largest companies in Spain) have published CSR reports (Obervatorio RSE-UGT 2012b). Most of them have followed the guidelines of the Global Reporting Initiative, although there often is incomplete information on sensitive issues, like job creation, equal opportunities, workers' training for employability or certain good governance indicators (such as pay transparency for senior executives or equal presence of men and women on the board of directors). However, on issues like environmental record, relationship with suppliers or corporate community engagement, they disclose more information (Obervatorio RSE-UGT 2012b).

Methods: unions interviewed

We interviewed seven members of the two largest unions in Spain: three from CCOO and four from UGT. Given that the organizational structure of both unions overlap in geographic and industry terms we interviewed union officials at the federal and regional level. These seven respondents were selected for their knowledge of current developments in CSR, reflecting experience in cities like Barcelona, Madrid, Seville, Valencia and Zaragoza. Two respondents were officials responsible for CSR nationwide (one of them in charge of CSR in the services and banking sector in Andalucía and a member of the State Council on CSR), two were responsible for CSR in Catalonia (where CSR seems to be more developed thanks to the joint activity of unions, employers and the regional government), two covered the metal industry (one in Catalonia and the other in Aragon, both familiar with the car industry) and the seventh was a high-ranking official of UGT's research centre for CSR. Interviews were carried out between January and December 2012, lasting on average 1.5 hours.

In addition to these interviews, we analysed relevant documents produced by the CSR centres in which the two main unions participate, legislation at the national and regional level, various documents issued by the State Council for CSR and the Experts' Forum, webpages by unions and universities with chairs in CSR, documents by managers' associations (like DIRSE) and regional administrations that have developed CSR centres or have created specific departments to deal with CSR matters.

Union understanding of CSR

The debate about CSR in Spain is centred mainly on two issues: how to define it and whether it should be made mandatory. First, different social actors have proposed several definitions, although it seems that the definition advanced by the European Commission is widely shared (Jiménez Fernández 2007). With some minor differences, unions perceive that CSR should go beyond compliance with the law in matters of equal opportunities, work organization, training and sustainability and/or corporate governance issues. CSR is generally understood by unions as a platform for improving working conditions and demanding transparency from companies, especially with respect to managerial salaries and benefits. Thus, it is associated with the idea of accountability and annual reporting on compliance with CSR principles. Strategically, CSR is also seen as an avenue for making contact with those SMEs which supply large multinationals, since MNCs involved in CSR practices may monitor (as do unions) working conditions and labour-related issues in SMEs. CSR is therefore perceived as a means of extending unions' presence in their organizational fields. More recently, a subtle addition can be detected as unions tend to present CSR as an issue that cuts across work-life balance and efficiency in the use of company resources and the environment. CSR is then related to business efficiency and sustainability, and improvement of working and living conditions.

The debate about CSR and its contents has been more tactical than strategic, since defining the policies associated with CSR indicates to social actors where they should be paying most attention and, consequently, paves the way for issues to be controlled and monitored by social agents, especially when the state or civil society create organizations for this purpose. Sometimes, letting others evaluate a company's environmental record or recruitment policies conflicts with perceptions of what the company should be or how it should behave. This is why some observers commented that even though some companies claim to follow CSR principles, their practices do not support those stated principles (Observatorio RSE-UGT 2012b).

The second issue at the centre of the debate is whether CSR practices should be made mandatory by the government or remain voluntary. Generally speaking, CCOO have favoured making it mandatory for companies to report on CSR practices or to enforce its regulation. UGT has been more prone to accepting that the company volunteers its reporting. The former option implies a need for regulation for which all governments and employers' associations have shown reluctance. The latter option seems to be more realistic. However, only large international companies have adopted CSR principles, while SMEs have tended to ignore them (Observatorio RSE-UGT 2012a). In the case of multinationals, public opinion, corporate image and trade union presence may play a role (in addition to genuine conviction) in explaining adherence to and deployment of CSR policies. In the case of SMEs, a lack of trade union presence, an unwillingness to incorporate CSR policies, the low cost of not following CSR principles, a lack of incentives, or a simple ignorance of CSR policies mean that these firms have remained largely free of CSR. When SMEs do incorporate some CSR policies this is usually linked to the values of their owners and/or their dependence on a larger firm which they supply (Fraj-Andrés *et al.* 2012). Furthermore, SMEs appear more prone to adopting CSR practices – such as equality plans or crèches – where regional administrations (notably Catalonia) have adopted a proactive role themselves. Consequently, a well-informed observer of the situation, Cándido Méndez, the general secretary of UGT, was reported by the Europa Press news agency on 27 January in 2010 as declaring: 'Only a minority of companies introduces CSR into their global corporate strategy'.

Union policies on CSR

Trade union interest in CSR policies began in the early 2000s (following the European Union Lisbon summit in 2000, where the issue was raised), at first introduced at union conferences (by 2002), then later integrated into organizational structures. Hence, UGT set up its CSR research centre and CCOO incorporated CSR functions into existing departments at the federal, regional and industry levels. Evidence of this interest is revealed in the growing number of courses offered to train worker representatives in the principles of CSR and how to introduce them into collective bargaining.

The role of unions in expanding CSR is seen as a function of different factors acting in isolation or in combination. State institutions like parliaments play a prominent role by creating regulation and regional administrations follow by creating specific departments in charge of promoting and monitoring CSR practices or allocating CSR to existing departments. Unions tend to participate in these initiatives as part of the social dialogue or collective bargaining with employers and government. Under this institutional umbrella, unions see the opportunity to introduce certain CSR-related issues into the agenda for collective bargaining, thus increasing the probability of extending CSR-type practices more widely across companies.

The chances of success are related in large part to the size and nature of the firm and ultimately of the industry. For instance, our interviewees reported that more CSR practices have been implemented in the car, chemical and finance industries – where large MNCs are concentrated – than elsewhere. As one interviewee remarked:

> CSR [policies] are secondary except for very large companies, usually multinationals, some with Spanish capital, others with foreign capital having plants in Spain; [...] these companies have the type of culture that promotes these types of policy or even when they do not promote them, when the union demands these CSR policies they are open to talk, discuss, negotiate, and in some cases you reach agreements, and in other cases you don't.
>
> (CCOO plant level worker representative)

A variation of this is the strength of the union federations in the public sector and the chemical industry, which report a higher concern for, and implementation of, CSR policies than in other industries. As one of these interviewees indicated:

> There are very large union federations, like those of the public servants or the chemical sector, which are quite powerful and get very favourable collective agreements in which you will find much more developed CSR policies than in the collective agreements of other industries.
>
> (UGT plant level worker representative)

Incorporation of CSR principles into union strategies for collective bargaining at plant and industry levels means that, at some point, certain CSR practices may be disseminated across companies, insofar as worker representatives are familiar with CSR and see its benefits. For that purpose, unions make an effort to train worker representatives in the principles of CSR. More recently, certain union federations have added socially responsible investment (SRI) to their range of CSR policies, especially with respect to pension funds. This is the case for COMFIA, the finance and clerical workers' division of CCOO (COMFIA, 2013), which first applied SRI to the workers' pension funds of a saving bank, Cajasol, in Andalucía.

Union engagement with CSR

Trade unions' familiarity with, and acceptance and promotion of, CSR initiatives is usually the result of three elements: the individual efforts of a certain member or official, exposure to CSR practices in large companies or participation in training schemes developed by unions. Among union representatives at plant level, the development of CSR seems to depend on the initiatives of individuals and the actual situation of the company. One of the interviewees put it this way: '[rather than being part of a CSR policy], the changes demanded in companies stem from the common sense of our workplace union representatives, who focus on a particular issue, rather than from demands organized or co-ordinated by the union' (CCOO plant level worker representative).

There is a shared belief among our interviewees that MNCs have helped to spread awareness amongst union representatives of certain CSR practices that are already being implemented in other countries at plant level. Additionally, involvement in European or global union federations has also contributed to awareness of the need for CSR policies amongst certain union officials. Hence it seems that internationalization (essentially Europeanization) is a leading pressure for learning about and disseminating CSR practices from countries where debates are more sophisticated. In this respect, some level of mimetic and normative isomorphism (DiMaggio and Powell 1991) might be observed in the near future in Spanish companies with respect to CSR. Regulation, emulation processes, corporate image advantages, the role of professionals and union pressures may all play a part in stimulating companies to adopt similar CSR practices.

Union attitudes toward CSR are positive for a number of reasons. First, keeping CSR on the agenda of the social dialogue with employers and governments gives unions room to introduce improvements into working conditions at plant level. Consequently, CSR is not seen as a means to undermine collective bargaining, but rather as a means to complement it. Second, institutionalization of CSR through the creation of offices and departments in companies and governments legitimizes the unions' support for CSR and reinforces their willingness to introduce changes in companies for the good of workers and consumers. Institutionalization grants unions a stronger presence in the public sphere to introduce changes and monitor them. Third, seen this way, CSR is aligned with the reformist outlook of the two largest unions and is sometimes seen as an appropriate response to some of the effects of globalization:

> Globalization is economic, but not social [...]. There is a global market, but social rights are not globalized. Markets are global, but so is production since there is a growing trend to subcontract the production of goods and services internationally. This forces trade unions to make new efforts [...]. The correct strategy to face the global economy is to make advances in CSR, combining the three pillars of sustainability: economic, social and environmental.
>
> (Representative of UGT's CSR research centre)

Fourth, CSR may help companies to survive, which is also in the interest of the unions. As one interviewee put it: '[CSR] is important for us because of the viability of the company; we have to work more on corporate governance, which is not just an internal matter for the company, since it affects its viability, and this is important for us' (CCOO federal and regional representative). Another remarked: 'CSR improves the economic performance of companies and their competitiveness. It needs to be considered as an improvement in working conditions, and work improvements increase productivity' (UGT plant level worker representative).

Fifth, CSR is an opportunity to expand union relevance in three ways: to create strategic alliances with other organizations (such as in the CSR research centre, in which CCOO participates), to penetrate the difficult world of SMEs and to establish co-operation with other international labour organizations. One interviewee observed:

> The union has centred on workers in plants, [...] but CSR will make it easier to take joint action from above at the international level and from the bottom at the supplier level [SMEs], especially when [large] companies begin to consider CSR criteria to work with suppliers. Then, this [CSR] might extend towards SMEs, and the union will also have access to small companies [from which it is usually excluded].
>
> (CCOO federal and regional representative)

However, a word of caution relating to SMEs needs to be mentioned. CSR is conceived as a set of practices that go beyond legal requirements. Expanding union activity related to CSR into SMEs (without the pressures that MNCs can apply to SME suppliers) may in many instances be utopian, given that SMEs tend to avoid compliance with laws and collective agreements without much cost.

> It is very difficult for the union to have companies abide by the law on basic issues like equality, occupational health and working conditions,

> or to have them to comply with the collective agreements in terms of salaries and working conditions. So, asking for good [CSR] practices making the companies going beyond what the law says is something that is beyond the unions' capacity.
>
> (CCOO plant level worker representative)

Sixth, unions have observed that those managers responsible for CSR may be more open to discuss labour issues than human resource managers used to be. This perceived change of attitude may help unions to advance strategies for a wider dialogue in which working conditions might be improved. According to one interviewee:

> an activist in the union at international level began using CSR arguments because when they had a dispute, an accident in the textiles industry, the unions went in and found that the company did not send the HRM people, but the CSR people. And they realized that CSR people were more prone to solving problems than those from HRM [...].
>
> (CCOO federal and regional representative)

Discussion

CSR seems to be a relatively recent issue for trade unions and governments in Spain, and certainly of not much interest in the context of growing unemployment and company closures. Where interest does exist, it sometimes depends on individual efforts to keep up with and monitor CSR practices. The largest two unions participate in CSR research centres, promote training and commission reports evaluating CSR practices, especially since the decision of the national government and some regional administrations to put it on the legislative agenda. They do so despite the social problems created by the financial crisis.

Notwithstanding the high expectations that CSR generated for most of the interviewees, it seems that the speed at which unions, employers, governments and NGOs have travelled to promote CSR practices has been dramatically reduced because of the crisis. All interviewees agreed that the crisis has put all these efforts on hold in two ways. First, as a result of the crisis and the subsequent labour reform of February 2012, employers' associations are no longer open to negotiations, which meant that when the reform came into effect the chance to introduce CSR initiatives into collective agreements was reduced. One interviewee stated:

> For a CSR policy to function, it is necessary to work together with the company. For the last three or four years, there has been no feeling of 'being in the same boat', because of the ideas of the employers' associations and the messages they send out about working more, less pay,

> less work-life balance. If there is anybody in Spain advocating CSR now, it's the unions.
>
> (UGT plant level worker representative)

Second, union interest at plant level has shifted towards basic issues like job security, preventing redundancies and solving growing workers' problems:

> if the crisis in this country gets any worse, people's needs will move into survival mode. If a few years ago we were defending health and safety issues at plant level, now we've dropped a notch, and we have to talk about keeping jobs or keeping salaries. Then, the gap between reality and CSR goals, which are voluntary practices that go beyond the law, will increase.
>
> (CCOO plant level worker representative)

A further interviewee indicated that: '[CSR] is delayed as a result of the deterioration of labour and social rights we are experiencing' (UGT federal and regional representative). However, this negative view of the crisis is complemented by a more optimistic one: 'The crisis, it was thought, looked like it was going to put an end to CSR, but it is the other way around since the argument is that the absence of CSR is what has created the crisis' (CCOO federal and regional representative). Hence the crisis is seen as an opportunity to realize that mistakes were made in the past and that new practices and values need to be introduced into the production system: 'The crisis is ensuring that nothing will be as it was before, and a central issue here is production. Products and production at any price will no longer be possible, and in this process CSR plays an important role' (UGT federal and regional representative).

Still, the fate of CSR is not seen as being associated with the crisis. Despite its uneven deployment and the lack of relatively good information about them, unions and other organizations are making an effort to disseminate CSR principles and practices. The fact that there are research centres, which are responsible for training and dissemination, university professorships, departments in companies and governments, certain laws and CSR issues on the bargaining agenda, is seen as an opportunity for the future. However, there is still an unresolved issue that might endanger future advances – the voluntary nature of implementing and reporting on CSR practices:

> Up to now, [CSR discussions] have been limited by the intransigence of the employers; their position was that since CSR is voluntary, they would do it in the way they wanted [...] and so there was no need to establish a dialogue. Furthermore, the union has also been a bit sceptical about CSR.
>
> (UGT federal and regional representative)

However, as one interviewee put it, it is one thing to adhere to CSR principles and practices, which are voluntary, and another thing to say that you practise CSR, participate in the appropriate forums – and then fail to monitor implementation:

> the big dispute with employers is that they do not want to be monitored. They argue that since CSR is voluntary, there should be no control. We say that it is voluntary to the extent that nobody forces any company to be socially responsible, but once the firm decides to commit to CSR principles, it has to meet some rules.
>
> (CCOO federal and regional representative)

Conclusions

The debate about CSR in Spain is still in its initial stages. There is some legislation promoting CSR. The Spanish parliament took the lead, but the regional parliament of Extremadura has gone further, passing a law in 2010 regulating CSR practices and creating incentives for companies to develop CSR policies. These limited initiatives are complemented by union activity both inside companies and as civil society actors developing research centres and disseminating practices. Other initiatives focusing on universities and large companies complete the picture of a limited development of CSR.

The approach of companies towards CSR is completely voluntary, as is the related issue of reporting. As a consequence, there is a lack of information about the actual scope and implementation of CSR policies. They are usually the outcome of a dialogue between companies and unions, although on many occasions the initiative lies solely on the company's side, especially in large companies. By contrast, SMEs are rarely involved in CSR policies, although there are some initiatives. The voluntary nature of reporting and the lack of a proper system of evaluation of CSR, however, blur the frontier between actual CSR initiatives and simple marketing campaigns. One interviewee, moreover, was keen to stress the importance of a foreign cultural legacy in the definition of CSR policies in his MNC, which has its headquarters outside Spain. The achievements of MNCs in terms of CSR seem more advanced than those of domestic Spanish firms, although some of the latter have developed CSR policies, such as the creation of nursery schools within the company.

Unions are progressively attaching more importance to CSR. However, there are only two unions which explicitly recognize CSR within their principles of action and which seem very much involved in CSR policies: CCOO and UGT. These two major trade unions share a similar outlook on CSR, although with certain minor differences regarding terminology and whether it should be mandatory or voluntary. While for CCOO CSR should be mandatory, UGT supports voluntarism. Since 2011, both unions have co-operated in the development of new joint projects aimed at fostering CSR in companies, with no differences reported between federal and sectoral levels. Their major function, however, lies in monitoring companies.

Within trade unions, formal structures relating to CSR exist at three levels: research, training and communications. Unions have created their own CSR institutes, sometimes in co-operation with universities (the UGT institute acts independently, while the CCOO one collaborates with the *Observatorio de RSC*). Unions also often co-operate with universities and academic institutions when conducting research. NGOs are also relevant actors who help to promote and monitor CSR in companies, but NGOs are far less involved at company level than unions. The picture that emerges, therefore, is that NGOs and/or consumers' associations tend to be less involved in CSR than the unions are. CSR has also promoted some co-ordination at the international level between unions.

Trade union interest in CSR is also demonstrated by the increasing number of training programmes that they have developed for their officials. Indeed, unions formally co-operate to promote CSR policies in companies and to train officials. CSR is important for the unions insofar as it involves an improvement of labour conditions or, at least, can affect them in a positive direction. Unions often succeed in introducing CSR topics into the 'social dialogue' agenda with employers' associations, so that they become part of the bargaining process at national level. In addition, CSR is seen as a platform for improving the participation of workers in the company. Particularly in recent years, CSR has represented a platform for introducing significant changes across many dimensions of labour relations, such as the quality of working life, gender equality, work-life balance and efficient energy use. Specific programmes have sometimes been developed, but so far they are isolated and are found mainly in those companies listed on IBEX 35, the index for the largest 35 companies on the Spanish stock market (Sánchez Richter 2008).

CSR has encouraged changes in how some companies operate, although it has not spread as widely as the unions might have expected. It seems, moreover, that the implementation of CSR is sector-based, with financial and service sector companies deploying more CSR policies than manufacturing or engineering companies. Unions (especially UGT's research centre) analyse the level of implementation of CSR policies in large companies and usually criticize the lack of coherence between what companies say and what they do. CSR is not perceived as a set of policies that undermines union legitimacy or bypasses their activities. Unions have a positive vision of CSR and regard it as an opportunity, agreeing that CSR policies may have a positive impact on company performance. In large part this is due to the fact that the Spanish parliament and government have been involved in creating the conditions for the development of CSR policies in companies.

In summary, we can see an uneven development in CSR practices, which may have been affected by the economic crisis. We highlight the positive vision of CSR policies held by unions which see a window of opportunity to improve the quality of working conditions. We have to recognize the key role of large companies and public policies in introducing CSR practices, although the present context seems to restrain their development. Trade unions seem to be involved at the upper levels (such as those created or promoted by the government to deal with CSR issues) but less so at the company level, where managers usually apply, with exceptions, the policies they consider appropriate to meet their image and marketing objectives.

Acknowledgement

The authors of this chapter want to thank Ángela Pérez Ostos and Adrián Rodríguez for their help in gathering information about legal issues associated with CSR.

References

Área de Estudios Sindicales de CC.OO (2010) *Anuario 2010*, Madrid: Fundación 1° de Mayo.

Beneyto, P. (2010) 'Afiliación y representación sindical en España: Expansión y límites', *Anuario de la Fundación 1° de mayo*, Madrid: Fundación 1° de Mayo, pp. 327–384.

Blanchflower, D. (2007) 'International patterns of union membership', *British Journal of Industrial Relations*, 45(1): 1–28.

COMFIA (2013) *Responsabilidad Social*. Available at: http://blog.comfia.net/responsabilidad-social (accessed 31 October 2013).

EFILWC (2010) *Trade Unions Strategies to Recruit New Groups of Workers*, Dublin: European Foundation for the Improvement of Living and Working Conditions.

DiMaggio, P.J. and Powell, W.W. (1991) 'The iron cage revisited: institutional isomorphism and collective rationality in organizational fields', in W.W. Powell and P.J. DiMaggio (eds) *The New Institutionalism in Organizational Analysis*, Chicago: University of Chicago Press.

Fraj-Andrés, E., López-Pérez, M., Melero-Polo, I. and Vázquez-Carrasco, R. (2012) 'Company image and corporate social responsibility: reflecting with SMEs' managers', *Marketing Intelligence and Planning*, pp. 266–280.

García-Olaverri, C. and Huerta, E. (2011) 'Los sindicatos españoles: voz e influencia en las empresas', *Working Paper Fundación Alternativas*, 175/2011.

Guillén, M. (2001) *The Limits of Convergence: Globalization and Organizational Change in Argentina, South Korea and Spain*, Princeton: Princeton University Press.

Hall, P.A. and Gingerich, D.W. (2009) 'Varieties of capitalism and institutional complementarities in the political economy: an empirical analysis', *British Journal of Political Science*, 39(3): 449–482.

Jiménez Fernández, J.C. (2007) *La responsabilidad social de las empresas. ¿Cómo entenderla? ¿Cómo afrontarla? Una perspectiva sindical*, Albacete: Altabán.

Miguélez, F. and Prieto, C. (1999) *Las relaciones de empleo en España*, Madrid: Siglo XXI.

Molina, O. and Rhodes, M. (2006) 'Conflict, complementarities and institutional change in mixed market economies,' in B. Hancké, M. Rhodes and M. Thatcher (eds) *Beyond Varieties of Capitalism: Contradictions, Complementarities and Change*, Oxford: Oxford University Press.

Observatorio RSC (2013) *Nuestro Mundo, Nuestra Responsabilidad.* Available at: www.observatoriorsc.org (accessed 26 October 2013).

Observatorio RSE-UGT (2012a) *Iniciativas de RSE en las Pyme*, Madrid: Secretaría de Acción Sindical de UGT. Available at: www.observatorio-rse.org.es/Publicaciones.

Observatorio RSE-UGT (2012b) *Culturas, Políticas y Prácticas de Responsabilidad de las Empresas del IBEX 35*, Madrid: Secretaría de Acción Sindical de UGT.

Observatorio RSE-UGT (2013) *Observatorio-UGT-Resonsabilidad Social de las Empresas.* Available at: www.observatorio-rse.org.es (accessed 28 October 2013).

Ortiz, L. and Coller, X. (2010) ' "Safe enclaves"? American multinationals and Spanish trade unionism', *Labor History*, 51(2): 193–209.

Renshaw, P. (1991) *American Labour and Consensus Capitalism*, London: Macmillan.

Rhodes, M. and van Apeldoorn, B. (1998) 'Capital unbound? The transformation of European corporate governance,' *Journal of European Public Policy*, 5(3): 407–428.

Royo, S. (2007) 'Varieties of capitalism in Spain: business and the politics of coordination', *European Journal of Industrial Relations*, 13: 47–65.

Royo, S. (2008) *Varieties of Capitalism in Spain: Remaking the Spanish Economy for the New Century*, Basingstoke: Palgrave Macmillan.

Sánchez Richter, M.E. (2008) *IBEX 35: Gobierno corporativo 2007. Juntas de Accionistas 2008*, Madrid: Confederación Sindical de Comisiones Obreras.

Santiago, Eva (2013) 'Regular las buenas intenciones', *El País, Extra Responsabilidad Social Corporativa*, 24 November 2013, p. 4.

Schmidt, V.A. (2009) 'Putting the political back into political economy by bringing the state back in yet again', *World Politics*, 61(3): 516–546.

Traxler, F. (1995) 'Farewell to labour market institutions? Organized versus disorganized decentralization as a map for industrial relations', in C. Crouch and F. Traxler (eds) *Organized Industrial Relations in Europe: What Future?*, Aldershot: Avebury.

11 Sweden

CSR as a non-union arena for union issues

Sabina Du Rietz

> This [CSR] is an issue that arrived during the 2000s. Before, our counterparts weren't even companies, they were public authorities.
>
> (SEKO, Swedish Union for Service and Communication Employees)

Introduction

The Swedish case illustrates the integration of corporate social responsibility (CSR) into a national context where one particular stakeholder, the trade unions, has held a key position as the preeminent counterpart to employers for the best part of a century, and where the national welfare system is the domain of the state rather than the private sector. While considered a co-ordinated market economy, Sweden has in recent years experienced structural developments in the workforce and in the labour market, such as outsourcing, and a shift in employment from the public to the private sector and to higher education. As a result, the balance between blue- and white-collar trade unions has shifted in favour of the latter. These developments have contributed to the emergence of a foreign concept – namely CSR – appearing as potentially both a threat and an opportunity for the unions.

Surprisingly, the union federation that has encountered the greatest challenges in terms of decreasing membership, LO (the Swedish Trade Union Confederation), is also the one which has allocated most resources to engage actively with CSR. At sectoral level, none of the unions interviewed for this chapter used the term CSR; instead they relied on the trade union vocabulary. They would use the term CSR only when dealing with multinational businesses or acting at the European Union (EU) level.

National business system

The Swedish business system is characterized by a combination of an international business orientation and a strong, centralized and supportive labour movement (Katzenstein 1985). Another feature is the long-standing relations between banks, notably SE-Banken and Svenska Handelsbanken, and industry. Owners and managers have traditionally stayed committed to their industry, even when these matured. Instead of diversifying and leaving their original core business, big Swedish corporations have developed into international and even global firms (Hellgren and Melin 1992).

Within the varieties of capitalism framework, Sweden is usually considered to be a co-ordinated market economy, with institutions reflecting higher levels of reliance on non-market co-ordination than in liberal market economies (Hall and Soskice 2001). Such a view finds support in the type of economy that emerged during the twentieth century. During their long period of power from 1936 to 1976, the Social Democratic Party set the framework for enterprises in a capitalist economy where productivity and profits increased the state's distributive power through taxes and budget transfers (Stråth 1996). The Swedish economy performed well during the post-war period and Sweden became one of the most affluent countries in the world by the late 1960s. The performance of the economy in the post-war period is commonly referred to as 'the Swedish model'. Although there is no commonly accepted definition of the Swedish model, Henrekson *et al.* (1996) highlight three features. First, an institutional set-up that encompasses unions and non-market-oriented regulations. Second, ambitious economic policies – such as stabilization, growth, industrial, labour market and welfare policies. Third, a very large public sector. However, many of the elements of the Swedish model have since been abolished or have disappeared (Henrekson *et al.* 1996).

The continuity of government policy over this period is particularly evident in one aspect: the belief in scientific methods to rationalize production and to organize society and the economy, such as social engineering or Keynesian economic policy (Stråth 1996). These economic policy doctrines were based on ideas developed by the Stockholm School of Economics in the 1930s and by trade union economists in the early post-war period. However, following the economic crisis of the 1990s, successive Swedish governments introduced a number of political initiatives influenced by Anglo-American economists, such as the establishment of an independent central bank, the abandonment of the full employment target and the deregulation of markets. All of these aimed to increase productivity and GDP per capita. As Sweden joined the EU in 1995, adjustment to EU economic policy was another source of influence on its policy regime (Erixon 2011).

Sweden today occupies a high position when countries are ranked in terms of macroeconomic stability, international competitiveness and sustainable growth (Erixon 2011). Sweden is home to a large number of multinational corporations (MNCs). This is reflected in the high proportion of outward foreign direct investment by Swedish companies, which amounted to 67.8 per cent of GDP in 2008 (Gjølberg 2010). Among the members of the Organization for Economic Co-operation and Development

(OECD), Sweden is still one of the countries with the lowest income differentials, the largest public sector, the highest labour-force participation rates and the strongest position for organized labour. However, from a national perspective, Swedish unemployment has remained at a high level. Between 2008 and 2010 it stood at 7.6 per cent on average, which was close to the average for all OECD countries (Erixon 2011).

Industrial relations system

Sweden has a high union density among both white-collar and blue-collar workers, with an average rate of 71 per cent (Medlingsinstitutet 2012). This comparatively high union density is often considered a result of separate white- and blue-collar unions and confederations. Union mergers rarely occur across this division. Other suggested explanations are the combined decentralization and centralization of industrial relations, a preference for self-regulation over state regulation and state-supported, union administered unemployment funds, known as a 'Ghent system' (Kjellberg 2007). Contemporary Swedish industrial relations are centralized in terms of sector-wide agreements between national unions and employers' associations. Another aspect of centralization is the ambition by both LO and the Confederation of Swedish Enterprises to bring about close internal co-operation between their affiliates. As a decentralized component of Swedish industrial relations, negotiations over wages and other employment conditions take their lead from the various industry agreements but are then conducted at local level (Kjellberg 2007).

Although high by international standards, the last two decades have seen a substantial decrease in trade union density. The unionized workers' share of all employees shrank steadily from 83 per cent in 1990 to 71 per cent in 2008, although it remained stable from 2008 to 2010 despite a deep recession. The reduction in union density accelerated during the centre-right coalition that came to power in 2006, from 77 per cent in 2006 to 73 per cent in 2007, because of raised individual contributions to the unemployment benefit system and the elimination of tax deductions for membership of a trade union (Erixon 2011). The decrease in trade union membership since the 1990s is most pronounced among young workers (Medlingsinstitutet 2012).

The high membership figures have facilitated a significant trade union influence on the Swedish economy, particularly by the trade union federation LO. During most of the twentieth century, LO was in partnership with the Social Democratic Party and hence had a significant impact on Swedish economic policy under Social Democratic governments, in particular in the post-war period. As an example, LO's chairman belonged to the party leadership and the party did not take any major decisions, even when in government, until these had been cleared with LO. However, in the 1990s problems confronting the partnership became increasingly visible. While the partnership tended to tie the hands of the government, it forced LO to accept responsibility for governmental decisions which undermined its authority vis-à-vis union members (Bergström 1991).

Among the factors contributing to a weakened position for LO at the end of the twentieth century was the change from centrally co-ordinated to sector-level wage negotiations in 1983. Sector-level wage negotiations reduced the role of LO in wage setting to one of an informal co-ordinator of blue-collar wage claims. When the co-ordinated wage bargaining system was reintroduced in the mid-1990s, LO failed to become a central actor again (Erixon 2011). Instead, the parties to the so-called Industrial Agreement, i.e. a number of sector-level trade unions and employers' associations, became the main actors. These changes led to a new form of centralization, a sectoral centralization for the entire manufacturing sector (Kjellberg 2007). These agreements were expected to serve as a wage norm for other sectors. The decentralization of wage negotiations to sectoral and local levels was seemingly more accentuated in Sweden than in the other Nordic countries (Erixon 2011).

One important reason for the Social Democratic Party collaborating with LO was the strength the party derived from the Swedish union movement. However, union capacity to perform this role weakened in the 1980s and 1990s as a result of the increased heterogeneity of the labour market (Bergström 1991). Manual workers constituted a diminishing sector of the labour force, with their share of total employment falling from 23 per cent in 1987 to 16 per cent in 2005. At the same time, total labour demand shifted towards skilled labour in the private sector, i.e. to workers not organized by LO (Kjellberg 2007). The shift towards private sector jobs was also a government concern; even leading social democrats supported the view that the public sector had become too extensive in the 1980s. In addition, the higher unemployment rate during the 1990s and 2000s reduced the strength of organized labour in general (Erixon 2011).

In contrast to trade union density, the density of employers' associations has remained relatively stable over the last 10–15 years. As a consequence, although private sector union density was comparable to private sector employers' association density in 2000, employer density has since surpassed union density. In 2010, 80 per cent of Swedish private sector workers were employed by a member of an employers' association, compared with a private sector trade union density of 65 per cent (Medlingsinstitutet 2012). The coverage rate of collective agreements has remained stable, however, despite a slight decrease since 2005. In 2010, 91 per cent of Swedish workers were covered by collective agreements, compared with 93 per cent in 2005. The decline is largely a consequence of developments in the private sector as all public sector workers are covered by such agreements (Medlingsinstitutet 2012).

The evolution of CSR

CSR is today an established phenomenon in Swedish business. It is promoted not so much by the traditional actors in the Swedish model – the state, employers and trade unions – but more by business itself and by intergovernmental organizations, such as the United Nations (UN) and the European Union (EU). Swedish companies develop CSR strategies within a context increasingly marked by the activities of actors like non-governmental organizations (NGOs), the media, consultants and investors (De Geer *et al.* 2009). Unsurprisingly, corporate social responsibility is not so much a new as a reinvented practice. Elements of social responsibility, where employers provided more than merely monetary remuneration for work, could be found in Sweden in different forms as far back as the nineteenth century. For example, the system whereby employers provided housing for their workers was not abolished until 1945 (De Geer 2009).

During the 1880s and 1890s trade unions were founded and among them particularly LO became the main driver for change concerning working conditions and the labour market. The unions pressurized employers to abandon their patriarchal role, demanding job protection and increased monetary remuneration, rather than housing and payments in kind (De Geer *et al.* 2009). The twentieth century was instead dominated by politics and the view that social issues are the responsibility of the public authorities. Laws and regulation – based on liberal or social conservative ideas – formed a public sector which became an alternative to the private sector assuming responsibility for meeting workers' needs. Efficient production became the main task of business, and its contribution to society would consist in sharing its resources through taxation. The Swedish model has been marked by a strict division of roles between the state, employers and trade unions. Issues directly related to conditions of work should be negotiated between the labour market parties, while social and economic policies, as well as the rules of the game of the labour market, were the domain of political decision-makers (De Geer *et al.* 2009). As a result, the Swedish model did not encourage concepts such as CSR.

Until the early 1990s Swedish companies appeared outwardly indifferent to social responsibility, yet in the latter part of the decade a range of labels – such as sustainability, corporate citizenship and business ethics – were increasingly adopted for communicating similar issues (Windell 2006). The adoption of these labels may be regarded as a response to a small but highly visible number of corporate scandals, both nationally and internationally. These scandals, although focusing criticism on particular companies, had the effect of presenting companies in general as being responsible for social and environmental issues. Additionally, UN policy and agreements at the time began to speak directly to corporations instead of affecting them through governments (Sahlin-Andersson 2006).

At the beginning of the twenty-first century, several of these labels were abandoned and CSR became the term most commonly used by the Swedish government and other organizations (Windell 2006). Building on the UN Global Compact and the OECD Guidelines for Multinational Enterprises, the Minister for Foreign Affairs, the Minister for Trade and the Minister for International Development Co-operation, Asylum Policy and Migration initiated a Swedish Partnership for Global Responsibility in March 2002, and invited the Swedish corporate community to take part (Sahlin-Andersson 2006). In November 2007, the Ministry of Finance launched accounting directives requiring state-owned companies to report their social and environmental impact according to the accounting guidelines of the Global Reporting Initiative (GRI) (Ministry of Finance 2012).

Among the Swedish unions, CSR was first discussed in an LO report of 2006. Seen as distinct from the traditional perspective and methods of trade unions, the CSR concept, according to the report, does not align well with the Swedish division between public welfare and employer responsibility. The view that companies should directly contribute to welfare services is especially criticized in the report. It is instead emphasized that welfare services should be financed through taxation (Landsorganisationen i Sverige 2006). Like the unions, employers' associations have not been a forceful actor in the CSR debate either. In 2002, the board of the Confederation of Swedish Enterprise claimed that Swedish legislation more than covered the core values underlying the UN Global Compact. CSR, in their view, is therefore relevant only to developing or newly industrialized countries. In 2008, the Confederation of Swedish Enterprise stated that CSR is a global issue, but the need for CSR is not global. The Swedish public sector is financed by a fiscal regime characterized by the world's highest taxes, so companies already contribute their share. To engage in additional CSR initiatives, the employers' association argued, would amount to paying for something twice (De Geer *et al.* 2009).

Methods: unions interviewed

Between December 2011 and December 2012, six interviews were carried out, including interviews with all the union federations and at least one, usually their largest, member union. However, the contacted SACO affiliate declined to participate.

The union federations are:

- LO, Swedish Trade Union Confederation – 1.3 million members in 14 affiliated unions which organize workers within both the private and the public sectors. Interview with a research officer in the international department, January 2012, 1.5 hours.
- TCO, Swedish Confederation of Professional Employees – around 1.2 million members, including students and retired workers, in 15 affiliated

unions. It organizes professional and qualified employees in both the private and public sectors. Interview with the Chief Officer for International Relations, December 2011, 1 hour.

- SACO, Swedish Confederation of Professional Associations – 600,000 members in 22 affiliated unions. Members are university graduates or professionals with a college degree working in both the private and public sectors. Interview with the Chief Officer for Social Policy, December 2011, 30 minutes.

The member unions are:

- IF Metall, Industrial and Metalworkers' Union, member of LO – 350,000 members. IF Metall organizes workers in mechanical engineering and plastics, pharmaceuticals, textiles and clothing, iron and glass, building materials, mines, vehicle repair and in sheltered employment. Interview with a research officer, December 2011, 1 hour 40 minutes.
- SEKO, Union for Service and Communication Employees, member of LO – 125,000 members. SEKO's members work in a range of sectors including public administration, energy, defence, postal services, maritime, aviation, telecommunications, healthcare, rail transportation and road and railways construction. Interview with the International Secretary, December 2011, 1 hour.
- Unionen, member of TCO – over 500,000 members. Unionen's members are professionals employed in the private sector. It is the largest union in the Swedish private sector and the largest white-collar union in the world. Interview with a research officer, December 2012, 1 hour 30 minutes.

In addition to these interviews (which totalled seven hours and 10 minutes), union documents on the CSR debate were studied and three seminars, organized by LO, TCO and Unionen, observed (five hours and 30 minutes). At the seminars aspects of CSR relating to trade union work were discussed. During these occasions, the union respondents explained their work to a larger audience consisting of union workers, CSR consultants, NGOs, company representatives, as well as occasionally a number of researchers.

Union understanding of CSR

The trade union respondents generally regarded CSR as a foreign concept, designed for companies rather than for unions. Some of them recognized that their work could overlap with CSR. Those unions which saw an overlap between CSR and their agenda often recounted participation in UN and OECD initiatives, such as discussions at the Trade Union Advisory

Committee of the OECD (TUAC). The respondents also recounted the changes in the business context that paved the way for such initiatives, which the LO respondent called 'the reality of globalization and the state's inability to protect its citizens'. According to the LO respondent, this development had already taken off in the 1970s when the increasingly multinational nature of businesses led to initiatives like the drafting of the OECD Guidelines for Multinational Enterprises, although the CSR concept has been used only over the last 10 years.

Among the union federations, LO is at one end of the spectrum (recognizing CSR and actively engaging with the concept), while at the other end is the academics' union federation, SACO (which has not discussed the topic). The degree of engagement reflects how the unions currently view CSR in relation to the traditional trade union agenda and whether or not they recognize a resemblance between their work and CSR. LO's engagement with CSR can be related to their view of CSR as overlapping with traditional issues and being potentially an undesirable alternative to dialogue between trade unions and employers. An early reference to CSR by LO appears in their 2006 report. Even by then it recognized an overlap in ideas (Landsorganisationen i Sverige 2006: 15):

> CSR is a concept that does not originate in the trade union movement's views and methods. However, large parts of the trade union movement believe that the concept that companies are not only responsible in terms of profit and value for shareholders but are also actors who create value for stakeholders is important to return to and apply today.

The LO respondent, who was part of the team who wrote the above report, viewed CSR practice as increasingly covering business issues rather than just corporate philanthropy, which was in her view essentially a good direction. She recognized an increasing overlap of CSR with the union agenda, while reporting that LO member unions have traditionally been sceptical towards CSR. CSR does not raise the bar for their members as much as for workers in other parts of the world. Thereby CSR can first and foremost support trade union discussions that are conducted outside of the national welfare state. LO also referred to the trade union tradition of solidarity among workers to motivate work conducted outside of Sweden, but admitted that it is still a challenge to address these issues using the mandate from and resources of the national members.

TCO, taking a stand somewhere between those of LO and SACO, conceived of CSR as responsibility that goes beyond financial returns, yet the respondent did not relate it to TCO's agenda. Instead, CSR is viewed as a 'pitfall', because there is a risk that companies focus on CSR instead of agreements with trade unions. Furthermore, among the range of CSR issues, environmental issues tend to receive more attention than social ones. Rather than using the concept of CSR to include workers in developing countries, the respondent said they would discuss such issues under the heading of human rights. TCO's approach towards CSR is less accommodating than that of LO, although TCO does recognize CSR and participates in initiatives when invited. Its motive for getting involved is primarily to ensure that CSR does not overshadow the trade union agenda.

Like LO, interviewees from its two member unions SEKO and IF Metall identified an overlap between their own core issues and CSR. Some CSR issues, in their view, are in their area of expertise. As the IF Metall respondent emphasized, the union wants to be a 'discussion partner' on 'their' issues, whether or not they are labelled CSR. Although viewing the concept of CSR as 'fluffy', the IF Metall respondent remarked that it does offer 'new ways for preaching the same message'. Hence the sector union respondents seemed to make a distinction between the concept of CSR and its content. Its content, that is, the individual issues, were recognized as affecting their members. This is reflected, for example, in what the Unionen respondent saw as her responsibility, namely, to monitor 'discussions of human rights in the workplace conducted in non-union arenas'. CSR is one such arena where issues that affect their members are discussed.

At the level of sectoral unions, pressure to consider whether there is an overlap between CSR and the trade union agenda seems to originate from companies and their adoption of codes of conduct that cover human rights and working conditions. The prevalence of CSR is, in the sectoral unions' view, not necessarily sector specific but depends on how international a sector is. It is also related to company size, as it is more common within large companies, whereas small businesses may practise CSR without labelling it as such. Of course, large companies are not necessarily international, and whether a sector is national or international is not set in stone. Some of the companies and sectors in which SEKO organizes changed during the 2000s from public authorities to private companies which became increasingly international.

The sectoral level respondents see a tendency to emphasize environmental issues when CSR is discussed, which is the CSR issue unions have engaged with least. However, they did not entirely disregard environmental issues either, as these are, they reasoned, part of the employees' day-to-day life. While CSR is criticized for its focus on environmental issues, trade unions are simultaneously inspired to engage with these issues in addition to their traditional social ones. Thus the SEKO respondent argued that issues are not necessarily either social or environmental as trade union issues may include environmental aspects too. At a seminar, the TCO chair brought up the question of the trade unions' responsibility for sustainable development and identified this as an area for future union engagement. 'We need to care for the environment, because without it there may be no jobs to protect', she argued.

In addition to making a distinction between the concept and the content of CSR, the respondents also referred independently to its implementation. The implementation of CSR was often found to be wanting, particularly in comparison with the trade unions' preferred way of working through two-party agreements. When asked about CSR reporting, the SEKO respondent remarked that follow-up mechanisms are a good thing, but that CSR reporting did not appear as rigorous as the follow-up mechanisms in global framework agreements (GFAs). Another frequently mentioned difference between the union agenda and CSR is the voluntary nature of CSR compared with the 'binding' agreements which trade union negotiations result in.

Union policies on CSR

Of all the respondents, LO had the longest time-line for official engagement with CSR. An indication of LO's extensive engagement is that it has had an officer specifically with CSR expertise since 2007. The only other union interviewed which had a designated officer to monitor CSR was TCO member Unionen. In terms of official policies, both LO and TCO were, at the time of the interviews, collecting opinions on CSR to formulate their official position on the subject.

The LO respondent envisaged that the LO policy document would be approved at the spring congress of 2012 and that it would include national guidelines (without reference to CSR) as well as international guidelines (containing the CSR concept). In practice, the LO policy took the shape of a model version of a global framework agreement (GFA) and was approved just before the spring congress. It was presented as a trade union alternative to the CSR way of working at a seminar with union officials, company and NGO representatives, consultants and researchers in November 2012. The design of the LO model agreement was inspired by existing agreements, and has since been used as inspiration for revising existing GFAs. The TCO policy arrived in June 2013. It states in the foreword that CSR concerns union issues but can never replace 'binding international norms, national legislation or collective agreements' (TCO 2013: 4). The document includes TCO's view on ILO conventions and the OECD guidelines, and emphasizes the need for GFAs. In the policy summary, the union concludes that its ambition is not only to influence the formulation of codes of conduct but to turn these codes into GFAs.

Another event that took place at the time of this study was an examination in 2013 of sustainability reporting by Unionen based on a sample of 25 Swedish companies. In the introduction to the report, the union states that its research aims to advise companies on how to improve their reporting on social issues and also to give guidance to local union representatives (Unionen 2013). In addition, Unionen planned a workshop for local union representatives on how to combine international union work with CSR. As is evident from the information presented above, the degree of activity and the number of initiatives increased over the duration of this study, that is, between 2011 and 2013. It is most likely that the number of union initiatives and resulting documents on CSR will increase further in the near future.

Union engagement with CSR

Apart from the two organizations with designated officers, LO and Unionen, the trade union respondents did not perceive a need to talk in CSR terms. Both IF Metall and SEKO experienced 'surprisingly little' pressure from their members to discuss CSR. The SEKO respondent thought that this might be a result of the fact that many of the sectors in which the union organizes, such as prison management and the police force, have only domestic operations. In Swedish they do not use the term 'CSR', but rather the individual trade union terms, such as gender equality, working conditions and education. The pressure to engage with CSR that does exist comes instead from the European level or from businesses with international operations.

At the international level, LO has started to use the term CSR. Globally exposed industries in particular, such as the paper industry, encounter the term. Thus the international aspect of CSR has significance for the union and LO's engagement with CSR has, the respondent claimed, facilitated its contacts with CSR advocates, such as the Swedish state and the EU. The other union federations interviewed, however, did not share this view. According to the TCO respondent, the union federations already have in place the necessary international contacts and rely on other international standards, such as those promoted by the ILO. Nevertheless, the TCO respondent saw the monitoring of concepts like CSR as within their role and recognized a responsibility to get involved, when asked, in initiatives such as the development of the OECD Guidelines.

At sectoral level, both the Unionen and IF Metall respondents identified pressure to discuss CSR and claimed this partly originates from NGOs. For example, IF Metall participates in the Clean Clothes Campaign Sweden, together with other sectoral unions and NGOs. Similarly, Unionen participated in a stakeholder dialogue with union and company representatives organized by NGO Swedwatch. Both IF Metall and Unionen participated in the work on ISO 26000 and, at the time of the interviews, engaged in dialogue with two large Swedish asset management firms regarding labour rights in the global labour market. Such dialogue is an example of what the Unionen respondent called 'non-union arenas where trade union issues are discussed'. In these examples, the unions had been invited, which is not always the case, as the Unionen respondent noted.

However, all the unions interviewed, apart from Unionen, rejected CSR tools such as codes of conduct and sustainability reports, and did not engage with them. While LO does have an officer with CSR expertise, their Negotiating Secretary, when asked during a seminar if they attempt to influence the design and implementation of CSR tools like codes of conduct, replied that they focus instead on GFAs. Rather than engaging with CSR approaches and tools, the unions thus promote their own alternative, GFAs. As the SEKO respondent expressed it:

> The companies are keen to talk CSR, but we want them to sign global framework agreements with us instead. What the companies often have, a CSR policy, is nothing we strive for. We would prefer to have a global framework agreement than a CSR policy.

A GFA refers to ILO conventions and prescribes how a company should act in its home as well as in foreign countries. The sectoral union respondents admitted that these can occasionally be too loosely formulated, but the agreements are considered working documents that the unions aim to 'tighten'.

Unionen, the only union that in some way engaged with CSR tools and practices, had previously reviewed codes of conduct for the joint project Fair Travel, where it collaborates, for example, with the Church of Sweden and the Swedish Hotel and Restaurant Workers' Union. Unionen's latest initiative consisted of an examination of Swedish sustainability reporting. When conducting the examination of corporate reports it effectively engaged with a CSR tool, one of the first Swedish unions to do so. The Unionen respondent explained their stance during the report release:

> I am among those who believe it is a good thing that companies take greater responsibility. We have to recognize reality. There are no unions or their equivalents in all of these countries.

Her argument was that it is better to engage with the CSR approaches and tools that do exist here and now than to wait for a future when union organizations would be in place in all the countries Swedish companies operate in.

Discussion

Sweden has high standards of legal protection for labour conditions and human rights. In addition, its public sector has in the past been extensive and, by international comparison, still is. When the mandatory level is already high and the unions' counterpart is not a company but a public authority, then CSR as a concept is not very useful. Nonetheless, the Swedish trade unions have worked with some issues that could be seen as falling under the heading of CSR, such as human rights in the workplace, for more than 100 years. However, since the 1970s, the characteristics of

Swedish industrial relations have shifted, even if this shift is minor by international comparison. The privatization of public services, a shift in demand towards skilled labour and the relocation of sections of the corporate workforce abroad have contributed to weakening LO's position in particular. In addition, a persistent high unemployment rate, from a national perspective, together with decreasing union density, have somewhat weakened the power of organized labour in general. In parallel with such developments, many trade unions have been losing members, because of recently increased contributions to unemployment insurance, one of their membership benefits.

In this context, the externally imposed concept of CSR, with its dispersed stakeholder and self-governance ideals, threatens to undermine further the role of trade unions as the pre-eminent opposite number to employers and the state as the guardian of public welfare. These recent developments, together with the historical stronghold enjoyed by Swedish trade unions, explain why all unions appeared to be, or admitted to having been, sceptical towards CSR. At the same time, trade unions are invited to attend an increasing number of international discussions on CSR initiated by the UN and the EU, as well as NGOs. For certain trade unions, this has resulted in a situation where demands for their participation in international discussions have increased, while the differences in labour rights between domestic and overseas employees of Swedish multinational companies are increasing more than before, and their membership base and income have actually decreased. The combination of lower membership and increased demands for participation across various initiatives is potentially a challenge for these unions.

While CSR is viewed by most unions as something that contains – or to some extent overlaps with – traditional trade union issues, it is also viewed as an externally imposed concept, particularly relevant for unions that organize in companies where the labour force is located abroad. Their concern is that CSR, based on voluntary participation and consideration of a range of stakeholders, could possibly become an undesirable alternative to the more rigorous bipartite negotiations the Swedish unions strive for. While the union respondents consistently referred to GFAs as binding, this binding status is, in fact, contested. Instead of highlighting such differences between GFAs and national agreements, the unions preferred to emphasize the similarities. Drawing on the trade union tradition of working with bipartite agreements, the Swedish unions seek to promote GFAs with companies as an alternative to CSR tools, such as codes of conduct and sustainability accounting.

Overall, the degree to which CSR is recognized as a new means to preach the same message seems to be related to the degree to which unions are affected by recent labour market developments. SACO, the union for university graduates, has enjoyed the largest increase in members and showed the least interest in and recognition of the CSR movement. In contrast, the union federation with the greatest challenges in terms of membership and competition from foreign workers, LO, has adopted a strategy of influencing the content and development of CSR. Between these two positions, TCO, although monitoring the CSR movement, remains hesitant to get involved in it. Despite this, TCO was in the process of forming an official standpoint on the subject. While SACO did not appear to perceive CSR as a threat, it does not engage with the CSR movement either and thereby foregoes opportunities to learn about it. As the respondent remarked, since SACO does not offer a forum for discussing CSR issues, it makes it less likely that member unions will raise the issue through the union organization. The trade union position is then not simply an adoption or rejection of CSR; their stance also has consequences for the development of the CSR movement in the Swedish context. The unions' engagement or lack of engagement may reinforce a view that CSR is only for blue-collar workers in developing countries. At the federal level, LO does engage with CSR, while LO's member unions, SEKO and IF Metall, do not. Although the CSR concept is addressed at the federal and international levels, for example in discussion with EU agencies and the Swedish state, at sector level CSR issues are dealt with under their individual headings, such as gender equality in the workplace, health and safety and so on.

Another theme in the findings is that the two organizations that officially dedicated resources to monitoring CSR, LO and Unionen, were more informed about developments and engaged more actively with the topic. On all observed occasions, the initiatives by these unions that mentioned CSR received an unanticipated amount of interest. For example, seminars had to be relocated to fit more participants and the organizers ran out of copies of the reports. The trade unions also show some interest in environmental issues that are not always viewed as relevant to the unions but which could be engaged with in terms of working conditions. Although the union respondents agreed that environmental issues tend to receive sufficient attention, they did see potential for their trade unions to engage more with environmental aspects.

Conclusions

While all the Swedish trade unions interviewed have at some point appeared at least sceptical towards CSR, their resistance to the concept appears to depend on how challenged their domain actually is. Structural developments in the workforce and in the labour market, such as outsourcing, a shift of jobs from the public to the private sector and to higher education, have not only affected the balance between blue- and white collar unions in favour of the latter, but have also contributed to a situation where a corporate concept, such as CSR, appears as potentially both a threat and an opportunity.

The approaches by the three union federations to CSR can be labelled 'not recognizing CSR', 'monitoring CSR' and 'actively influencing the CSR debate'. Surprisingly, the union federation encountering the greatest challenges in terms of decreasing membership, LO, is the one that has allocated most resources to engage actively with CSR and shape its development. At the sectoral level, none of the unions used the term CSR but relied instead on trade union vocabulary, the exception being when dealing with multinational businesses or acting at the EU level. When CSR is viewed as overlapping with trade union issues, it is also seen as 'a new way to preach the same message' and possibly bring attention to new issues, such as environmental challenges.

The unions with an officer dedicated to monitoring CSR have identified not only threats but also opportunities in its emergence. In the respondents' view, it is the tools and manner of implementation that make CSR unattractive rather than its perceived content. The voluntary aspect, as expressed for example in the EU strategy for CSR, clashes especially with traditional Swedish trade union methods of operating within legal frameworks and signing 'binding' contracts. To match the geographic coverage of CSR, trade unions need to defend labour conditions outside their home country. Such activity can be justified through the trade unions' solidarity agenda. The challenge for most of the unions is that their nationally based membership is decreasing while the challenges arising from the growing foreign workforce of Swedish companies and their suppliers are increasing.

References

Bergström, H. (1991) 'Sweden's politics and party system at the crossroads', in J.-E. Lane (ed.) *Understanding the Swedish Model* (pp. 8–30), London: Frank Cass.

De Geer, H. (1982) *Job Studies and Industrial Relations: Ideas about Efficiency and Relations between the Parties of the Labour Market in Sweden 1920–1950*, Stockholm: Almqvist & Wiksell International.

De Geer, H. (2009) 'Den svenska historien, modellen och förståelsen för CSR', in T. Nilsson (ed.) *125 år med corporate social responsibility* (pp. 103–143), Stockholm: Centrum för näringslivshistoria.

De Geer, H., Borglund, T. and Frostenson, M. (2009) 'Reconciling CSR with the role of the corporation in welfare states: the problematic Swedish example', *Journal of Business Ethics*, 89: 269–283.

Erixon, L. (2011) 'Under the influence of traumatic events, new ideas, economic experts and the ICT revolution: the economic policy and macroeconomic performance of Sweden in the 1990s and 2000s', in L. Mjøset (ed.) *The Nordic Varieties of Capitalism* (pp. 265–330), Bingley, UK: Emerald.

Gardell, B. (1976) *Arbetsinnehåll och livskvalitet: en sammanställning och diskussion av samhällsvetenskaplig forskning rörande människan och arbetet*, Stockholm: Prisma i samarbete med Landsorganisationen i Sverige.

Gjølberg, M. (2010) 'Varieties of corporate social responsibility (CSR): CSR meets the "Nordic model"', *Regulation and Governance*, 4: 203–229.

Hall, P.A. and Soskice, D. (2001) *Varieties of Capitalism: The Institutional Foundations of Comparative Advantage*, Oxford/New York: Oxford University Press.

Hellgren, B. and Melin, L. (1992) 'Business systems, industrial wisdom and corporate strategies', in R. Whitley (ed.) *European Business Systems: Firms and Markets in Their National Contexts* (pp. 180–198), London: Sage.

Henrekson, M., Jonung, L. and Stymne, J. (1996) 'Economic growth and the Swedish model', in N. Crafts and G. Toniolo (eds.) *Economic Growth in Europe since 1945* (pp. 240–289), Cambridge: Cambridge University Press.

Katzenstein, P.J. (1985) *Small States in World Markets: Industrial Policy in Europe*, New York: Cornell University Press.

Kjellberg, A. (2007) 'The Swedish trade union system in transition: high but falling union denisty', in C. Phelan (ed.) *Trade Union Revitalisation: Trends and Prospects in 34 Countries* (pp. 259–286), Oxford: Peter Lang.

Landsorganisationen i Sverige (2006) *Ägaransvar och ägarmakt: en rapport från LOs ägarmaktsprojekt*, Stockholm: LO-distribution.

Medlingsinstitutet (2012) *Avtalsrörelsen och lönebildningen år 2011*, Stockholm: Medlingsinstitutet.

Ministry of Finance (2012) *Statens ägarpolicy och riktlinjer för företag med statligt ägande*, Stockholm: Finansdepartementet i samarbete med Grayling.

Sahlin-Andersson, K. (2006) 'Corporate social responsibility: a trend and a movement, but of what and for what?', *Corporate Governance*, 6: 595–608.

Stråth, B. (1996) *The Organisation of Labour Markets: Modernity, Culture, and Governance in Germany, Sweden, Britain, and Japan*, London: Routledge.

TCO (2013) *TCOs policy för socialt ansvar i det globala arbetslivet – mänskliga rättigheter, globala avtal och facklig organisering*, Stockholm: TCO.

Unionen (2013) *Granskning av hållbarhetsredovisning i 25 svenska storföretag*, Stockholm: Unionen.

Windell, K. (2006) *Corporate Social Responsibility under Construction: Ideas, Translations and Institutional Change*, Uppsala: Företagsekonomiska institutionen, Uppsala universitet.

12 United Kingdom

Scepticism and engagement in union positions on CSR

Michael Gold, Chris Rees and Lutz Preuss

> We've never defined what corporate social responsibility is.... But, in a way, before the term was even invented, we were ... as a trade union ... making companies behave as if they had a corporate social responsibility policy.
>
> (GMB)

Introduction

In many respects, the general attitude of trade unions in the UK towards corporate social responsibility (CSR) might, at least on the surface, be characterized as lying somewhere between lack of interest and cynicism. Most unions do not appear to engage actively with the concept of CSR or to have formulated specific policies on CSR, and many union officers express considerable scepticism about how far the pronouncements of employers in this area represent genuine statements of principle as opposed to public relations exercises. Of course, issues concerning the responsibilities of business, especially towards employees as key stakeholders, have a long history and are central to trade union concerns, and yet, in the UK at least, these issues tend not to have been associated explicitly with the discourse of CSR. We demonstrate here how this might be explained with reference to the way in which CSR has developed within a distinctive national institutional setting.

The relative lack of regulation and the primacy given to shareholder value in the UK national business system, coupled with the voluntarist and conflictual system of industrial relations, have acted against the development of high-trust employment relationships and co-ordinated regulation concerning the social obligations of business. As a result, CSR has developed more as a response to deregulation and corporate scandals, driven by responsibly minded business and non-governmental organizations (NGOs), than under pressure from trade unions. That said, this picture has been changing in recent years, as unions have become more likely to utilize CSR arguments to promote their own agendas, sometimes in liaison with NGOs, and have become more engaged with the international dimensions of the concept.

National business system

The UK occupies a particular place in typologies of national business models across Europe. In their classic account, Hall and Soskice (2001) classify the UK as a liberal market economy (LME), as opposed to a co-ordinated market economy (CME), like Germany. Indeed, the UK has been described as 'the principal European LME' (Hanké *et al.* 2007: 27). Amable (2003) terms the UK a market-based economy, as distinct from social democratic, continental European and southern European forms of capitalism. These classifications reflect the fact that the UK national business system is, relatively speaking, characterized by short-term finance, deregulated labour markets, generalist education and strong product market competition, rather than the long-term co-operative relations between firms and the active role of the state characteristic of CMEs (Whitley 1992).

The internal structure of UK firms tends to be characterized by far-reaching powers for CEOs and boards of management, leading to a high degree of flexibility to alter work processes. Corporate governance is heavily influenced by the role of the stock market, which is reflected in 'the weak formalization of constituencies other than shareholders in firm decision-making' (Vitols 2001: 338). UK firms tend to access finance through bank credits and securities that are sensitive to short-term movements in productivity. Hence managerial short-termism has been the result, with corporate policy designed to increase share value at the expense of longer-term investment in the company (Grinyer *et al.* 1998). The deregulated, flexible nature of the business system, the lack of formality and the prominence granted to business leaders in the national business system arguably underpin certain features of English culture, which is noted for its individualism, sense of 'fair play' and ability to 'muddle through' (House *et al.* 2004).

These key institutional and cultural complementarities have created a number of advantages and disadvantages for the country's firms. A key weakness of the UK system has been the strategy of British firms to compete through holding down wage costs rather than investing in new technology. At the same time, British firms have found it comparatively easy to take advantage of new commercial opportunities, such as the Single European Market. The flexibility of the national business system has also led to a move of labour from manufacturing into services more extensive than that, for example, in France or Germany (Hall 2007).

Industrial relations system

The most striking feature of the industrial relations system in the UK today is the predominance of the company and the workplace as the focus for collective regulation – where it exists at all – of both procedures and pay and conditions. Legislation has established a basic individual and collective regulatory framework, to which a national minimum wage, improved trades union recognition procedures and family friendly employment policies have been added since 1997. Despite elements of state planning in the post-war period up until the election of the Conservative government in 1979 under Margaret Thatcher, the role of the state today is limited. It has helped to establish employment policy in areas like active labour market policies and life-long learning and, over the years, has created regulatory agencies at national level to monitor particular policy areas, such as the Equality and Human Rights Commission. There is accordingly no tradition of continental-style corporatism in the UK. Rather, the system is based on 'voluntarism' – that is, autonomous relationships between the parties, in which legislation has rarely played more than a minor role.

Multi-employer bargaining, sometimes known as sector-level bargaining, has declined dramatically in recent years, and there has never been intersectoral regulation through peak employers' and union confederations. The result has been a process of what has been described as 'disorganized decentralization' (Traxler 1995) as companies and workplaces have moved centre-stage in collective bargaining and industrial relations regulation. In the industrial relations arena, then, there is a reliance on market relations providing managers with greater freedom to determine corporate strategy and to hire and fire personnel than in most other European countries (Marchington *et al.* 2011). The relationship between employer and worker is therefore principally contractual, and has been termed a 'conflict model' (Coupar and Stevens 1998: 146). Notwithstanding the rhetoric of human resource management and 'partnership' approaches, it has seldom developed into 'high-trust' relationships. In non-unionized workplaces – only 14 per cent of those in private manufacturing or services now have any union members (Van Wanrooy *et al.* 2013: 14) – workers can do little to remedy poor employment relations, so conflict has increasingly taken the form of individual disputes referred to employment tribunals rather than collective forms, such as strikes (Dix *et al.* 2008). Industrial relations within small and medium-sized enterprises may be characterized as heterogeneous, depending on sector, structure of ownership, management style and so on (Curran and Blackburn 2001). Overall, labour in the UK is regarded as a variable cost, to be laid off or made redundant, often as an easy way to reduce costs in a crisis and maintain share value. There is no premium on commitment, and – given the fluidity of its relationship with its workers – the company is unlikely to invest much in training them. In terms of the education and training system, a generalist education thus dominates (Heyes and Rainbird 2009).

British unions historically developed along the lines of craft, industrial, general and white collar unionism, although waves of mergers in recent years have reduced, if not eliminated, these divisions. Though many unions are still specialist, two of the largest are broadly general, that is, membership is open to any type of worker: Unite the Union (1.52 million members) and GMB (0.6 million). The third of the largest unions is Unison (1.37 million members), which represents members in public services and utilities, whether employed in private companies, public authorities or the voluntary sector (Certification Officer 2012: 56). Declining membership, changes in the employment structure and ideological opposition in particular by Conservative governments since the 1980s have led to a relatively weak union movement (Marchington *et al.* 2011). Membership peaked in 1979 when there were 13.29 million members (around 52 per cent of those eligible). By 2012 membership had fallen to 7.26 million, a decrease of about 45 per cent since 1979. At the same time, the total number of trade unions has declined from 502 unions in 1983 to 154 in 2012. However, only eight unions now account for 5.3 million members, each with a membership of over 250,000. Some unions buck the trend of decline. Prospect, for example, which organizes mainly engineering and management staff, had 121,000 members in 2012, a rise of 16 per cent over the previous year. Overall, in 2011, 30 per cent of workplaces with five or more workers had members of a union, with 21 per cent having a recognized union (Van Wanrooy *et al.* 2013: 14). However, these figures are considerably higher in the public sector and in larger organizations.

The Trades Union Congress (TUC) is the umbrella organization that represents the union movement in the UK. Fifty-four unions are affiliated to it, representing almost six million workers. All the largest unions are affiliated apart from the Royal College of Nursing and the British Medical Association. The TUC is the forum in which its affiliates decide general policy, organize campaigns on employment-related issues, represent union interests at national and international level and operate a range of educational and training programmes. It also lobbies government, but this role has fluctuated greatly since 1945, with its period of greatest influence – under the 1974–1979 Labour government – eclipsed by subsequent governments, both Conservative and New Labour. It should be noted too that the TUC plays a significant role in the European Trade Union Confederation, founded in 1973 to represent unions at EU-level across the now 28 member states. The Confederation of British Industry is the principal organization representing employers at national level, but as collective bargaining, where it exists, has decentralized, employers' associations too have dwindled in numbers; there are currently 60 (Certification Officer 2012: 50–51).

The evolution of CSR

Discussions about the responsibility of employers to a broad range of stakeholders beyond shareholders – such as workers, local communities and environmental interests – have a long pedigree in the UK stretching back to the early nineteenth century. The societal transformation brought about by the Industrial Revolution led to moves amongst progressives to create alternative forms of production and ownership, such as model villages for company employees, as well as to the emergence of the co-operative movement and the development of Fabianism and Guild Socialism (Fox 1985). Religious movements, such as the Quakers, who launched the first ethical investment trusts in the country, formed another significant strand to these moves (Sparkes and Cowton 2004). These developments all reflected concerns among enlightened employers, trade unionists and political and social theorists to ensure that productive activity should benefit not just owners and shareholders but also workers and society more generally. However, with the rise of the welfare state during the twentieth century, the provision of such services like education, health care and social housing was increasingly transferred to central and local government and financed through taxation. As a result, the corporate role narrowed to focus on community philanthropy (Moon 2005).

The 1980s were a watershed for the evolution of CSR in its modern sense. The early 1980s witnessed high levels of unemployment and societal unrest, culminating in riots across a number of UK cities. The privatization and deregulation policies of the Conservative governments under Thatcher led to a decline in the government's role in providing key services, such as energy, mass transport and utilities, and a correspondingly greater visibility for business (Moon 2005). The need for a more serious engagement with CSR was also fostered by a number of corporate scandals, like large-scale pension fund irregularities at the Maxwell publishing empire or the bankruptcy of Polly Peck International. Not least, these events led to the emergence of the country's largest CSR network, Business in the Community (Grayson 2007). As a further influence on the evolution of CSR, a new wave of companies emerged that sought to do business with a difference, such as the Body Shop, which started its operations in 1976.

During the 1990s, the range of concerns addressed under the banner of CSR widened considerably, from community involvement to products and processes, employment relations as well as environmental responsibilities (Moon 2005). The public outcry that followed the occupation of Shell's oil storage platform Brent Spar by Greenpeace activists in 1995 when the company threatened to sink it in the North Sea led to the publication in 1998 of Shell's report *Profits and Principles*, which is still a milestone in corporate stakeholder engagement and reporting on social and environmental issues (Mirvis 2000). The decade also saw the emergence of a more visible role for NGOs in the CSR arena. For example, Amnesty International set up its UK Business Group in 1991 with the aim to make the business community more aware of human rights issues around the world (Chandler 2009). The international dimension of CSR was further strengthened through the significant growth of the Fair Trade movement (Davies 2007).

The New Labour government under Tony Blair, which came to power in 1997, regarded CSR as a means to promote more responsible corporate activity without the need for the heavy use of regulation that had characterized previous Labour administrations. In 2000, it created a Minister for CSR (abandoned by the Coalition government under David Cameron in 2010) in the then Department of Trade and Industry, followed in 2004 by the CSR Academy to help diffuse good practice in CSR. This decade also saw the proliferation of multi-stakeholder initiatives. As an example, the Ethical Trading Initiative (ETI) is a joint initiative of businesses, trade unions and voluntary organizations to improve working conditions in international supply chains. A cornerstone of the ETI's work, its Base Code, is based on the principles of the International Labour Organization (ILO).

For some commentators, the 'UK as a whole is widely considered to be a leader in the field of corporate social responsibility' (Ward and Smith 2006: v). There is widespread evidence of the institutionalization of CSR in UK companies. At least large corporations are today expected to have key CSR tools in place, such as codes of conduct or CSR reports. The country is home to a number of influential NGOs in the CSR arena, such as Amnesty International and Christian Aid. The UK also has a sizeable CSR support industry, including providers of independent research into corporate environmental and social performance, such as the Ethical Investment Research and Information Service (EIRIS), or the sustainability consulting departments of major accounting firms, like Accenture and Ernst & Young. In line with the arm's length approach that characterizes the national business system of the UK, government policy on CSR has focused on developing interest in the topic, facilitating the exchange of best practice, providing incentives for CSR and encouraging public–private partnerships (Albareda *et al.* 2007).

Methods: unions interviewed

We carried out six interviews between January 2012 and March 2013: two at the TUC and one each at the country's three largest unions (Unite, Unison and GMB) with a further one at Prospect, a union whose members are concentrated amongst engineering and management staff. These unions organize in metalwork/engineering, utilities and textiles, the three principal sectors covered in this book.

- Trades Union Congress (TUC) – the national union federation, representing 54 unions and almost six million workers. Interviews with a senior policy officer and a policy officer in the EU and international relations department;
- Unite – one of the so-called 'big two' unions; 1.52 million members – mainly in manufacturing, chemicals and pharmaceuticals. Interview with a research officer;

- Unison – the other of the 'big two'; 1.37 million members – mainly in local government and health, also water, gas and electricity industries. Interview with the head of international relations;
- GMB – a general union with almost 602,000 members working across all sectors of the economy. Interview with the international officer;
- Prospect – 121,000 members, mainly engineering and management staff in the ICT, defence and energy sectors. Interview with the international development co-ordinator.

Additional information was gleaned from internal union documents, such as CSR agreements or briefing documents for union officials.

Union understanding of CSR

None of the unions we interviewed had their own definition of CSR. However, one of our TUC interviewees stated:

> We see [CSR] as basically being about companies managing and taking responsibility for their social and environmental impacts, and managing them appropriately.

In discussing this approach with the unions, three points became clear. The first is that central to the unions' understanding of CSR is the nature of *stakeholder relationships*, particularly with workers and unions. The TUC believes that the business community had earlier adopted a narrower approach, based largely on philanthropic activity, but that now it too accepted a broader understanding of CSR. The principal issue was that companies should take responsibility for the impact of their activities on workers, communities and the environment, particularly through supply chain management.

The second is that the unions tend to distinguish between their understanding of CSR in *domestic* and *international* contexts. Their understanding of CSR as such generally revolves around international issues – such as ensuring corporate compliance with ILO conventions and other international regulations and campaigns on, for example, fair trade – rather than domestic issues. A common theme that emerged was that the unions were already dealing domestically with the issues that commonly pass as CSR, for example, ensuring decent labour standards, union rights and health and safety: 'We just don't actually call it CSR', explained our Unite interviewee, as these items form the bedrock of traditional union bargaining agendas.

The third point is that some unions remain *sceptical* about CSR. The GMB interviewee, for example, argued:

> I start off from the premise that we live in a capitalist society and the reasons that any enterprise exists is to make money. That's what

> they're there for. In fact, they've got a legal obligation to their shareholders, have they not? If they think that by appearing to be good corporate citizens, it helps the bottom line, then they'll do it. If they don't think so, then they won't do it. And of course, I think there are some that are in between the two, so it's difficult to generalize.

One of our TUC interviewees also expressed scepticism. As the business community regards CSR as voluntary, this leads to:

> ... a sort of pick and choose agenda ... and the idea that, because it's voluntary, companies can focus on anti-corruption or labour standards or community – they don't have to do all of them. And I think that is a view that we simply reject.

Such a voluntary approach may be regarded as purely a public relations exercise on the part of the company. This interviewee argued that a company has to accept overall responsibility for its impact on workers, communities and the environment, and cannot choose to focus purely on, for example, anti-corruption or philanthropic initiatives: 'I think there's been a lot more recognition now that CSR is really about how a company makes its money, not what it does with it. It's about how it generates its profits'. In an international context, union rights, employment conditions and environmental protection all form part of the CSR agenda. Central to the TUC's understanding of CSR is that a workplace cannot be regarded as 'clean' on labour standards unless there is a union present that *agrees* the standards. Indeed, only one union that we interviewed, Prospect, had actively engaged with companies on CSR, driven from below by membership pressures, a point we return to.

Union views on social and environmental reporting were similarly mixed with respect both to its value and to whether it should be made mandatory or not. On the one hand, there was the case for social reporting in that it allows comparisons between companies through transparent benchmarking standards, which could have a significant impact on company performance. Accordingly, there are grounds for clarifying and standardizing indicators and making the process mandatory. On the other hand, unions argued that transparency does not necessarily lead to changed behaviour. A number of companies already publish social and environmental reports, and these have not necessarily led to improvements in corporate action. In addition, it can be difficult to develop adequate indicators of impact. Mandatory reporting may therefore be seen as a necessary but not sufficient condition for guaranteeing change. Unions themselves remain divided on the issue of mandatory reporting. While our Prospect interviewee felt that companies might resist and not do it well, our GMB interviewee, by contrast, was in favour.

It would appear, then, that the predominant union attitude towards CSR is changing. While CSR is seen as focusing principally on international rather than domestic issues, the notion that it involves companies in accepting wider responsibility for the impact of their activities on workers, communities and the environment, particularly through supply chain management, has become established. In particular the TUC suggested that companies are now more likely to involve their workforces in CSR initiatives than they were in the early 2000s, and there are instances where unions have found it expedient to frame demands using CSR-type discourse, a point we also explore below. Overall, it believes that the CSR debate has become more sophisticated in the recent past because there has been increasing consensus over definitions of the issues based on documents like the *Guiding Principles on Business and Human Rights*, endorsed by the United Nations Human Rights Council in 2011. However, some (but not all) unions in the UK still view CSR as a cynical shield to deflect criticism from real company practices. These unions are likely to remain sceptical unless good practice across the range of CSR issues is verified by a union.

Union policies on CSR

Very few explicit CSR initiatives have been submitted as resolutions by affiliated unions to the TUC Annual Congress. Areas covered by the CSR agenda are generally tabled with reference to alternative terms, such as international development work, 'green workplace' representation and the role of pension fund trustees in securing corporate responsiveness to community needs. Similarly, GMB, Unison and Unite do not generally receive resolutions for their own conferences making direct reference to CSR, though the term has become more mainstream in Prospect. The unions tend to pursue their own angle on CSR in terms of policy, taking into account the interests and nature of their own membership. Unite, for example, has established a policy on its own pension fund that CSR-type issues must be reported quarterly to its trustees, but otherwise considers its approach to CSR to be quite reactive.

These unions do not have a single officer who co-ordinates CSR activity. As Unison pointed out, the union has a range of officers who deal with environmental matters, international issues, employment rights, pensions and so on. Any one of these might cover relevant dimensions of CSR, but would do so from the perspective of a specific campaign. For example, if a company flouted redundancy consultation periods, then the relevant union officer would raise questions about failures of corporate responsibility, but not specifically under the banner of CSR:

> We probably have a stance on most things – you know, it runs from nuclear disarmament through to freedom of association and everything

> in between and beyond that. But has anyone ever sat down and said this is our policy on corporate social responsibility? Probably not. But if you looked at the various bits of our work, there are elements there which clearly are part of that.

Prospect proved rather different, however, because pressure from its membership – concentrated in engineering and technical specialisms – has generated lively interest in CSR, and the union has even published its own negotiator's guide on the subject (Prospect 2008). Energy companies, in which Prospect organizes, had been developing CSR policies without consultation with their employees. In response to member demands, the union became involved with the CSR policies of a major power generating company, and later with those of other energy companies and research institutes. The union then received funding from the UK government's Department for International Development (DFID) to develop a network of representatives to monitor supply chains and raise awareness of CSR issues. Furthermore, union branches in organizations including an electricity supply company, a marine planning organization and a veterinary services supplier approached Prospect for assistance in developing appropriate CSR policies, even though the issues identified for examination were not necessarily initially identified as CSR. In these ways, CSR has opened up new policy and dialogue initiatives with employers.

Given the analysis above, it should come as no surprise that there is very little trade union training specifically on CSR issues. The interviewee at Unite stated:

> We've got our own education department ... and I'm sure CSR practices and details of CSR issues certainly come into a lot of the training programmes without being actually called CSR.

Indeed, one of our interviewees at the TUC concurred that 'a lot of ordinary bargaining and training for bargaining that goes on you could call CSR'. The TUC itself tackles the issues obliquely. For example, it has produced a bargaining guide on procurement so that union members, particularly in the public services, know how to insert CSR requirements into their employer's procurement policies and procedures. It is also producing a guide to all the different international instruments that are potentially available for CSR purposes and how they can be used to support union organization globally. Unionlearn, the TUC's training wing, trained almost 48,000 workplace representatives in 2012 in courses covering core CSR issues like green representatives, health and safety, and equality representatives amongst many others. In particular, and importantly for the CSR agenda, Unionlearn trains workplace learning representatives, who then promote further training and skills within their own workplaces in a cascade. Prospect has developed more specific training in CSR, covering areas like the ETI and procurement supply chains, with professional CSR consultants. It used outside speakers on the grounds that CSR comes with its own discourse that has to be learnt to engage with the corporate world. The union now runs stakeholder engagement training, covering international development and corporate accountability as well as environmental issues.

Union engagement with CSR

Unite provided a striking example of the way in which it had engaged with CSR discourse to defend domestic jobs. When companies produce business plans to justify factory closures and redundancies, Unite would respond by submitting amendments. Though the union does not have a policy on CSR, it would include CSR-related arguments in setting out its alternative business plan to gain leverage over the company. For example, a large food multinational had proposed outsourcing one of its products from the UK to Poland, even though 95 per cent of its consumers were in the UK. Unite argued the environmental case against the proposal: 'Common sense would say, if you've got your market in the UK, then you produce what you can in the UK to save costs and environmental impact.' Similarly, it campaigned to improve working conditions in the white-meat sector, and achieved better results when it pursued its objectives through the supermarkets by stressing the alignment of union objectives with their own CSR commitments, such as the ETI Base Code. Overall, however, Unite's engagement is driven case by case, rather than through any particular policy on CSR.

CSR achieves greatest visibility in relation to the international activities of trade unions. For example, unions are frequently able to bring pressure on companies when they fail to comply with their own CSR guidelines. Dutch colleagues of the GMB had produced an alternative report which exposed the vacuity of the CSR policies of a major multinational consumer goods company, while a Central American subsidiary of a US company, said to be producing labour-standard compliant clothing, turned out to be in receivership and had not paid any wages for three months. In such cases, the union will go public to bring the company to the negotiating table. The TUC is, meanwhile, lobbying the European Commission to ensure that EU businesses operating in Colombia – a country notorious for intimidation and assassination of trade unionists – must comply with the *Guiding Principles on Business and Human Rights*, particularly the principle of freedom of association. The context for this campaign is a forthcoming EU trade agreement with Colombia into which the TUC hopes to insert a union protection clause.

Most interviewees were, however, circumspect over the impact of CSR in defending their members' interests. Our interviewee at Unite, for example, declared:

> I think ... we have had a few successes in companies who have looked to close down factories and make many people redundant, and we've saved the plant and saved the jobs, but it couldn't be put down to any one issue. In fact, I'd probably say that the CSR side of things was minimal in the actual end result because, a lot of the time, we'd end up dealing with private equity or venture capitalists from their offices in Mayfair. So you'd go to a meeting in Mayfair, you'd provide the business brief, 'All very well, thank you very much, it's all very good – can you save us money?' and if we turn round and say, 'Well ... the bottom line is we can save £1.5 million per year by making the adjustments we're talking about,' then they'll say, 'Right, we'll sign it off and we're happy.' I tend to think that CSR ... is in the back of those people's minds.

Prospect, however, provides a qualified contrast to this view. In one electricity supply company, for example, the union secured an agreement that allows trade union delegates, through the European Works Council, to audit standardized CSR reports, which has helped to secure improvements in stakeholder engagement within the company. Prospect had made progress with an agricultural college over developing a joint CSR policy too, but admitted some setbacks. For example, new management at a marine planning organization withdrew facilities for Prospect's work on CSR because they did not see it as a union issue. Thus, our interviewees were all able to give examples of various successes with the 'embarrassment factor', where they contrasted companies' CSR commitments with their actual behaviour in labour relations.

Pension funds should also be mentioned as a means by which unions engage with CSR. Trustees of the Prospect pension fund have discussed ethical investments, while Unite was the key driver in tabling shareholder resolutions at the AGMs of two major UK retail companies on broadly CSR themes. It also collaborates with the pressure group, Fair Pensions, on other issues, such as the tar sands campaign in Canada. GMB disinvested from a major grocery company following a dispute over union recognition, while Unison has had a capital stewardship programme in place since 2007. In addition, the TUC, Unison and Unite have recently drawn up their own joint trade union voting and engagement guidelines – entitled Trade Union Share Owners (TUSO) – to allow co-ordination of their voting activity at the annual general meetings of major companies (TUC/TUSO 2013).

Unions work closely with NGOs, though their objectives may differ and their relationships may be quite complex. For example, Prospect stressed that – in contrast to the aims of some NGOs – for them CSR was not just about the environment and sustainability but also about union engagement. One of the TUC interviewees stated:

> There has been an uneasy relationship historically [between unions and NGOs] because unions are all about slow, clunky democracy. It

> might take us a while to come up with a point of view, but we're saying it on behalf of our members, whereas NGOs tend to pluck it out of thin air and, you know, it's the three or four people who are in the organization. So, it's taken a while to culturally understand each other, politically understand each other.

However, there is too a kind of symbiotic relationship as NGOs are able to pursue agendas that the unions may find more difficult. An NGO, concerned about its profile with donors, may be able to condemn corporate practices in public, while a union, with its members' interests in the company at heart, may find itself more constrained. As the GMB interviewee put it: 'it's not the campaign, it's the result. We want to get something out of it, not just to be seen to be saying the right thing'. That said, all the unions work with the major international NGOs and there are a variety of fora for joint co-operation. For example, the ETI has both an NGO and a trade union caucus, and the TUC itself has an international development group on which NGOs are represented.

UK unions are furthermore linked into the European and global labour movements through the European Trade Union Confederation (ETUC) and their affiliation to the relevant European industry federations and global union federations (Croucher and Cotton 2009). Though resolutions on CSR are occasionally tabled at these levels, most co-operative activity appears to centre on bilateral links (for example, Prospect with the Kenyan Central Organization of Trade Unions on energy generation) or through European Works Councils (as cited by Prospect in relation to the electricity supply company, noted above, and a further case in a telecommunications company).

Discussion

Prior research demonstrated that many UK unions perceive CSR as a threat as it transfers more power and discretion to managers (Preuss *et al.* 2006). Indeed, our own findings reveal a continuing, underlying mistrust towards CSR based on the fear that it is little more than a public relations exercise that may undermine union workplace organization. Our respondents emphasized that only unions have the capacity to represent and bargain on behalf of their members, and that therefore only they could genuinely deal with CSR-type issues. This perception is not surprising given the identification of the UK as an LME. As discussed at the start of this chapter, the primacy of shareholder interests embodied in the UK system of corporate governance had led to the view that labour was a variable cost to be laid off or made redundant in the short-term interests of the company. The result was an industrial relations system traditionally based on adversarial relations between workers, their unions and employers.

However, our findings also point to a more differentiated picture. Though scepticism of CSR remains strong, unions may sometimes use CSR to repackage well-established demands under a more fashionable heading in an attempt to gain leverage over a company. Unite, for example, campaigned against plans to offshore the manufacture of a food product on broadly environmental grounds, while a CSR approach to labour issues has informed the ethical procurement policies advocated by GMB in the public sector. The TUC too has been in the forefront of arguing for a broad approach to CSR to counter what it perceives as the 'pick and choose' policies of multinational companies that favour the easier items, such as philanthropy, over labour standards. Prospect, in running its own training on stakeholder engagement, insists that its members use the corporate discourse of CSR in order to gain maximum impact with employers. Unions do, therefore, act pragmatically in accepting the broad realities of the CSR agenda – even if the multinationals exert a strong influence over the agenda to start with.

In addition, the unions accept CSR-type arguments more readily in international than domestic arenas. They make extensive use of ILO regulations, OECD guidelines and the ETI Base Code, amongst other such frameworks, frequently working alongside NGOs and global union federations to campaign worldwide for decent labour standards. These frameworks sometimes long predate current concerns over CSR – the ILO, after all, was founded in 1919. What CSR does is to open up a sphere of discourse that allows unions to pursue their own objectives under a new, more fashionable banner. Fair pay and restrictions on excessive overtime are no longer sidelined as merely union demands, but are rather brought forward as strategies for multinationals designed to demonstrate internationally acceptable standards of stakeholder engagement in accordance with UN guidelines. These strategies gain particular influence at a time of global anti-capitalist awareness as multinationals strive to demonstrate legitimacy with consumers, governments, NGOs and workers, organized or not, all of whom are increasingly networked through social media.

This chapter indicates that these influences, however, are not uniform, and vary by sector, levels of labour intensity, brand vulnerability and membership profile of the unions concerned. We would suggest, for example, that the higher the technical skills profile of the union's membership, the more likely the union is to engage explicitly with CSR as pressure emerges from below. Unions are also likely to develop a behind-the-scenes approach towards multinationals over certain CSR-type issues in contrast with a more confrontational approach that may be favoured by NGOs. We must therefore guard against a determinist approach – that unions in the UK are likely to reveal adversarial attitudes towards CSR *because* the UK is an LME – and adopt a more nuanced position. The UK's LME framework sets certain parameters to the development of union attitudes, policies and levels of engagement, but many other factors allow unions a considerable degree of agency in developing CSR-type approaches to address their traditional interests.

Conclusions

Multinational companies in the UK have shifted their emphasis in recent years from a position where they tended to regard CSR as a voluntary 'add-on' to one where they acknowledge to a greater extent their responsibility for their social and environmental impacts. There is renewed interest in CSR as a consequence of the financial crisis and, as the public demands greater corporate transparency, the interest in CSR is likely to increase. Furthermore, CSR – coming after a long period of anti-union policy by Conservative governments in the 1980s and 1990s – has given unions the opportunity to raise issues, such as relating to employment practices in supply chains, which companies find more difficult to dismiss in the context of CSR than union rights.

Unions tend to see CSR initiatives as a tool that companies may use to deflect criticism from their real practices. Unions also believe that they are already covering many of the issues, but do not refer to them as CSR. However, there is also evidence of some openness towards engagement with CSR though this is generally designed to support traditional bargaining agendas, such as Unite's use of CSR-type discourse as leverage over a multinational's plans to offshore production. Union engagement with CSR, such as it was, focused much more on international rather than domestic dimensions of company practice. The TUC pointed out with satisfaction that a consensus appeared to be developing around the understanding of the labour standards aspects of CSR – particularly in relation to supply chains – based on the *UN Guiding Principles on Business and Human Rights*.

Furthermore, union engagement with CSR issues depends on a variety of contextual factors, such as sector and its level of labour intensity, the company's brand vulnerability and the union's membership profile. There is also evidence of a certain division of roles between unions, which often try to influence companies privately, and NGOs, which help to expose corporate malpractice in public. The principal question is how effective CSR will prove to be. One company may respond to public anger over its tax evasion, but another by contrast may not. Or companies may respond in industrialized countries, but feel less of a need to do so in emerging economies. Companies that embody decent terms and conditions in the UK may not necessarily embody them elsewhere in the world.

References

Albareda, L., Lozano, J.M. and Ysa, T. (2007) 'Public Policies on Corporate Social Responsibility: The Role of Governments in Europe', *Journal of Business Ethics*, 74(4): 391–407.

Amable, B. (2003) *The Diversity of Modern Capitalism*, Oxford: Oxford University Press.

Certification Officer (2012) *Annual Report of the Certification Officer 2011–2012*. London: Certification Office. Online. Available: www.certoffice.org/CertificationOfficer/files/1c/1c9b8633–3611–4a3c-b55e-23fad475d2e3.pdf (accessed 5 April 2013).

Chandler, G. (2009) 'The Amnesty International UK Business Group: Putting Human Rights on the Corporate Agenda', *Journal of Corporate Citizenship*, 33: 29–34.

Coupar, W. and Stevens, B. (1998) 'Towards a New Model of Industrial Partnership: Beyond the "HRM versus Industrial Relations" Argument', in P.R. Sparrow and M. Marchington (eds) *Human Resource Management: The New Agenda*, London: Financial Times/ Prentice Hall, pp. 145–159.

Croucher, R. and Cotton, E. (2009) *Global Unions, Global Business: Global Union Federations and International Business*, London: Middlesex University Press.

Curran, J. and Blackburn, R. A. (2001) *Researching the Small Enterprise*, London: Sage.

Davies, I.A. (2007) 'The Eras and Participants of Fair Trade: An Industry Structure/Stakeholder Perspective on the Growth of the Fair Trade Industry', *Corporate Governance*, 7(4): 455–470.

Dix, G., Forth, J. and Sisson, K. (2008) *Conflict at Work: the Pattern of Disputes in Britain since 1980*, ACAS Research Paper Ref. 03/08, London: Advisory, Conciliation and Arbitration Service. Available at: www.acas.org.uk/media/pdf/f/j/Acas_Research_Conflict_at_work_03_08-accessible-version-July-2011.pdf.

Fox, A. (1985) *History and Heritage. The Social Origins of the British Industrial Relations System*, London: Allen & Unwin.

Grayson, D. (2007) *Business-Led Corporate Responsibility Coalitions: Learning from the Example of Business in the Community in the UK*, Cranfield: Doughty Centre for Corporate Responsibility, Cranfield University.

Grinyer, J., Russell, A. and Collison, D. (1998) 'Evidence of Managerial Short-Termism in the UK', *British Journal of Management*, 9(1): 13–22.

Hall, P.A. (2007) 'The Evolution of Varieties of Capitalism in Europe', in B. Hanké, M. Rhodes and M. Thatcher (eds) *Beyond Varieties of Capitalism: Conflict, Contradictions and Complementarities in the European Economy*, Oxford: Oxford University Press.

Hall, P.A. and Soskice, D. (eds) (2001) *Varieties of Capitalism: The Institutional Foundations of Competitive Advantage*, Oxford: Oxford University Press.

Hanké, B., Rhodes, M. and Thatcher, M. (2007) 'Introduction: Beyond Varieties of Capitalism', in B. Hanké, M. Rhodes and M. Thatcher (eds) *Beyond Varieties of Capitalism: Conflict, Contradictions and Complementarities in the European Economy*, Oxford: Oxford University Press.

Heyes, J. and Rainbird, H. (2009) 'Vocational Education and Training', in M. Gold (ed.) *Employment Policy in the European Union*, Basingstoke: Macmillan.

House, R.J., Hanges, P.M., Javidan, M., Dorfman, P. and Gupta, V. (2004) *Culture, Leadership and Organizations: The GLOBE Study of 62 Societies*, Thousand Oaks, CA: Sage.

Marchington, M., Waddington, J. and Timming, A. (2011) 'Employment Relations in Britain', in G.J. Bamber, R.D. Lansbury and N. Wailes (eds) *International and Comparative Employment Relations*, London: Sage.

Mirvis, P.H. (2000) 'Transformation at Shell: Commerce and Citizenship', *Business and Society Review*, 105(1): 63–84.

Moon, J. (2005) 'United Kingdom: An Explicit Model of Business-Society Relations', in A. Habisch, J. Jonker, M. Wegner and R. Schmidpeter (eds) *Corporate Social Responsibility across Europe*, Berlin: Springer.

Preuss, L., Haunschild, A. and Matten, D. (2006) 'Trade Unions and CSR: A European Research Agenda', *Journal of Public Affairs*, 6(3/4): 256–268.

Prospect (2008) *Corporate Social Responsibility: Negotiator's Guide*, October. London: Prospect.

Sparkes, R. and Cowton, C.J. (2004) 'The Maturing of Socially Responsible Investment: A Review of the Developing Link with Corporate Social Responsibility', *Journal of Business Ethics*, 52(1): 45–57.

Traxler, F. (1995) 'Farewell to Labour Market Institutions? Organized versus Disorganized Decentralization as a Map for Industrial Relations', in C. Crouch and F. Traxler (eds) *Organized Industrial Relations in Europe: What Future?*, Aldershot: Avebury.

TUC/TUSO (2013) *Trade Union Voting and Engagement Guidelines*, March. London: Trades Union Congress. Press release available at: www.tuc.org.uk/economic-issues/corporate-governance/pensions-and-retirement/member-trustees/new-share-owner-group.

Van Wanrooy, B., Bewley, H., Bryson, A., Forth, J., Freeth, S., Stokes, L. and Wood, S. (2013) *The 2011 Workplace Employment Relations Study. First Findings*, London: Department of Business, Innovation and Skills. Online. Available at: https://www.gov.uk/government/uploads/system/uploads/attachment_data/file/175479/13-535-the-2011-workplace-employment-relations-study-first-findings1.pdf (accessed 23 April 2013).

Vitols, S. (2001) 'Varieties of Corporate Governance: Comparing Germany and the UK', in P.A. Hall and D. Soskice (eds) *Varieties of Capitalism: The Institutional Foundations of Competitive Advantage*, Oxford: Oxford University Press.

Ward, H. and Smith, C. (2006) *Corporate Social Responsibility at a Crossroads: Futures for CSR in the UK to 2015*, London: International Institute for Environment and Development.

Whitley, R. (1992) *European Business Systems: Firms and Markets in their National Contexts*, London: Sage.

13 European trade unions and CSR

Common dilemmas, different responses

Chris Rees, Lutz Preuss and Michael Gold

Introduction

This book has examined the relationship between corporate social responsibility (CSR) and trade unions across 11 European countries: Belgium, Finland, France, Germany, Hungary, Lithuania, Poland, Slovenia, Spain, Sweden and the United Kingdom. In this final chapter we offer a summary of the areas of distinctiveness within these countries as well as some conclusions addressing common themes that have emerged across many of them. Whilst national differences in attempts by unions to define and engage with CSR have been identified before, our book provides a more comprehensive coverage going beyond individual or small numbers of countries. Our aim has been to undertake a 'mapping exercise', profiling national differences through the lens of comparative institutionalism and sketching contemporary trade union perspectives and positions.

The chapter begins with two sections summarizing our key findings on the development of CSR across the 11 countries and trade union responses to it. By way of conclusion, it then draws attention to particular themes that emerged as significant during the course of the research. These include the relationship between CSR discourse and traditional trade union agendas, the contrasts between domestic and international dimensions of CSR, and the relationship between trade unions and non-governmental organizations (NGOs). Finally, the chapter suggests how trade union attitudes towards CSR across Europe can best be characterized, in broad terms, and offers some indication of how trade unions might usefully engage with this area in the future.

National variation in the development of CSR

Our approach throughout the book has been to understand CSR in national context, to situate the development of CSR within specific economic and political regimes, and against the background of particular historical developments, rather than to follow the more popular conception of CSR as a generalist corporate blueprint for particular practices. We have considered within 11 different national settings how notions of CSR are generated, maintained and challenged.

In mapping these national patterns, we can see certain broad groupings emerging from our study. One of these might loosely be called the 'Nordic model', based on our findings from Finland and Sweden. In both these countries institutionalized patterns of interaction between employers and trade unions have been established over a long period, there is an acceptance of collective regulation, and trade unions have a strong legitimate status, with mandatory and codified rights. In recent years, CSR has become increasingly important for Finnish companies, and both companies and public authorities in Finland have promoted the application and communication of CSR in various forms, such as codes of conduct, standards, audits and reports. Deregulation of the national business system and increasing globalization are important reasons for this. Despite certain reservations, Finnish trade unions in general have a highly positive attitude towards CSR. This can be explained with reference to the national context. The unions view themselves as having a strong legitimate status in the Finnish institutional system, and they do not appear to be experiencing any marked sense of threat from CSR. Moreover, key features of the country's value system have been identified as pragmatism, high risk-aversion, co-operation, trust and honesty. These are considered to be important social resources, even if it is now acknowledged that Finns' values have become more individualistic and efficiency-oriented, and they can be seen as providing broad guiding principles for responsible business activities.

Sweden, like Finland, is commonly identified as a co-ordinated market economy (CME), with institutions reflecting higher levels of reliance on non-market co-ordination than those in more liberal market economies (LMEs). Whilst many of the prerequisites for the so-called 'Swedish model' have been challenged and eroded, Sweden remains one of the European countries with the lowest income differentials, the largest public sector, the highest labour-force participation rates and the strongest position for organized labour. Sweden has long been marked by a clear division of roles between the state, employers and trade unions – with issues directly related to conditions of work being negotiated between the labour market actors, while social and economic policies have been the domain of the state. Consequently the 'Swedish model' did not encourage concepts such as CSR, and until the early 1990s Swedish companies outwardly appeared to be rather indifferent towards their social responsibilities. However, since the latter part of the 1990s the concept can now be considered an established phenomenon in Swedish business, promoted not so much by the traditional economic actors – the state, employers and trade unions – but more by business itself and by intergovernmental organizations, such as the United Nations and the European Commission.

Another country commonly depicted as a CME, or as an example of 'continental European capitalism' (CEC) (Amable 2003), is Belgium. As in the case of Finland and Sweden, these characterizations stress the importance of relatively stable political and social relations, and trade unions and employers' associations remain powerful organizations. However, unlike Finland and Sweden, Belgium presents some particular features in relation to economic, linguistic, political and regional divides, which have led to successive reforms of the state structure since the early 1970s. Over this period Belgium has evolved from a unitary state into a federal state with distinct communities, regions and language areas. CSR in turn reflects this complexity, with initiatives organized at both national and regional levels. From 2000 to 2008, CSR was strongly promoted by the federal government and other stakeholders, with the number of CSR networks and initiatives increasing significantly and including a broad range of stakeholders such as business, government, trade unions and not-for-profit organizations. In 2006 the federal government adopted the Belgian CSR Reference Framework which was established through a multi-stakeholder consultation, a landmark document providing a common basis for all organizations in the country.

Germany is often described as the archetypal CME, with close relationships between companies, their suppliers and customers, internal decision-making structures and processes that are strongly consensus-based, and a longer-term orientation towards company finance. The industrial relations system is highly institutionalized, with legal codification of union rights, both at the company and industry levels. The principle of 'social partnership' within a corporatist structure provides a framework for collective bargaining. Consequently the importance of trade unions for Germany's national business system remains strong. It is notable, however, that, compared with other European countries, Germany still appears to be relatively uncharted territory in terms of the concept of CSR. German firms do indicate certain types of engagement that can be described as CSR, but much of what is commonly considered as CSR is determined by civil society and enforced by the state. Given the German institutional and cultural context, the idea that firms themselves should develop their own standards of corporate responsibility has not become firmly established. This can be explained with reference to the argument that voluntary CSR practices will tend to be more common in liberal economies, where they act as a substitute for institutionalized forms of stakeholder participation, whereas in countries like Germany – where codified co-determination and strong employment rights already exist – one is likely to see less developed forms of voluntary CSR activity, and CSR will thus remain more 'implicit' than 'explicit' (Matten and Moon 2008).

Various authors have portrayed Spain as either approaching the CME model whilst lacking some of its formal elements, or alternatively as part of an intermediate category dubbed 'Latin capitalism', 'mixed market economy' or 'state-influenced market economy', in which the state is seen as a leading and influential actor (Rhodes and Apeldoorn 1998; Molina and Rhodes 2006; Schmidt 2009). Certainly the driving forces behind the implementation of CSR practices in Spain – which are still in their early stages – are national and regional governments, economic actors like large companies and, especially, the two largest trade union federations, UGT and CCOO. The agreements between governments, employers' associations and unions that are central to the Latin or mixed capitalist model are the umbrella under which particular CSR initiatives are taken. The law encourages the voluntary implementation of CSR policies, and independently from government there are various other initiatives in which trade unions play an important role. Perhaps the most relevant is the CSR Research Centre, in which NGOs, universities, CCOO and other experts collaborate to produce and exchange ideas to promote CSR initiatives. Spain's economy seems now to be moving towards the (weak) LME pole as a result of a number of deregulatory reforms that the conservative government has implemented since it took power in 2011. This transformation has affected the dynamics and the role of unions and employers' associations in the national business system, perhaps leading towards what has been termed 'disorganized decentralization' (Traxler 1995).

Like Spain, the main characteristic of the French national business system is commonly seen as the central role of the state. The state is a principal investor, a significant owner of key enterprises, and a major influence over the development of individual companies through strong business legislation. The French national business system has been represented as an example of the 'continental European model' (Amable 2003), or as occupying an intermediate position between the Anglo-American and the German models. Whatever the label, French unions are highly institutionalized and considered legitimate by the state and employer organizations. The state has a strong influence over the strategies and actions of French trade union representatives in the field of CSR. An example is the decision of the government to involve unions and other stakeholders in the national strategy on sustainable development. Being regularly consulted by the government on economic, social and environmental issues, the major French unions have been encouraged to develop their own proactive strategies towards CSR, even though major differences in approach remain between them. The most visible activity of the French public authorities in the field of CSR concerns the development of mandatory social and environmental reporting, which guarantees extensive information about corporate social and environmental strategies, practices and performance, hence again encouraging trade union activity in the field of CSR.

The UK occupies a particular place in typologies of national business models across Europe, and is often considered to be the principal European LME. There is no tradition of continental-style corporatism in the UK. Rather, the system is based on 'voluntarism' – that is, autonomous relationships between the parties, in which legislation plays a relatively minor role. The UK business system is generally identified with short-term finance, deregulated labour markets, generalist education and strong product market competition, rather than the long-term co-operative relations between firms and the active role of the state characteristic of CMEs. Issues concerning the responsibilities of business, especially towards employees as key stakeholders, have a long history and are central to trade union concerns, and yet have not necessarily received the same degree of attention within the discourse of CSR. Again this can be explained with reference to the way in which CSR has developed within a distinctive national institutional setting. The primacy given to shareholder value in the UK, coupled with the voluntarist system of industrial relations, have acted against the development of high-trust employment relationships and the co-ordinated regulation of the social obligations of business. As a result, CSR has evolved more as a response to deregulation and corporate scandals, driven by responsibly minded businesses and NGOs, rather than under pressure from trade unions. That said, since the 1990s the range of concerns addressed under the banner of CSR has widened considerably.

As well as covering northern and western Europe, our book has also encompassed a number of countries from eastern Europe. Certain commonalities are evident across these countries, alongside distinct national peculiarities, which are again explicable in terms of particular historical and institutional legacies. In Hungary, CSR is, on the one hand, frequently equated with the social welfare role of enterprises before the end of socialism, and, on the other hand, has been more commonly associated in recent years with inward foreign direct investment (FDI). Prior to 1989 enterprises in Hungary controlled a significant proportion of workers' lives, in terms of organizing housing, holidays and leisure activities, which defined the parameters of social responsibility quite differently from western European perspectives. The country is now a major recipient of FDI in the manufacturing sector, and was a regional first mover in offering attractive packages to encourage MNCs to make pioneering investments during the uncertain period following the fall of communism. Most of this FDI comes from CME economies – such as Austria, Germany, Luxemburg and the Netherlands – and there is thus an opportunity to assess how far home country CSR practices are successfully transmitted to host country subsidiaries. In essence, our trade union respondents felt that the import of institutions from CME countries had not been a success, due to their mismatch with domestic economic circumstances, the minimal role for trade unions, and the underdevelopment of civil society more generally. This supports the argument that where host country institutions are weak, MNCs are able to introduce home country practices more selectively. CSR practices at enterprise level in Hungary are therefore largely driven by foreign definitions of the term which are not necessarily in line with long-established domestic understandings of 'social responsibility'.

In Lithuania trade unions are also relatively weak and CSR is, as in Hungary, associated almost entirely with foreign companies. Lithuania is often labelled as a liberal market economy (LME), based on its high degree of labour market flexibility, lack of collective bargaining, short-term investment, high job mobility and weak employee commitment. Overall the country is marked by a lack of both transparency in its business operations and integrity of its social institutions, which has led Lithuanian society to regard notions of social welfare and well-being as mere rhetoric and to trivialize violations of the public interest, all of which significantly undermines the development of CSR. Negative attitudes from employers and the wider society towards trade unions also persist from the Soviet past when they gained a reputation for ineffectiveness. Lack of recognition hinders unions from gaining wider support for their activities, and their engagement with CSR is therefore, not surprisingly, weak. Trade unions also lack understanding of CSR as a set of tools that they might engage with to help employers improve business performance, which in turn might strengthen their position in social dialogue. Accordingly, they tend to view foreign multinational companies, as well as the processes of social and environmental harmonization in the European Union, as the most likely drivers of change.

Slovenia is one of the relatively successful new European Union member states, and one of the few transition countries to join both the EU and the Eurozone with a fairly robust economy. The country has been characterized as a CME, which is rare among the post-communist transition countries. Slovenia also has a strong trade union movement, dating back to the Yugoslav model of company self-management, and high trade union density compared with other transition countries. There is relatively high employment protection, social dialogue with centralized wage bargaining, and long-term capital market and bank-based finance for companies. However, while workers' participation has been formalized to some extent, there is a lack of transparent corporate governance practices in Slovenian companies. Since 2007 the corporatist model of industrial relations has been significantly eroded in the face of widening social cleavages. This has resulted from a combination of the right-of-centre government policies in force until 2008, the global economic crisis, the pressures of Eurozone membership, the recent decline in union density, and corporate governance issues within Slovenian companies. The concept of CSR has entered into debate only recently. Despite the emphasis placed on CSR by EU institutions, trade unions in Slovenia are not a visible stakeholder in CSR. Whilst some positive initiatives have been emerging, at a national level these are relatively insignificant compared with other EU countries.

Finally, CSR is also a relatively new concept in public discourse in Poland. As in other eastern European countries, trade unions began to explore the field of CSR fully only after the country joined the EU in 2004 and, although they have advanced considerably in their engagement with the concept, they are still at the early stages of the process. Poland can be described as a case of 'embedded neoliberalism' (Bohle and Greskovits

2012), where a struggle between marketization and social protection takes place. The industrial relations system is pluralistic, with low density of union and employer organization, as well as moderate coverage of collective agreements. In the early phase of transformation CSR did not make a breakthrough into the mainstream of public discourse, but following EU accession attitudes began to change, and CSR became quite a fashionable concept, although this fashion rarely translated into action. In the latter part of the 2000s, a trend to integrate CSR into corporate strategies became visible, although the arrival of the global economic crisis has called further progress into question. In Poland the origin of capital is an important factor differentiating the approach of companies towards CSR. Companies with foreign capital, especially multinationals, tend to display a higher level of CSR awareness than domestically owned firms. However, multinationals are also subject to criticism from trade unions, which note a reluctance on the part of international businesses to include employment and labour-related issues in their reporting activities.

Our starting point for mapping the nature and development of CSR within particular European countries has been to draw broadly upon the comparative institutionalist approach. In these terms we can see considerable diversity across the 11 countries represented in the book, with distinct differences emerging between so-called liberal and co-ordinated economies, and particular political and economic legacies impacting upon the understanding and implementation of CSR in post-socialist economies. However, whilst labels such as LME and CME are useful as ideal-typical constructs, they also mask considerable variety and nuance within national patterns, and the nature of CSR, as well as trade union approaches towards it, cannot simply be read off from the standard national system typologies. The status of the concept of CSR, and its degree of embeddedness in civil society, varies according to a range of factors: the strength of state intervention, the power of industrial relations actors, the level of foreign direct investment, the degree of engagement with European-level debates, and the extent of non-governmental initiatives. All these factors combine to fashion a particular role for trade unions in each country, and influence both their ability and their willingness to engage with CSR.

Trade union engagement with CSR

Drawing upon a comparative institutionalist approach allows us to examine how the boundaries between business and society are constructed in different ways in different national settings. Seen through this theoretical lens, CSR comes to be considered not merely as the private concern of companies, but rather as a broader 'mode of governance' (Brammer *et al.* 2012) which reflects specific national institutional configurations. In many countries, trade unions play a significant role within this process of governance. Having sketched some of the key features of each of the 11 countries in the previous section, along with their implications for the role of trade unions in CSR, we now examine union perspectives and strategies in more detail. We consider what unions make of the rise of CSR, the extent to which they engage with corporate initiatives in this area, the degree to which they have developed their own explicit CSR policies, and their connections with national and European-level policy developments.

We began above with the Nordic model represented in our study by Finland and Sweden. In Finland our trade union respondents emphasized that unions should adopt a proactive stance of engagement with CSR, in addition to their traditional focus on collective bargaining, and reportedly did not feel unduly threatened by CSR. On the whole, attitudes towards CSR in the Finnish trade unions were the most positive in our sample, with CSR often regarded as a potential contributor to the development of working life and to dialogue between management and employees. Topics like wellbeing at work, continuing professional development, employee participation and flexible working were all typically considered relevant to CSR. Several interviewees agreed on the legitimacy of the European Commission's definition of CSR, and most Finnish trade unions adopt EU terminology in talking about CSR.

In Sweden our trade union respondents would, like their Finnish counterparts, explicitly use the term CSR when dealing with multinational businesses or acting at the intergovernmental level, and some of them recounted participation in EU, UN and OECD initiatives. The prevalence of CSR – which they generally regarded as a 'foreign concept' – depended, in their view, not on sector but on enterprise size and international orientation. However, there were a range of positions on CSR among the union federations, from LO (which actively engages with the concept) at one end of the spectrum, to SACO (which has not even discussed it) at the other. The degree of engagement reflects how far the unions perceive any overlap between CSR and traditional trade union concerns. In this regard, a number of respondents pointed to the voluntary nature of CSR compared with the 'binding' agreements which trade unions prefer. Consequently the Swedish trade unions seek to promote global framework agreements (GFAs) with multinational companies rather than voluntary CSR tools such as codes of conduct and sustainability accounting.

This scepticism towards voluntary CSR was more pronounced among our Belgian trade union respondents, among whom we find a clear expression of distrust towards the concept, or rather towards the way it is perceived to be used by companies. International conventions, such as those adopted by the International Labour Organization (ILO), are seen as sufficient in terms of freedom of association, the right to collective bargaining and all other fundamental principles and rights at work. The added-value of CSR is consequently questioned. Indeed our respondents described CSR as a concept that had been defined solely by, and for, companies, and suggested that the name itself does not encourage workers to participate in the debate, but instead is rather exclusive. Moreover they felt that CSR too often remains at the level of rhetoric, providing a convenient way for companies to present themselves as 'responsible organizations', and serves as a 'marketing tool' with little substance and meaning. None of the Belgian trade unions we studied has, or has had, any formal internal structures to deal with CSR. The concept is discussed to some extent, but perhaps in a rather superficial way and only within the upper levels of the union hierarchy.

Trade unions in Germany also insist that CSR commitments should be laid down in binding agreements between companies and unions, in order to prevent companies from being allowed to define responsible behaviour for themselves. There is considerable scepticism towards the more management-centred approach to CSR, which unions see as mere 'window-dressing'. According to our respondents, many companies boast of their ability to ensure the quality of their products throughout their supply chains, and yet are unable to make binding statements concerning compliance with employee rights. Unions complain, in particular, that the verification of companies' compliance with voluntary agreements, or with social or environmental labels, is practically impossible. As a result, they too advocate GFAs, as binding and traceable agreements between companies and global union federations, individual unions or European works councils. They insist that only once international labour standards and the additional standards of the ILO have been fully observed and enforced can voluntary commitments by companies make an additional contribution. From a CSR perspective, trade unions are also just one stakeholder among many, which can conflict with their understanding of themselves as unique stakeholders *sui generis*, derived from the legal foundations of the German industrial relations system. In general, German trade unions have adopted a position that involves actively addressing CSR *issues* without necessarily explicitly relating them to the *concept* of CSR.

Our evidence suggests that trade unions in Spain adopt a broadly favourable stance towards CSR, at least in terms of perceiving it as an opportunity to render companies accountable for their sustainability claims. CSR is generally understood by the unions as a platform for demanding transparency from companies, especially with respect to managerial salaries and benefits. At the same time, Spanish unions acknowledge that CSR provides an opportunity for companies to improve their public image, and to promote a set of principles that may not necessarily lead to genuine improvements in their business practices. Evidence of a longer-standing trade union interest in CSR is revealed in the growing number of courses offered to train worker representatives in the principles of CSR and their introduction into collective bargaining. Several unions have set up research centres to help disseminate and monitor appropriate corporate policies. Trade unions' promotion of CSR initiatives is usually the result of three elements: the individual efforts of a certain affiliate or official, exposure to CSR practices in large companies, and/or participation in training schemes developed by unions.

All the major trade unions in France report involvement in the negotiation of agreements at company level related to sustainable development or CSR, whether these are transnational company agreements, national or site agreements. Apart from CGT-FO, all unions emphasize the importance of the legislation on mandatory reporting of companies' social and environmental impacts, and aim at its improvement. The *Environment Grenelle* process led the unions to develop a clear perspective regarding the way in which they perceive CSR and their respective strategies inside and outside their organization. All the unions we studied have developed a communications policy and a discourse on CSR at the intersectoral level, mainly to allow their members to respond to potential requests for information from companies. However, French unions' engagement in disseminating the principles of sustainable development and CSR among their members differs according to their strategies. As the union that aims to be the most proactive in this field, CFDT has developed a large number of initiatives at both sectoral and regional level. The intersectoral level includes training sessions to help members understand the challenges and consider possible activity in the area of sustainable development and CSR.

In the UK there are also a number of trade unions reporting a fairly advanced level of engagement with CSR. The CSR debate has become more sophisticated in the recent past due to an increasing consensus over definitions of the issues based on documents like the UN *Guiding Principles on Business and Human Rights*. Central to the unions' understanding of CSR is the nature of stakeholder relationships. The TUC believes that the business community had earlier adopted a narrower approach, based largely on philanthropic activity, but that it has now accepted a broader understanding of CSR that includes workers and unions. The principal argument here is that companies should accept responsibility for the impact of their activities on workers, communities and the environment, particularly along their supply chains. Union engagement with CSR issues depends on a variety of contextual factors, such as sector, levels of labour intensity, the company's brand vulnerability and the union's membership profile. Pension funds should also be mentioned as a means by which some unions, like Prospect and Unite, engage with CSR. However, many unions in the UK still consider CSR to be used primarily as a shield to deflect criticism from company practices, and they are likely to remain sceptical unless good corporate practices across the range of CSR issues are open to formal trade union verification.

In Hungary CSR is still largely perceived as a concept imported from abroad. Where there is recognition of company-level social responsibility this tends to be in the continuation of popular socialist-era programmes, such as generous pension or health care schemes. As such, there is a developed sense among workers of what the 'social responsibilities' of firms should be, based on pre-1989 paternalistic company policies. Beyond this, the uptake of 'Western-style' CSR is hampered by a limited domestic discourse, weak unions, a sparse NGO presence, as well as a pre-established discourse in MNC subsidiaries. There was a general recognition among our respondents, although not an unchallenged one, that German companies paid more attention to worker involvement and took their social impact more seriously, but this was not necessarily linked to CSR. Regardless of how CSR is perceived, however, there is very little action taken by unions to engage with the concept. None of the Hungarian unions we studied has specific policies on CSR, and neither was CSR discussed as a topic nor used as a reference point internally, perhaps reflecting the lack of a domestic debate over the term more generally.

Our findings concerning Lithuanian trade unions' understanding of CSR, as well as their engagement with it, indicate that they tend to associate CSR either with personal duty and exemplary role-model behaviour towards people and the environment, or with a company's approach towards employee representation, the environment and sound accounting principles. The tendency of the Lithuanian unions to speak about CSR from a normative perspective is notable, and most definitions of the concept were infused with a morally-laden vocabulary denoting obligation. Few substantive actions have been taken from a CSR perspective by union representatives, and trade union policies with respect to the promotion of CSR still seem to be lacking. CSR remains a genuine challenge when bearing in mind the small size of companies that dominate the Lithuanian business system. With respect to the integration of CSR into their structures, none of the unions we studied had a CSR-related policy or a CSR officer.

CSR is a fairly recent phenomenon in Slovenia. The interviews with our trade union respondents revealed a familiarity with the basic idea of CSR, although usually there was no reference to the concept itself but rather to specific areas that come under the CSR umbrella. There seems to be no common definition of the term, and trade unions feel no special affinity with it. Overall, CSR as a concept was not seen as particularly effective and, as one interviewee said, it is generally regarded as no more than 'words on paper', reflecting a high degree of scepticism towards corporate pronouncements in this area. Slovenian unions have no official documents or policies on CSR-related issues, apart from some basic materials prepared for member education purposes at seminars and conferences. That said, our respondents tended to see CSR as a very important issue for trade unions, and one that should be better understood by their members. A number of them agreed in principle with the 'business case' for CSR and equated this with the long-term success of organizations, which they saw as beneficial for all parties – owners, managers and employees.

In Poland, the concept of CSR is similarly not well known among rank-and-file trade union members, and union leaders – whose knowledge is more advanced – often treat CSR with caution, seeing it as a long-term threat rather than as an opportunity for organized labour. Considering the essentially adversarial nature of Polish industrial relations, this reluctance to embrace CSR is hardly surprising, as trade unions often suspect there is a hidden agenda on the part of employers engaging in CSR activities. Unions have consequently emphasized the importance of mechanisms that allow for the verification of CSR claims, such as CSR labels, mandatory information and auditing. For a number of our respondents, CSR is again seen as an essentially 'foreign' concept, which they tend to perceive as a non-affordable luxury, or even as mere capitalist propaganda. The approach of companies towards CSR is perceived as highly instrumental, with business interested in CSR only insofar as it provides a viable vehicle for public relations. None of the Polish unions we studied treats CSR as a strategic priority, as manifested by the lack of relevant CSR policies or documents. However, whilst the involvement of trade unions in CSR in Poland is moderate, the influx of EU funds which became accessible after EU-enlargement has boosted the interest of trade unions in CSR-related initiatives.

In terms of trade unions' understanding of CSR, their degree of engagement with corporate initiatives in the area, and the importance they attach to the concept internally, our study suggests that many unions consider CSR as an imported or foreign concept, as more relevant for larger companies, and as characterized by a degree of informality and superficiality which severely weakens its impact. Consequently most unions will tend, not surprisingly, to direct their energies towards negotiating more formal agreements around CSR-related issues, rather than relying on the voluntary initiative of firms. We also found that CSR as a specific concept has in most cases not become integrated into the unions' own policy development processes. There are variations across countries, with trade unions in some cases being more likely to have developed training courses around CSR issues or to have collaborated with NGOs, as well as government bodies, in the establishment of CSR campaigns and research initiatives. Overall, however, we find that where trade unions do engage more fully with the concept of CSR, their primary aim is to use it as a vehicle to promote their more established concerns, such as those relating to labour rights, employment protection and the quality of work.

Emerging themes

So far in this concluding chapter we have sketched the nature of CSR in each country in our study and provided a broad outline of how trade unions have conceptualized and engaged with the concept. Whilst the book emphasizes national distinctiveness and stresses the need to frame understanding of these issues within specific historical and institutional trajectories, there have also been several common themes recurring throughout the country chapters.

Trade union attitudes towards CSR – threat or opportunity?

One of these themes might be described as the fundamental dichotomy at the heart of trade union attitudes towards CSR, wherein the discourse of CSR and its manifestation in corporate policy are seen at the same time as both a threat and an opportunity. The threat arises from the potential for the rhetoric of CSR to be appropriated by companies merely as a means to improve corporate image, with little substance in terms of practice, and indeed with the possibility of providing a smokescreen which cloaks damaging activities. The opportunity lies in the potential that CSR commitments afford to trade unions for positive engagement with companies around issues which overlap and complement their more established concerns and priorities.

In every country we see our trade union respondents expressing some variant or mix of these two positions, with an emphasis towards one pole or the other depending upon their particular circumstances, political viewpoints and experiences. Even in those countries where trade unions are the most positive in terms of regarding CSR as largely in tune with their aims and objectives, there are nevertheless concerns expressed. In Finland, for example, many of our respondents suggested that CSR could be used as a cover for unacceptable practices, or as a means to undermine or bypass established channels of trade union representation and collective bargaining. Likewise in Sweden the emergence of the 'foreign concept' of CSR is perceived by many trade unionists as challenging the role of trade unions as the pre-eminent 'opposite number' to employers and the state. We found a particularly strong expression of scepticism and mistrust of CSR amongst our Belgian trade union respondents. They suggested that, despite the rhetoric of stakeholder engagement, in reality CSR may be having a negative impact on social dialogue, providing a legitimate bypass for companies to avoid engaging with trade unions. A respondent in Slovenia raised concerns over the consequences for workers' pay if companies devote increasing resources to caring for the environment. And in Germany the view was forcefully expressed that voluntary CSR agreements, whilst on the surface appearing to benefit workers, could at the same time undermine obligatory standards or encourage a movement towards deregulation. Our German respondents, like many others, stressed that companies should firstly implement international labour standards, such as those agreed by the ILO, and only then engage in voluntary CSR initiatives.

Whilst a degree of scepticism towards CSR was universal, we also found cases where trade union attitudes tended, in broad terms, towards the more positive end of the spectrum. In Spain, for example, a number of our respondents stressed that the CSR agenda gives unions scope to push for improvements in working conditions at plant level, and as such CSR may be less a means to undermine collective bargaining and more a complement to it. Some unions considered that CSR offered them an opportunity to expand their relevance in three ways: creating strategic alliances with other organizations (such as through CSR research centres); penetrating the difficult world of SMEs; and establishing co-operation with other, in particular international, labour organizations. In Slovenia too, our respondents tended to view CSR not as something that would undermine their activities, but rather as an important issue for trade unions that should be more broadly understood by their members, with the business case for CSR being generally accepted.

This more positive stance towards CSR is in some cases specific to particular trade unions, reflecting decisions on the part of senior officials to pursue the CSR agenda with greater purpose in an effort to align it more squarely with their wider aims. The role of such trade union 'champions' was referred to in several of our chapters, including Belgium, Slovenia, Spain and the UK. Two examples stand out. The first is that of Prospect in the UK. Here membership pressure led union representatives to actively engage with companies on CSR. Some energy companies, in which Prospect organizes, had been developing CSR policies without consultation with their employees, and the union became involved in response to member demands. The union then received funding from the UK government's Department for International Development (DFID) to develop a network of representatives to monitor supply chains and raise awareness of CSR issues. As a result CSR has opened up new policy and dialogue opportunities, and the union has developed specific training in CSR, covering areas like the Ethical Trading Initiative (ETI) and public procurement. This activity has since extended to stakeholder engagement training, covering international development and corporate accountability as well as environmental issues. The second example of a union CSR 'champion' comes from Belgium, and stands out as an exceptional case in that national context, as most Belgian trade unions expressed a high degree of cynicism and antipathy towards CSR. ACV-CSC Leuven is a case where the interest and drive of one particular official has led to the union paying considerable attention to the concept of CSR. According to this official, CSR challenges trade unions to broaden their horizons and can help them to change their established models and develop their activities in imaginative ways.

In broad terms, the evidence provided by our respondents would suggest that most trade unions have a somewhat dichotomous attitude towards CSR, viewing it simultaneously as both a threat and an opportunity. The balance between the two depends upon various factors, such as the political stance of unions, the extent to which unions see any overlap between CSR and their traditional concerns, levels of trust between unions and companies, as well as the particular priorities and strategies of individual unions and union officers.

Differences between the domestic and international context for CSR

Whether CSR is considered a threat or an opportunity for trade unions is also partly linked to developments in the international sphere, and to perceptions in some countries of CSR as a 'foreign concept' that represents a challenge to domestic understandings of the proper role of business in society. A further common theme running through our country analyses has been the different challenges posed by CSR in the international as opposed to the domestic context. Respondents in every country referred to the contrast between a domestic understanding of the responsibilities of business that has evolved historically over a considerable period, juxtaposed with a more recently emerging international agenda – set both at the intergovernmental policy level and through the activities of inward-investing MNCs – which compels unions to adopt new positions and strategies.

Finnish unions, for example, whilst confident in their established position within their own country, do not feel they have the same institutional support in the international arena. In the domestic context, formal regulations and collective agreements, together with key Finnish social values such as trustworthiness, provided the framework for social responsibility in companies, whereas in the international context different standards and recommendations are encountered, and neither intergovernmental regulation nor common values in employee–employer relationships could be relied upon. Consequently Finnish unions are increasingly networking, negotiating and acting in co-operation with foreign unions, NGOs and multinational corporations.

A number of unions stressed that they place considerable emphasis on pushing international firms to negotiate formal GFAs, which are considered far preferable to the frequently more informal and voluntary nature of CSR initiatives. So in Sweden the officer with the CSR brief at LO, when asked if his union attempted to influence the design and implementation of MNC codes of conduct, replied that he focused instead on encouraging companies to sign GFAs, as these refer to ILO conventions and prescribe how a company should act in its home as well as in foreign countries. The sectoral union respondents in Sweden acknowledged that these agreements are often rather loosely formulated, but they are considered to be 'working documents' that the unions can progressively aim to 'tighten'. In the UK, trade unions' understanding of CSR also generally revolves more around international issues – such as ensuring corporate compliance with ILO conventions and other international regulations and campaigns on, for example, fair trade – rather than domestic issues. UK unions make extensive use of ILO regulations, OECD guidelines and the ETI Base Code, amongst other such frameworks, frequently working alongside NGOs and global union federations to campaign worldwide for decent labour standards.

Some of our respondents emphasized how the nature of CSR and the challenges it poses also vary according to company size, with large organizations tending to have the most developed CSR policies. In Slovenia, according to our interviewees, the widest differences in levels of CSR implementation are related to company size and overall business success, with larger and more successful companies more likely to take CSR-related issues seriously. In Lithuania, as in Hungary, CSR is a recent phenomenon that has so far gained most attention and engagement from large foreign companies which are more experienced players in global markets and possess greater resources to implement CSR strategies. The effect of company size is also evident in Spain, where only large international companies appear to have adopted CSR tools, with SMEs tending to ignore them. In the case of MNCs, public opinion, concerns over corporate image and trade union presence may all play a role – independently from genuine conviction – in explaining deployment of CSR policies. In the case of SMEs, by contrast, a lack of trade union presence, the low cost of non-compliance with CSR principles, or simple ignorance of CSR policies has led to most SMEs remaining largely CSR-free. This of course represents a challenge for those unions who see benefits in CSR tools and would wish to encourage their adoption in smaller enterprises, especially as many of the economies in our study have high proportions of SMEs.

There is also a shared belief among our interviewees that MNCs have helped to spread awareness amongst union representatives of CSR practices that are already in operation at plant level in other countries. Additionally, involvement of trade unions in their European industry federations or global union federations has also contributed to greater awareness of CSR issues among union officials. Hence it seems that internationalization processes are fostering a degree of trade union learning through the dissemination of CSR practices from countries where the debates are more sophisticated. The development of international framework agreements initiated in the early 1990s by large French companies (such as Danone and Rhodia) has, for example, offered opportunities for unions to negotiate on CSR. From this point of view, certain companies and unions might be viewed as 'institutional entrepreneurs' (Greenwood and Suddaby 2006) that have contributed to a dynamic conducive to CSR. Many of these frameworks long predate current concerns over CSR, but CSR appears to open up a sphere of discourse that allows unions to pursue their own objectives under a new, more fashionable banner.

Relations between trade unions and non-governmental organizations

In considering how trade unions engage with the discourse of CSR at the international as well as the domestic level, we have encountered numerous instances where collaboration between unions and non-governmental organizations (NGOs) has occurred. Such collaboration is a further common theme that pervades most, but not all, of the previous country chapters. Whilst unions can clearly benefit from these relationships, co-operation with NGOs can also be problematic, and in a small number of countries it is effectively non-existent.

In Finland, our trade union respondents considered active co-operation with NGOs, both domestically and internationally, as crucial. Several NGOs or other movements and campaigns were mentioned, such as Finnwatch, Fair Trade and the Clean Clothes Campaign. Similarly in Sweden, Unionen was involved in a project called Fair Travel, a collaboration with the Church of Sweden and the Swedish Hotel and Restaurant Workers' Union, aimed at evaluating codes of conduct of companies in the travel industry. In the UK trade unions also work alongside NGOs in various campaigns, such as the ETI, a joint initiative of businesses, trade unions, NGOs and the UK government's Department for International Development to improve working conditions in international supply chains. In Spain, NGOs, universities, the union CCOO and other experts jointly set up a CSR research centre to exchange ideas, promote initiatives and monitor corporate practices. To some extent, collaboration with other stakeholders seems to have enabled certain trade unions to address one of their main concerns about CSR, centred around its voluntary nature, by pressing companies to make firmer commitments to responsible business practices.

Whilst the examples above were generally seen as positive initiatives on the part of unions, other examples were provided of tensions between unions and NGOs. For example, some of our German respondents detailed how NGOs tend to put pressure on companies by disseminating negative information about them, whereas unions do not wish to undermine corporate reputations, as doing so could endanger jobs, both in Germany and abroad. Similarly, in Slovenia, KNG cited the example of a potential conflict between the union and an NGO that arose from unsupported claims made by local environmentalists. In France we found evidence of trade unions developing a variety of positions towards NGOs. While CFDT, CGT and CFTC co-operate closely with NGOs, CFE-CGC and CGT-FO do not, and in fact criticize their growing role in relation to social regulation. CFE-CGC argues that NGOs tend to focus on protecting the environment, whereas trade unions have a specific mandate to defend workers' interests, and these two are not always mutually compatible. The union insists, moreover, that NGOs lack legitimacy and representativeness. For CGT-FO, NGO leaders often represent only themselves, while unions communicate with their membership and have transparent processes for appointing leaders and developing strategies. These major differences explain, according to our CGT-FO respondents, why traditional bilateral social dialogue between employers and unions should not be widened to include NGOs.

Scepticism towards collaborating with NGOs was particularly evident in two cases. In Belgium, where mistrust of CSR was strongest among all the countries in the sample, unions said that they had received invitations to participate in stakeholder fora organized by the government, either at the regional or national level, or by multi-actor networks on

CSR. However, they all admitted that they had not responded positively to the invitations as they saw no need to attend, and had very low expectations about the outcomes of the discussions. There was a similar situation in Lithuania, where our trade union interviewees also did not have much experience in co-operating with NGOs. Although they considered NGOs to be conducting important work, they regarded their activities as very different from that of trade unions, so union/NGO collaboration might divert attention from union/employer dialogue towards wider and more diluted forms of campaigning. Moreover, they saw the sheer number of NGOs as an obstacle to engaging in productive partnerships with them.

In summary, most trade unions we studied perceived relevant NGOs as partners. Several of our respondents commented on the potential for a symbiotic relationship between unions and NGOs, as NGOs are able to pursue agendas that the unions may find more difficult. An NGO may be able to condemn corporate practices in public, while a union, with its members' interests in the company at heart, will find itself more constrained but able to pursue a 'behind-the-scenes' approach. In this connection, unions stressed their ability, unlike NGOs, to secure direct access to corporate decision-makers. In some countries, such as Germany, our respondents expressed a particularly strong preference for the 'internal way', for management-union discussions of CSR projects. Differences also emerged in the type of campaigns and initiatives that unions and NGOs engage in. While NGOs were praised by our union respondents for their ability to monitor companies' activities abroad and to rally around environmental topics, the unions were more likely to engage in those initiatives – such as the ETI or the various Clean Clothes Campaigns – that are more closely aligned with their traditional interests in safeguarding employment rights and working conditions.

Final reflections

This book has attempted to provide a snapshot of contemporary patterns of trade union engagement with CSR across Europe, and to contribute to a clearer picture of the varying ways in which CSR is both shaped by, and embedded within, wider institutional arrangements. We have utilized a broadly comparative institutionalist perspective to draw attention to the historical and political determinants of CSR within different countries, and to highlight how the concept is understood by key social agents. With this standpoint in mind, we have not interrogated the CSR policies of particular companies, nor attempted to judge the effectiveness of more general CSR frameworks and initiatives. Rather, our intention has been to provide an overview of current trade union thinking on CSR across a diverse range of countries, and to explore the kinds of challenges and opportunities which unions feel the concept poses to them and their members.

Our overall conclusion is that trade unions across Europe hold highly ambiguous attitudes towards CSR, in a combination of favouring CSR in principle but at the same time remaining sceptical about its implementation and effectiveness. In terms of their own policies in this area, our findings indicate that a majority of unions have not developed internal initiatives, do not have full-time officers with a specific CSR brief, and do not tend to present issues to their members in CSR terms. This ambiguity towards CSR may be explained by various factors: the concept is ill-defined in general, CSR principles may not be very strongly embedded in national conceptions of the proper role of business in society, and – perhaps more than anything else – the way the term is used (and at times abused) within companies deters trade unions from active engagement with it. Together, these factors contribute to a broadly sceptical attitude towards CSR on the part of trade unions. CSR might be perceived as a fine concept in principle, but as too general and too vague in its application, and many of our trade union respondents do not see its relevance to the issues and problems that their members face in their day-to-day jobs. Rather, CSR is frequently perceived merely as a corporate marketing tool, more focused on the reputation of the company than on genuine improvements in working conditions or more responsible business practices. Moreover, unions report that CSR may threaten their role, challenging their power in social dialogue as well as their legitimacy with respect to other stakeholders.

However, despite a generally sceptical attitude and a lack of formal policy positions on CSR, our findings also reveal a considerable degree of trade union engagement with the concept. Unions responded positively to state initiatives in France and Spain to shape the national discourse on sustainable development. Elsewhere, several unions have used CSR to repackage well-established demands under a more fashionable heading in an attempt to gain leverage over companies. We have also reported evidence of a diverse range of considerable union initiatives around CSR in some countries, perhaps most notably in Finland, France, Lithuania, Spain and the UK. In terms of the European-level CSR agenda, and the greater scope for trade union engagement that comes from European funding opportunities, we observe a degree of pragmatism on the part of unions, in particular in Poland. Furthermore, many trade unions collaborate with NGOs across a wide range of joint campaigns and initiatives, albeit maintaining a degree of caution. Despite the broad picture of scepticism of CSR activities, most trade unions remain embedded within a web of various CSR-related initiatives involving a variety of stakeholders.

The debate on the responsibilities of business in a globalized economy has received renewed and urgent attention during the financial crisis. As the public demands greater corporate transparency, we would expect interest in CSR-related issues to increase. From a trade union perspective, the crisis has highlighted once more that unions cannot rely on the private voluntary activities of firms to realise responsible and sustainable business practices. Rather they will need to be pro-active across a number of fronts – engaged in efforts to promote transnational labour standards, working with MNCs in the development of international framework agreements, building effective coalitions with NGOs and other civil society organizations, and lobbying at the European level for improvements in the regulation of corporate governance.

In the light of their concerns over the voluntary nature of CSR, it is not surprising that we have found trade unions giving more attention to other means of pursuing their agendas. Most of our interviewees preferred to focus their efforts on negotiating more binding agreements, such as GFAs, and put CSR relatively low on their list of ways to improve working conditions. In countries such as Germany, where trade unions have established a strong position in the institutional framework, we find suspicion of CSR labels and standards to be particularly marked, accompanied by a clear emphasis on seeking more formal agreements with companies. A range of concepts have been advanced within the European labour movement in recent years which imply a broader and more substantial alternative to CSR. For example, Eurocadres (2006) has championed the idea of 'responsible management' and the ETUI has more recently advocated the 'sustainable company' (Vitols and Kluge 2011) as a potential way forward. The latter concept embraces a variety of features, such as employee representation at all levels of an organization including the board, controls over executive remuneration, employee share ownership and strengthened international framework agreements, as well as strong regulation in governing financial markets and environmental protection, amongst other issues.

We may question whether the concept of CSR is the most appropriate umbrella term for trade unions to frame their campaigns and demands around the social responsibilities of business. This is because CSR remains largely a management initiative, drawn up with management aims and objectives in mind. Much like other management fashions in the past – such as productivity bargaining, the 'flexible firm' and 'employee empowerment' – unions are required to react to agendas that they did not themselves create. That is not to suggest that CSR lacks importance as a topic, on the contrary. The ambivalence in union attitudes reflects a genuine desire to strengthen corporate responsibilities, together with the equally genuine concern that management wants the answers on its own terms, to improve its public relations or to head off criticism that it relies, for example, on sweated labour. Whilst the concerns that underpin CSR remain critically important, as they focus on company relationships with their social environment and in particular with their range of stakeholders, our study suggests that trade unions might do well to find more robust alternatives around which to campaign – alternatives which, unlike '*corporate* social responsibility', place their own priorities at the top of the agenda, more effectively combine an emphasis on strong regulation, collective self-regulation and civil society pressure, and chime more readily with wider calls for a more 'responsible capitalism'.

References

Amable, B. (2003) *The Diversity of Modern Capitalism*, Oxford: Oxford University Press.

Bohle, D. and Greskovits, B. (2012) *Capitalist Diversity on Europe's Periphery*, Ithaca/London: Cornell University Press.

Brammer, S., Jackson, G. and Matten, D. (2012) 'Corporate social responsibility and institutional theory: new perspectives on private governance', *Socio-Economic Review*, 10(1): 3–28.

Eurocadres (2006) *A Curriculum for Responsible European Management (REM)*, Brussels: Council of European Professional and Managerial Staff.

Greenwood, R. and Suddaby, R. (2006) 'Institutional entrepreneurship in mature fields: the big five accounting firms', *Academy of Management Journal*, 49(1): 27–48.

Matten, D. and Moon, J. (2008) '"Implicit" and "explicit" CSR: a conceptual framework for a comparative understanding of corporate social responsibility', *Academy of Management Review*, 33(2): 404–424.

Molina, O. and Rhodes, M. (2006) 'Conflict, complementarities and institutional change in mixed market economies,' in B. Hanké, M. Rhodes and M. Thatcher (eds) *Beyond Varieties of Capitalism: Contradictions, Complementarities and Change*, Oxford: Oxford University Press.

Rhodes, M. and van Apeldoorn, B. (1998) 'Capital unbound? The transformation of European corporate governance,' *Journal of European Public Policy*, 5(3): 407–428.

Schmidt, V.A. (2009) 'Putting the political back into political economy by bringing the state back in yet again', *World Politics*, 61(3): 516–546.

Traxler, F. (1995) 'Farewell to labour market associations? Organized versus disorganized decentralization as a map for industrial relations', in C. Crouch and F. Traxler (eds) *Organized Industrial Relations in Europe: What Future?*, Aldershot: Avebury, pp. 3–19.

Vitols, S. and Kluge, N. (eds) (2011) *The Sustainable Company: A New Approach to Corporate Governance*, Brussels: European Trade Union Institute.

Index

Page numbers in *italics* denote tables.